Mothering and Literacies

Edited by

Amanda B. Richey and Linda Shuford Evans

DEMETER PRESS

Copyright © 2013 Demeter Press

Individual copyright to their work is retained by the authors. All rights reserved. No part of this book may be reproduced or transmitted in any form by any means without permission in writing from the publisher.

Published by:
Demeter Press
c/o Motherhood Initiative for Research and
 Community Involvement (MIRCI)
140 Holland St. West, P.O. 13022
Bradford, ON, L3Z 2Y5
Telephone: 905.775.9089
Email: info@demeterpress.org
Website: www.demeterpress.org

Demeter Press logo based on Skulptur "Demeter" by Maria-Luise Bodirsky
<www.keramik-atelier.bodirsky.edu>

Printed and Bound in Canada

Front cover artwork: Rachel Epp Buller, *Swirling Stories,* 2010. Monoprint. Collection of the artist.

Library and Archives Canada Cataloguing in Publication

         Mothering and literacies / edited by Amanda B. Richey and Linda Shuford Evans.

Includes bibliographical references.
ISBN 978-1-927335-14-7

Cataloguing data available from Library and Archives Canada.

*We dedicate this book to mothers—
those that contributed and the legions of others who negotiate
mothering and literacy on a daily and ongoing basis.*

Table of Contents

Acknowledgements
xi

Foreword
Alison Piepmeier
1

Introduction:
An Invitation to Dialogue
Linda Shuford Evans and Amanda B. Richey
3

I. LITERACIES OF PREGNANCY, BIRTHING, AND ADOPTION

Chapter 1
High-Risk Pregnancy
Miriamne Ara Krummel
19

Chapter 2
Loving Mothers: International Guatemalan Adoption
and Digital Literacies
Laura Newhart
32

Chapter 3
"We Can Get Old or We Can Get Dead":
Celebrating Fifteen Years of the Midwifery Coalition
of Nova Scotia's Newsletter
Erin Hemmens
51

II. LITERACIES AND SCHOOLING

Chapter 4
Advising for Inequity: Literacy Advice to Mothers
Suzanne Smythe
65

Chapter 5
Reclaiming Literacy:
A Kindergartner Teaches Her Mom to Read
Jill Bryant
83

Chapter 6
"You Are Your Child's First Teacher":
The Construction of Maternal Subjectivity
in Family Literacy Programs
Stacey Crooks
99

III. MOTHERING AND VISUAL LITERACIES

Chapter 7
Social Representations of Motherhood Through
the Practice of Art Journaling
Jessica Smartt Gullion and Ariel Cooksey
119

Chapter 8
Visual Literacies of Mothering
Rachel Epp Buller
133

IV. MOTHERING AND LITERACIES IN CROSS-CULTURAL CONTEXTS

Chapter 9
"My Girls are Going to Make It in the Future":
Intertwined Discourses of
Mothering, Literacy and Desire
Blaire Willson Toso
145

Chapter 10
From Traditional to Transmedia Storytelling:
Constructing and Deconstructing
Motherhood Across Cultural Contexts
*Elizabeth Trejos-Castillo, Paulina Vélez,
and Marta Cecilia Gutiérrez-Restrepo*
163

Chapter 11
Rethinking Literacy Research/Training
with Marginalized *Mujeres*
Cinthya M. Saavedra and Cara L. Preuss
182

Chapter 12
Literacy and Motherhood Abroad:
The Case of Japanese Overseas Mothers
Masako Kato
196

V. PUBLIC DISCOURSES AND LITERACIES OF MOTHERHOOD

Chapter 13
Mothers-For-Natural-Hair: The Afro-Cyberella's
Social Media Guide to Afrocentric Hair
Lauren Cross
221

Chapter 14
Hidebound Prohibitions and Electronic Literacies: Separate
Spheres Ideology and the Surveillance of Mommyblogs
Elizabeth Howells
237

Chapter 15
King Solomon's Semiotic Chains/Inner Division
and the Literacy of Motherhood
Teresa Winterhalter
253

Chapter 16
"What's a Mom To Do?":
Negotiating Public Health Literacies
Through the Traffic between Motherhood and
Mothering in School-based HPV Vaccination Programming
Michelle Wyndham-West
270

Contributor Notes
289

Acknowledgements

We would like to thank Demeter Press, specifically Andrea O'Reilly, for seeing the potential for a project that put mothering and literacies in the same (figurative) room and allowed us to sit in there with the great company of other writers, scholars, and artists. Moreover, we thank and acknowledge the talented and thoughtful women who contributed to this volume.

Amanda: I thank my co-editor Linda Evans for her friendship and collaboration. I also owe a debt of gratitude to my family—partner Hicham and children Noor and Lena—for being constant sources of comfort, love and inspiration.

Linda: I thank my co-editor Amanda for bringing me on board with this project. I am indebted to my parents, Ray and Rose Shuford, who always made literacy a priority and supported my "book habit" throughout my childhood. I am also grateful for my children, Abby and Zach Evans, who have taught me so much about both mothering and literacies, and my partner Bob, who has supported me unwaveringly and kept me well-fed during the final edits.

Foreword

ALISON PIEPMEIER

BEING A MOTHER is a high-stakes endeavor. Many of the essays collected here address the expectations our culture has for mothers—and *mothers* in particular, even though our cultural rhetoric is often the gender-neutral "parents." The expectations are high. It does not really matter what your life looks like—the idea is that you will read to your child, stimulate your child's mind, make every moment of every day a learning moment.

In the introduction, Amanda Richey shares,

> When I was a doctoral student in literacy and a mother of babies, I often found myself on a dissonant journey of going straight from a discussion of empirical research about family literacy (i.e., the importance of reading to children from birth) in a night class, to my home where inconsolable babies were clamoring to nurse. I would then read a board book for the requisite 20 minutes through red, blurred eyes.

Another author, Jill Bryant, articulates the same anxiety: "The unexpected pressure of being a parent and feeling responsible for the growth and development of my own child made the stakes seem much higher."

I feel those pressures. They can be particularly challenging when it comes to literacy. I see the ways in which it's used to evaluate children. The stakes are particularly high for children with intellectual disabilities, like my daughter. These children's ability to speak, read, or write can be used to determine where they will be placed in a school system, what services they will receive, and indeed whether they should be born in the first place. I feel that when I write the words *speak*, *read*, and *write* they should all be in scare quotes—and *Mothering and Literacies* gives me tools to unpack those terms and use them differently.

Mothering and Literacies invites us to recognize literacy as a socially constructed category, one of those overloaded terms which demands a whole series of questions: What does it mean? Whose definition? Who benefits? Who is being marginalized or ignored? The book is quite encouraging: it is not a book that is encouraging me, as a reader, to feel guiltier—to try harder—to pull out the white board this morning and get my daughter to read a few words. Instead, it is a book that is inviting me to be skeptical of the expectations that surround me, and to recognize that much of what I am already—even automatically—doing with my daughter is encouraging her to learn, to be "literate," to be a thoughtful and happy member of her community.

Can my daughter speak? Her words are difficult to understand to those who do not know her well—indeed, often even to me—but she speaks. More importantly, she communicates broadly, using her body, her clothing, her dance moves, her dolls. As the scholars in *Mothering and Literacies* demonstrate, our parenting is better—as is our scholarship—when we are attentive to the varying forms communication takes. This is a book that asks us to consider the many ways in which mothering and literacy are intertwined, and it offers both support and a host of good ideas.

—Alison Piepmeier
College of Charleston
Women's and Gender Studies

Introduction

An Invitation to Dialogue

LINDA SHUFORD EVANS AND AMANDA B. RICHEY

WHEN THINKING ABOUT how we wanted to introduce this volume we envisioned a dialogue—that is, a way for us to negotiate and construct our understanding of the work as a whole and what we brought to it. Linda, a bilingual education scholar with 33 years of teaching and mothering under her belt, brought a wealth of literacy experience upon which mothering-as-discourse could be circumspectly posed. Amanda, still with preschoolers running around her "office" (really, just a well-worn spot on the sofa with a coffee table nearby), and a desire to interrogate the disconnect between "home" and "school" literacies, brought a tentative acknowledgement that mothering *was* literacy, and a highly politicized form at that.

Juxtaposing literacy and motherhood was bound to expose contradictions and powerful chunks of memory. Indeed, the authors in this volume—among them writers, poets, visual artists, professors, performers, and mothers—reveal that there is no simple definition of either. Through deft prose these authors tell the stories of self and motherhood, literate networks of meaning that traverse multimodal spaces. We read and feel here stories of memory and imagined spaces where literacy is not confined by skill-based sets of knowledge or top-down campaigns to "cure" illiteracy or increase literacy delivered from mother to child. Here, instead, we see how women wield literacy—and where we once saw deficits, we now see agency.

What does it mean to investigate the literacy practices of women, especially mothers of young children who are often the object of mothering-discourses-as-institution? First, we understand that literacies are multiple, local, and contextual (Barton, Hamilton, and Ivanic; Gee; Street, *Literacy in Theory, Social Literacies, "What's 'New' in New Literacy Studies?"*), but that there are "limits" to only examining "local" literacies without referencing the agency of individuals or power and hegemony in a decidedly globalized society (Brandt and Clinton).

Several studies in the past 20 years have used the New Literacy Studies framework (see: Gee; Street, *Literacy in Theory and Practice, Social Literacies*) to examine the literacy practices of women and, specifically, mothers. Relatively early studies such as Jenny Horsman's examination of the literacy lives of women in Nova Scotia—a challenge to the "myth of illiteracy" (15)—examined how women who had been labeled "illiterate" actually exercised various and powerful literacy practices in their daily lives. Another early seminal work by Janice Radway explored how women read romance novels and how these readings were a sort of "declaration of independence" from the demands of childrearing and family life in the patriarchal structures of the heteronormative family (11). More recent examinations of the literacy practices of women have paved the way for a deeper engagement with the ideological implications of family literacy campaigns in cross-cultural contexts.

The chapters in this book are stories of literacies and motherhood that reflect larger contested stories of institutional and sociocultural relationships of power, privilege, and meaning-making. They ask us questions about the seemingly uncritical aspects of educational "success" and implicit neutrality of the pursuit of literacy. These aren't stories of "suffering" or simplistic "success" stories, but stories of agency borne of the "strong objectivity" (Harding 149) of grounded knowledges in specific contexts. From the cyber networks of "Afro-Cyberellas" to the powerful informal literacies of an evolving newsletter for midwives in Nova Scotia, these narratives reflect larger stories—marginalization of families in schooling, agency of women who harness multimodal and varied literacies, and the wisdom of women who weigh options for children and make difficult, but insightful choices.

As we read, considered, discussed, and arranged the stories by the authors in this volume, we learned a lot about and from each other. While each chapter is written with a tone appropriate to its message—personal to more academic—all are imbued with a sense of exploration of the humanity of mothering and its connection to literacies. Additionally, each author posits definitions of both mothering *and* literacies that are borne of particular contexts and histories, reflecting the self- and socially-constructed nature of each. In light of this, we felt that capturing some of our own co-constructions as editors of this book would provide a backdrop to the rich explorations offered by the authors in this volume.

DIALOGUE BETWEEN AMANDA AND LINDA

Amanda: As I think about the connection, or the disconnection, between motherhood (a social condition with gendered meaning, over-coded and under-researched) and literacy/-ies (a system that has been codified in popular culture and each and every major institution), I wonder: Is the connection forced? Is it essentializing to ask how mothers and literacies intersect in our culture?

Likewise, when I think about literacies and motherhood, I think about how families, especially those who are underserved and marginalized by the institutions of schooling, are blamed for low literacy (or branded illiterate, or considered "differently literate," i.e. only orally literate, etc.) and how we so very rarely connect our academic postulating to real lives. How can this volume rectify this? Or where is the pragmatic linkage between the two?

Linda: I, too, wonder about the connections and distinctions between literacies and motherhood, much in the same way that I ponder the distinctions between math and science or literature and social studies. Based on the notion that we can understand phenomena by taking them apart and studying their constituent parts (the foundation for evidence-based research currently so prevalent in our education literature), we dissect our academic content, our students, our notions of teaching and learning, and our very lives, compartmentalizing them into separate research studies, separate courses, separate subject areas, and separate teaching and learning strategies. It's no wonder, then, that we separate motherhood from literacies and relegate mothers to a tangential role of either aiding what schools do or, more frequently, getting in the way, falling short. We stratify and marginalize the notion of motherhood by placing literacies in the center of what is considered "success" in life. When formal institutions such as schools are the center of the discussion, everything else is relegated to a supporting, hindering, or irrelevant—invisible—role.

With English as the epicenter of learning in the U.S.—instead of actual critical knowledge of the world—it is inevitable that mothers of English learners, themselves often in various stages of acquiring English, are found lacking. With no recognition of the value of native languages in learning, despite several decades of solid research showing that literacy only need be acquired once and is best acquired in a language that the learner comprehends, the non-English languages of mothers are ignored at best and demonized at worst.

Also, with middle class as the benchmark for normal, it is inevitable that families of poverty or lower socioeconomic status—often the case for English learners and their families—are seen as deficient, needing to be "fixed" by imbuing the children with middle class values and ways of knowing and being, and yes, middle class literacy practices.

Rather than seeing different literacy traditions and mother/child connections as contributing to the ideal "literacy," all but what can be segmented and identified empirically is discarded and disregarded in the schooling process. The very distinction between "real life" and schooling is troubling and something I feel that we should be up in arms about. What is schooling but a *part* of life?

When we segment our children, the very life force of a civilization, into "students" and "children," and we speak about what happens outside of school as "life" (or worse, we don't speak of it at all), we are treating children as widgets on an assembly line and arrogantly ignoring the value of the teachings and interactions they have with those most connected to them—their family members—and with the world outside the walls of the school.

For whether the institution of education likes it or not, our children are whole, and that whole is the sum of ALL of the influences, experiences, attitudes, beliefs, and people that exist in their worlds. Life cannot authentically be compartmentalized.

I feel that one hallmark of this volume is a breaking down of the artificial structures that disempower literacy influences in children's and mothers' lives. It is a reclaiming of the whole child, a celebration of the power of mothering, and an opening of a dialogue filled with emotion, thoughtful debate, recountings of anguish and joy, and a multitude of questions regarding literacy practices and mothering.

Amanda: To "break down artificial structures" means that we must question status quo definitions and that includes our own academic institutions' structures, definitions, and boundaries. In teacher education where I now find myself working—and here I think of Paolo Freire's concept of educators doing "culture" work—we speak of the "involvement" of parents and family in their children's literacy and learning. A great deal of time is spent lambasting the deficit ideologies that have allowed us to label children and their families "at risk," yet we seem to be caught in a web of hegemonic dead ends. In the United States, standards-based education reform has merely been shifted and tweaked, with only incremental gains. (As I write this, Chicago Public School teachers are in their second week of striking, and negotiations involve redefining the standardized-scores-based teacher evaluation system.) Perhaps this is why this conversation is "too hot" for a teacher education context where the institutional need is for more alignment, more standardization, more answers—less dismantling/deconstructing, less critical thinking, and less questioning the "way things are."

If this volume is new and somehow makes a fresh conceptual partnership between mothering as an institution and literacy as a set of social practices and contested skills/knowledges, then we must make a strong case for this. What do you bring to this "stage," Linda? How did you/do you experience the tension between literacies and mothering?

Linda: Well, mostly I bring more questions than answers based on my experiences as mother and educator. I come to this project with 33 of my 55 years of age as an educator specializing in literacy, 27 of them as a mother. My daughter Abby is 27 and my son Zach is 21. This project prompted me to look back on my experiences of mothering two bright children through their schooling experiences, and caused me to question once again some of my choices while participating in that endeavor. I say once again because I actively questioned every aspect of parenting as I was living it!

As a highly literate, White, middle-class educator, I was afforded choices. I had entrée to my children's schools; I felt comfortable in schools and knew how they worked. I kept a low profile on what might have been, to the schools and teachers, potentially the most threatening aspect of my character—my job as a university professor of literacy. Unlike skin color, accent, or socioeconomic status, I could minimize the evidence of my job, knowledge base, and beliefs simply by not speaking up. This is what created the most tension for me as I raised my children—my dual roles of mother and educator.

The most vivid intersection of these roles came when my son was in second grade and the program Accelerated Reader (AR) was introduced in his school. My daughter, six years older than my son, had gone to that school, so I knew most of the teachers and thought I knew how things operated there. When my son, then eight years old, told me that by virtue of his standardized reading scores he was not allowed to read certain books, or rather that those books wouldn't "count," I told him that he was mistaken, that AR was optional and designed for those kids who needed encouragement to read more. One day he came home and tearfully told me that he didn't have enough "points" for the grading period because he hadn't read and taken a quiz on enough books that counted, that were AR-approved books.

The problem was that for Zach to read on his assigned grade level—sixth grade—he had to exclusively read chapter books, which are lengthy, have few pictures, and present themes designed for the interests of older students. At age eight, Zach had the attention span and interests of an eight-year-old. I read chapter books to him at home, but listening to a book is a different task than reading one, and what became a bonding, storytelling time for the two of us morphed into an academic pursuit with consequences for not completing a ten-question multiple-choice test with at least 80 percent accuracy.

My son went from being excited about reading to declaring "I hate reading," the antithesis of what any school program should aim to achieve. After protesting, talking to his teacher, and questioning the school, I did what I had to do. I asked for a list of all the AR books, selected the chapter books with the largest number of points, and read those with/to Zach. He took the tests, passed them, and after only a couple of large-point books he was free to read whatever he wanted for the rest of the nine weeks. In other words, we scammed the system. Unfortunately, he would not show a love for reading again until late in his high school years when he found material in his literature and social studies courses that was relevant and compelling to him. He subsequently attended a liberal arts college where reading and writing in the humanities was how he spent most of his time.

One might say that all's well that ends well, but what of all of those years in between? What of all that my son might have been reading, writing, thinking about had he not been reading-adverse for so long? But for me the greater question is this—What became of all of the bright children of all backgrounds who didn't have parents who could help them scam the system? What happened to the children without the English skills to read the number of books to gain the number of points to help them fit in with their peers and to "succeed?" AR was a one-size-fits-all, literacy-is-what-schools-decide-it-is program that came to symbolize for me the malpractice of focusing on literacy as a subject or skill rather than as part of a child and a way of life. And what of my role? I could have done more, but even I, with my degrees and my knowledge, fell into the complicity of allowing schools to define the value of our family literacy practices, *even when I knew better*. I questioned it at the time but didn't have the clarity to follow through with it. I'm still pondering that!

Amanda, you ask the question: "Why do we relegate this discussion of mothering and literacies to gender and women's studies more often than education or social sciences?" I come to this project from the perspective of education and social sciences, but I am not as well-versed in gender/women's studies context. What does the literature offer in terms of understanding the connections between literacy and mothering, or, conversely, does it speak about the disconnect between the two?

Amanda: Adrienne Rich's seminal work *Of Woman Born: Motherhood as Experience and Institution* set the stage for a variety of ways to explore motherhood. As a poet, academic *and* mother, her connection to motherhood (in all its visceral joys and disappointments) was personal, but she noticed that it stood in contrast to what she began to see as the "institution" of motherhood. Drawing this distinction allowed Rich (and others) to parse (recognize, name, question) the "institutional" discourses of mothering and parenting from the experiential factors (the agency of mothering and having a mother self). Suzanne Smythe, (Chapter Four in this volume) foregrounds these discourses in her critical discourse analysis of a century of literacy advice to mothers. Knowing that institutional constructions of motherhood have powerfully shaped and infiltrated mothers' agency and relationships with schooling (i.e., "You are your child's best teacher"; "Teach the parent, reach the child," etc.), it is all the more important to listen to and understand how women who mother actually *do* literacy. That is, when given the concept of literacy as a negotiable—what will we do with it? How will we redefine and reshape such well-worn contours?

Meanwhile, motherhood continues to receive plenty of scholarly *and* popular treatment. The proliferation of "Mommy memoirs" or "momoirs" (see Hulbert for a discussion of this) and "mommyblogs" continue to document the multiple ways we conceive of and enact motherhood in a digital era—a set of discursive practices intimately tied to the consumption and production of text (see Mace). Extending this discussion, Elizabeth Howells (Chapter Fourteen) explores the discourses of popular mommyblogs as locations for spheres of ideology and "surveillance." Moreover, there appears to be no end to the iterations of how-to books that attempt to brand mothering perfection (see Chua and Druckerman for recent examples). Alas, the conversation continues as we delve into these realms as a matter of import and analysis.

Linda: As I ponder the implications of the intersection of motherhood and literacies, I recognize that as the mother of two preschoolers, you are squarely in the middle of many of the issues explored in this book. Your children also are of multicultural, multiethnic, and multilingual backgrounds. What have you struggled with and/or learned so far on your journey as a mother and a literacy educator?

Amanda: As mothers, we are also expected to be educators. "The most important teacher." "Teach the parent, reach the child." So go the familiar sayings. I've written before that mothers-as-educators are expected to be "conduits, perfectly greased knowledge shoots that deliver information and developmentally appropriate brain-boosting activities at just the right times" (Richey 25). Twenty minutes of reading a day. Homework help. Moral education. Our parenting is teaching and our teaching, parenting. When our kids "fail" at school, often we are blamed, or our blame is collapsed into a familiar euphemism, spoken in hushed tones: "home life." The question is asked, whispered even: *But what about the home life of this child?*

When I was a doctoral student in literacy and a mother of babies, I often found myself on a dissonant journey of going straight from a discussion of empirical research about family literacy (i.e., the importance of reading to children *from birth*) in a night class, to my home where inconsolable babies were clamoring to nurse. I would then read a board book for the requisite 20 minutes through red, blurred eyes. I identify with the journey described by Jill Bryant (Chapter Five) as her kindergartner, Maya, "teaches" her how to reclaim literacy through the experiential realm of mothering.

In my pre-academic life, when I was a living in a multilingual/literate culture and struggling to learn languages myself, I questioned the autonomous model of literacy (Goody) and the requisite women's literacy campaigns that were invariably associated with the international NGOs that operated in Morocco. What inspired me at that time was the *Neddy,* an all-woman space where women defined their own literacy learning and their own goals. Visiting one Neddy on the edge of the Sahara desert in Merzouga, Morocco, I met women who spoke five languages fluently, taught kindergarten, and operated an elaborate store with handmade textiles, jewelry, and other items. Here was found a revival of the ancient glyphs of *Tiffinagh,* the written version of Tamazight (an indigenous language of the Berbers, or Amazigh, of North Africa) long considered to "only" be a spoken language, a "dying" language. The women wove the hearty glyphs on blankets, rugs, scarves, and shawls, creating a potent form of literacy—one that benefited their families and advanced, very publicly, Tiffinagh as a legitimate language—a purposeful language that was worth reviving and enacting upon household items (evoking the complex beauty/literacy of quilting in the American south). I remember the images of the Neddy now because I wonder why we ignore or avoid the power of women and mothers-defining-literacy in our discussions of family literacy. As a mother, I recognize this omission and I seek out spaces where that power might be actualized so that I may participate. As an academic, I see how those omissions have limited our understandings of literacy, and thus, impacted the success and instruction of children in dramatic ways.

LITERACIES OF PREGNANCY, BIRTHING AND ADOPTION

The first group of manuscripts in the collection offers highly personal aspects of literacies and mothering that begin at the beginning—pathways to motherhood. We join Miriamne Ara Krummel as she recounts the literacies she encountered during her high-risk pregnancy. We then explore with Laura Newhart aspects of digital literacies as part of the international adoption process. We look more broadly at print literacy as a change agent as we follow Erin Hemmens' retrospective on the evolution of the Midwifery Coalition of Nova Scotia's newsletter as it parallels the evolution of the organization.

LITERACIES OF SCHOOLING

As children grow, their worlds expand from the womb to their mothers' arms to the institutions and expectations of schooling. The expectations come from both the mothers themselves and from the institutions' beliefs about a mother's role in formal education of children. We learn from Suzanne Smythe the historical nature of nineteenth and early twentieth century literature that formed the foundation of the modern-day movement to "educate mothers to educate their children" by regulating mothering practices in an effort to produce children who come to school perfectly prepared for the school's definition of literacy. We grapple alongside Jill Bryant, a literacy expert, as she reevaluates her lifelong literacy ideologies as her young daughter learns to read. We also feel the weight of responsibility expressed by Stacey Crooks as she queries the implications of the mantra: "You are your child's first teacher."

MOTHERING AND VISUAL LITERACIES

In this section of this collection, authors turn to the visual to answer the question: How do we read and write motherhood and mothering? With a grounding in social representation theory, Jessica Smartt Gullion and Ariel Cooksey advocate for recognition of the creative practice of art journaling not only as a viable tool in academic work on mothering, but also as a tool bridging the solitary and public natures of motherhood. Rachel Epp Buller observes that visual literacies on mothering already proliferate publicly in the imagery found in art history, picture books, parenting magazines, and popular media outlets, among others. Buller sparks our imaginations with descriptions of how she "makes visible the roles of women and girls, mothers and daughters, as bearers of oral and other histories" through her artwork. While acknowledging the value of modern print literacies of "momoir," "mommyblogs," and social media, she asserts that visual literacies provide a means to capture the strands of unwritten knowledge in a form that can be "read" by all.

MOTHERING AND LITERACIES IN CROSS-CULTURAL CONTEXTS

The interrogation of the interconnectedness of mothering and literacies becomes even more multidimensional across cultural and linguistic contexts as authors explore the discourses that impact mothers' views of and participation in the literacy development of their children. Blaire Willson Toso introduces us to Olivia, a woman of Mexican heritage whose own literate identity and ambitions are challenged by the desire for her daughters' success and by the pressures of the Mexican-American community to conform to its notion of "good mother." We next join Elizabeth Trejos-Castillo, Paulina Vélez, and Marta Cecilia Gutiérrez-Restrepo as they explore the changes in the transmission of cultural discourses regarding mothering due to the impact of media literacies, particularly the Internet, in the U.S. and Latin America. Cinthya Saavedra and Cara Preuss both use and explore *pláticas*, or conversations, as points of critical reflections across their own individual studies of literacy initiatives and the (dis)empowerment of Mexican mothers. Finally, Kato turns the spotlight to Japanese mothers negotiating the role of mother tongue literacy and the (re)construction of motherhood as they face the pressures of cultural norms from both their home and host countries.

PUBLIC DISCOURSES AND LITERACIES OF MOTHERHOOD

Finally, we turn our attention to the portrayal of motherhood in the public forum and follow our authors through an examination of what is being written by whom and to what end. Lauren Cross takes us into a different public discourse with potent controversies when she explores the meanings and agencies ascribed to Afrocentric hair care and the potential for using modern technologies to create "new cultural discourses through social media platforms." Elizabeth Howells takes us into twenty-first century discourses as she recounts the conflicted history of "mommy-blogging" and the resulting "discursive explosion," with many attributes in common with pre-technology literacies of mothering. Teresa Winterhalter affirms this notion that even as modern literacies hold the promise for creating new meanings and conditions for the cultural transformation of identities, this promise has yet to be realized, as evidenced by the public discourses from and around prominent women in today's media. Finally, Michelle Wyndham-West recounts a study of Canadian mothers trying to piece together "their public health literacies" in an attempt to sort through and critically analyze the barrage of information about the HPV vaccination offered for girls by local middle schools. She provides a stark contrast between the notion of mothering—a chaotic construct occurring in-the-moment and on-the-ground—and the tidy notion of motherhood, which embodies the "good mother" as sanctioned by society.

WORKS CITED

Barton, David, Mary Hamilton, and Roz Ivanic, eds. *Situated Literacies: Reading and Writing in Context.* London, England: Routledge, 2000. Print.

Brandt, Deborah, and Katie Clinton. "Limits of the Local: Expanding Perspectives on Literacy as a Social Practice." *Journal of Literacy Research* 34.3 (2002): 337. Print.

Chua, Amy. *Battle Hymn of the Tiger Mother.* New York: Penguin Press, 2011. Print.

Druckerman, Pamela. *Bringing Up Bebe: One American Mother Discovers the Wisdom of French Parenting.* New York: Penguin, 2012. Print.

Freire, Paulo. *Teachers as Cultural Workers: Letters to Those Who Dare Teach.* Boulder, CO: Westview Press, 1998. Print.

Gee, James Paul. *Social Linguistics and Literacies.* London: Taylor & Francis, 1996. Print.

Goody, Jack, ed. *Literacy in Traditional Societies.* Cambridge, MA: Cambridge University Press, 1968. Print.

Harding, Sandra. *Whose Science? Whose Knowledge? Thinking from Women's Lives.* Ithaca, NY: Cornell University Press, 1991. Print.

Horsman, Jenny. *Something on My Mind Besides the Everyday: Women and Literacy.* Toronto: Women's Press, 1990. Print.

Hulbert, Ann. "The Real Myth of Motherhood: Reconsidering the Maternal Memoir-Cum-Manifesto." *Slate Magazine.* Web. October 10, 2012.

Mace, Jane. *Playing With Time: Mothers and the Meaning of Literacy.* London, England: Routledge Press, 1998. Print.

Radway, Janice A. *Reading the Romance: Women, Patriarchy, and Popular Literature.* Chapel Hill, NC: University of North Carolina Press, 1984. Print.

Rich, Adrienne. *Of Woman Born: Motherhood as Experience and Institution.* New York: Norton, 1976. Print.

Richey, Amanda. *(M)Other Literacies: Transgressive Identity and Education in Women's Narratives.* Dissertation, Tennessee Technological University, 2011. Print.

Smythe, Suzanne. *The Good Mother: A Critical Discourse Analysis of Literacy Advise to Mothers in the 20th Century.* Dissertation, University of British Columbia, Canada, 2006. Print.

Street, Brian V. *Literacy in Theory and Practice.* Cambridge, England: Cambridge University Press, 1984. Print.

Street, Brian V. *Social Literacies: Critical Approaches to Literacy in Development, Ethnography, and Education.* London, England: Longman, 1995. Print.

Street, Brian V. "What's 'New' in New Literacy Studies? Critical Approaches to Literacy in Theory and Practice." *Current Issues in Comparative Education* 5.2 (2003): 77-91. Print.

I.
Literacies of Pregnancy, Birthing and Adoption

1.
High Risk Pregnancy[1]

MIRIAMNE ARA KRUMMEL

APRIL 5, 2005. I walk into our apartment—our home—after a full day of teaching. The little red light on the phone is blinking. Someone has left a message. I drop the keys on the dining room table and turn to the cordless phone. Ever-thirsty these days, I fill a glass with water to entertain myself while the phone system runs through the tedium of the programmed script: provide password, two saved messages, one new message.

I choose the option to listen to the new message. I hear the recorded voice of my OB/GYN, Dr. Evelyn Chao, on the other end of the receiver. The message is for me. My pulse rate increases: her words send my head into a spin. My hand runs to my abdomen as I try to protect my fetus. To calm me, to calm her.

What did I just hear?! With slightly numbed fingers, I scramble to touch 3 and then 4 to play the message again. Then I attempt to contact Dr. Chao at her office in Miami Valley Hospital. The phone rings and rings. A recorded message asks me to leave my name and number. So I do. Scared, frightened, powerless, I ask to be called back as soon as possible.

Then, I wait. I sit by the telephone and stare at its lifelessness.

I am not the sort to paint—or even to create—a nursery. Having a bassinet peopled with three little, colorful, stuffed objects is enough preparation for me. Each cuddly toy combines a little bit of what I am with a little bit of what I imagine the fetus might become. These future friends of the fetus exist in between two worlds, defined by outside observers, representing the unknown, manifesting the limitless possibilities of the imagination. One resembles the mythical unicorn; another, a zebra; a third, a hairless, sexless, swaddled baby.

Dubbed "Shem," the Hebrew word for "name," the fetus is becoming less unknown and more familiar at this point in the pregnancy. I can now expect afternoon and evening kicks. A personality is emerging. These spirited knocks and demanding taps proclaim, "Hey! Notice me! I am here!" Shem Fetus is not so much expressing a need to leave her warm and comfortable quarters as she is making known a definite desire to establish independence. My life changes imperceptibly. I take daily breaks with Shem, and at these moments, we listen to *Mozart for Mommies and Daddies*, a shower gift that I had initially seen as a gag gift and that I now cherish. (The male colleague who gave me this CD and I share a deep affection for classical music.)

Shem Fetus has begun to link to both my conscious and my conscience. I am falling in love with her.

The numbers recorded on the three-hour Glucose Tolerance test indicate that I have gestational diabetes. I cannot translate this diagnosis. While I am no stranger to illnesses (I have had multiple sclerosis since 1994), I feel incredibly worried about and protective over the fetus that is growing in my uterus. I do not know how gestational diabetes will transform my pregnancy, or—for that matter—change my carefully maintained MS-body, endanger the health of my fetus, alter my way of life. The person on the other end of the line—an answering service operator who reads from a prepared script—cannot assuage my fear.

Troubled by the word "diabetes," I demand some logic to this diagnosis: *What does this mean?* I query the woman on the other end of the line as if she can offer me medical solutions or emotional security. Something. Anything. I need some grounding. *I eat well and exercise as much as I am able. How can I have diabetes? What does this diagnosis mean?*

The voice on the other end of the line cannot help me. She assures me that she can only read what is written on the piece of paper that sits before her eyes.

"The three-hour Glucose Tolerance yielded very high numbers," she remarks so matter-of-factly, so calmly, in a tone of voice that is the antithesis of the nervous anxiety ripping through my body, birthing sensations of scattered numbness—electronic shocks in my extremities. The news is causing a temporary flare-up of the MS because of the intensity of my worry (Krummel). The voice of the message service continues to read her script.

Apparently, after one hour my blood delivered a 184 ("180 is top," I am told); after two hours, my blood was recorded as 182 ("155 is top"); after three hours my blood produced a better number—140 ("140 is top"). *What does this mean?* I ask again: I am stuck in this refrain, demanding answers from a woman who probably knows less about dealing with a (dis)abled body than I.

"On Monday morning, call Sharon or Lucy." *But it's Thursday night. I need to know what I should do now and whether my fetus is okay!* Pushed to deal with me, the voice on the other end of the line locates the best answer she can deliver: "Avoid breads. Worst case scenario is that you will have to take insulin. On Monday morning, call Sharon or Lucy." *But I need to know what I should do and whether my fetus is okay.* "On Monday morning, call Sharon or Lucy." I hang up and call my husband. Maybe he will offer some sort of balm. Or throw me a life preserver.

Toppled by the pressure of another illness, I wait for him to come home. When he does, we search the Web for answers. We wait in the unknown and unclear. We worry about Shem's kicks which become more furious and insistent.

The diagnosis of gestational diabetes changes everything. Everything. Coupled with what is considered my "advanced maternal age" (I am 38 years old) and my diagnosed multiple sclerosis (when I was 28), the gestational diabetes confirms that my pregnancy is now "High Risk."

My OB/GYN drops me from her care. Dr. Chao explains to me that I now need a full-time OB/GYN and that she runs a part-time practice. I read her refusal to care for me as indicating that my high-risk-disabled body is too high-maintenance for her; she prefers low-risk-abled bodies. I am cut loose and have to locate a new OB/GYN at the beginning of the last trimester of my first pregnancy.

Until this moment in the pregnancy and because of the ultrasound machine, I have believed that I am growing a healthy fetus (Sonek, 18 Feb. 2005). But now I need to review, to reconsider what I know. And that is very little: I feel Shem's kicks. I have assumed, because of the regular thumping, that she is strong. I understand also that I am responsible for her. My body is the place where she is growing.
But my body is failing her ... and me ... again.
The doctor's concern frightens me.
I reassess: I am 28 weeks pregnant without an OB/GYN and with gestational diabetes. And worried. Having successfully battled against MS for a decade, my fighting spirit seems suddenly to be lagging. I have forgotten how to negotiate the world as a "crip." Suddenly, I am troubled by the unknown. Being diagnosed with gestational diabetes differs from the diagnosis of multiple sclerosis. Even though I have fought and survived the undercurrents of misogyny and antisemitism, I am not prepared for this new struggle. Misogyny and antisemitism have been my own battles. Ten years fighting the ins and outs of multiple sclerosis have been personal negotiations with this disease (Krummel). Warrior marks tell of the depth of these battles. But all of these conflicts have been my own. I want to protect the fetus—not yet in the world—from the struggles of life.

For me, the gestational diabetes becomes another battle I have to fight ... and try to win. For me and for the fetus that grows inside of me. Without drugs, without insulin. Already trained to nurture my high-maintenance body, I convert what I learned about caring for the MS to what I need to know about tending to the gestational diabetes. I continue the pattern that has already been established after ten years of babysitting a disability: I possess my disease (Krummel). I accept my hybridity, and just add another hyphen—and a new word after that hyphen—to my already complex identity (Radhakrishnan). No one sees me as a whole person: I am only spectrally present—a victim of stereotyping, a collection of diseases that make me occupy space in a high-risk body (defined by sex, age, MS, Raynauld's syndrome, gestational diabetes, and a genetic carrier of Gaucher's Disease).[2] So thoroughly hyphenated as an older-gestationally-diabetic-circulation-impaired-Gaucher-carrying-woman-with-multiple-sclerosis, I am a walking disease vector, carrying a potentially overlarge fetus that might become a macrosomic baby.

And while I never perfectly master the art of maintaining the ideal blood sugar, I do learn to negotiate this new disability. Fear chastened by reason. One day—while attending a medieval studies colloquium at Ohio State University—I eat half a bagel with hummus and my blood sugar number soars. The higher number sends me into an emotional tornado. I immediately worry about the fetus before I calm down and recognize that this too is manageable. A lesson learned. Hereafter, I assiduously monitor my blood sugar and carefully follow the diet plan (International Diabetes Center). I contain the gestational diabetes with both diet and exercise. After this episode, I cut bagels into quarters; I add more protein to my meals; I try to take a walk after I eat. Although my blood-sugar numbers are sometimes high, they are usually within the target range. I study my daily habits of eating and exercising and try not to repeat the events that led to the higher-than-acceptable blood sugar levels. I am, in essence, mimicking a pattern I had established in the early years of my multiple sclerosis: watch, look, listen, record, and change the pattern that initiated exacerbations (Krummel).

I learn new things: how to balance, save, and reuse carbs. My specific plan (tailored for my body's needs) allows me two carbs and a protein for breakfast, three carbs and a protein for lunch, three carbs and a protein for dinner. I dutifully measure cereal; I carefully count the blueberries; I add three tablespoons of nuts. I restrict sugars, committing myself to reading the nutrition information on all packages, forever attentive to—and worried about—carbs, especially. I become mindful of the serving size limits and their exchanges: one slice of raisin bread equals ½ cup of bran cereal; 24 Oyster crackers equals ½ cup of corn; 17 small grapes equals one cup of Cranberry juice (American

Diabetes Foundation). I place only allotted amounts of foods on my plate. I drink a lot of water and more tea. If I construct a morning snack that includes one protein but does not require a carb, I can save that carb for lunch and have two slices of bread (and eat a sandwich!). I make the pricking of my fingers a game of shifting from one hand to another and from one side of a finger to the other side of that finger. I maintain careful records of everything: diet, exercise, sleep.

And I find my continued distrust of the doctors' decrees to be spot on. Even though I prove that I can competently manage the gestational diabetes, some of the OB/GYNs in the new group of doctors I locate are showing neither respect for my wishes nor trust in my carefully (and personally) monitored regimen. I expect the doctors' disdain. I have read about the medicalization of birth. As *The Birth Book* aptly warns me, birth (really, a natural process and an activity that women have evolved to accomplish) has "become so medicalized" that the process has been stolen away from women, them, us by the "obstetric establishment" (Sears 22).

Recognizing that my body is viewed through a layer of distrust and confusion, my partner and I prepare a birth plan that follows the recommended rituals: we introduce ourselves and express our desires—all the while duly noting (as we have been reminded frequently in the literature) our realization that our dream birth might become impossible to attain (Balaskas 156-57; Sears 234-36). I want to communicate my humanity to the medical establishment in language that they will understand and appreciate, but I recognize that my partner and I are made out to be "terrorists" (a word used by William and Martha Sears in *The Birth Book*) in our birth—trying to hijack the delivery of our first child.[3] Imagine that: a woman trying to own her birth process.

29 June 2005. The one doctor in the group who respects my birth plan and who speaks to me like I am a rational, educated adult, is the one who delivers my daughter. I am lucky. My first and only visit with this OB/GYN is quite a remarkable event, and because of all my experiences to the contrary, I am amazed that he, Dr. Daniel McGovern, thinks as I do. This OB/GYN, despite the

38-week ultrasound's measurement that the fetus weighs 7 lbs., 3 oz. (Sonek 27 June 2005), places his hands on my expanding uterus, and declares, "The fetus weighs no more than five pounds."

Oh, for real, I think, *this man can't be serious. Does he honestly believe that his hands can unmake documentable science authorized by medical technology?*

The answer is, "yes."

July 7, 2005. 3:00 a.m. I awaken Matt after I realize that my water has broken. There is no significant pain, so at 5:00 a.m., we first call the doctor and then phone my mother who takes the next flight out from LaGuardia Airport to Dayton International (Kettering Medical Center, 3). We are told to go to the hospital immediately, but we wait, talk, and eat some breakfast. (A little bit of arrogance and a lotta bit of a mistake.) The choice to wait makes the medical personnel angry, especially the admitting R.N., Emily Rodgers, who meets us in the delivery room, our first contact with the maternity and delivery system. Emily Rodgers chastises us. We have, in her interpretation of the world, behaved irresponsibly; she treats us like disobedient children.

I try to reassure Nurse Rodgers, *I know nothing should enter the vagina after the water breaks. I am informed about the risks* (Curtis and Schuler 207).[4]

The attending OB/GYN, Dr. Pashmina Kumar, does not agree and prescribes amoxicillin. I protest. But Dr. Kumar feels that my breach of protocol (by not going immediately to the hospital when my water broke) warrants her demanding that the drug must be administered.

In essence, the medical establishment expects to seize control of my birth because of my act of rebellion (remaining at home for breakfast). I can no longer be trusted to direct my own delivery. But I will not turn over my fetus without a fight. I protest more. Sharon leaves the room to call Dr. Kumar. Matt and I wait.

The R.N. returns.

A deal is drafted. The dose will be cut in half. If the fetus is delivered within the next seventeen hours, I will not have to take the second dose. Everyone—Sharon, Matt, Rifke (my mother who has just arrived from New York City)—looks at me. Their various expressions suggest some version of the question: *What will she decide?*

My decision is a large one and not easy to make. Part of this arrangement with the Kettering Hospital people—and my being checked into Kettering Memorial Hospital, in general—involves accepting a heparin lock. I learn this. But I resist a hep-lock. I review the history: initially, I planned—and hoped—to give birth in a natural birthing center (Family Beginnings) in Miami Valley Hospital. That ended when my health insurance company terminated their relationship with Miami Valley. Now I am here in Kettering Memorial, and the hospital personnel make it clear that this direct line to my vein is not negotiable. The medicalization of Shem's birth increases, and I am being deprived of more and more choices. *What do I do? Should I tell Matt, "We are leaving this hospital!" And if I do say this, where will we go?*
My preparation for Shem's birth had not figured in hep-locks. I am caught unprepared.

Moments pass.

Okay. Deal.

Deprived of agency and choice, I assent to this medicalization. I have to, after all. There is no choice in the matter.[5] The half dose of amoxicillin is administered. The hep-lock line is forged.

13:26. The doula, Rebecca Ireland, arrives. (Rebecca actually represents more control by Kettering Memorial. While Rebecca is a doula, she is also one of the three doulas in the employ of Kettering Hospital.)
The R.N. measures my cervical dilation. I am not dilating beyond one centimeter, and the R.N. expresses concern about the lack of dilation. Pitocin is prescribed by Dr. Kumar. I refuse Pitocin. I do not budge on this one. Pitocin creates artificial contractions, and I translate the use of Pitocin as an unnatural intervention into my and Shem's labor. Dr. Kumar and Nurse Rodgers are not respond-

ing well to my opposition. Rebecca demurely suggests walking; the R.N. consents to her request. And so, Rebecca and I roam the halls of the Mother/Baby Suites of Kettering Memorial Hospital for forty-five minutes. When we return to the delivery room, I am measured again. Cervical dilation has progressed to four centimeters. Still, the hep-lock line graduates to an IV. Rebecca—ever so cautiously and with great care—negotiates twenty-minute ambles around the maternity ward for me. So the hep-lock line is made more mobile—put on wheels—every forty minutes so that I can walk for twenty. These short strolls are all that the hospital staff permits Rebecca and me.

14:45. The birth pain begins. The intervals between the pangs are still quite long—approximately one hour lapses between them. A routine develops: freedom for twenty-minutes, followed by monitoring for forty. Rebecca and I take twenty-minute walks, roaming the halls of the labor and delivery floor with my portable IV stand. After we return to the hospital room, I am once again hooked into two monitors—one follows the fetus's movements and the other charts my heart rate and pulse.

While the monitors do their work, I reflect on what is about to happen. I really have never thought about the final act of giving birth to a macrosomic fetus. But the final moment of truth is arriving. And despite the medicalization, I remain drug-free and continue without Pitocin, without a desire for an epidural, and with no wish for an episiotomy.

July 8, 2005. The "Labor Progress Report" from Kettering Medical Center documents my final three hours so starkly. 00:16. "Using breathing techniques and doing well." 02:59. "Feels pressure." 03:09. "OB called for delivery." 03:34. "OB in room."

My story is different.

The final 45 minutes of the parturition are nerve-wracking. One part fear and two parts resistance and pain. Fear, groomed by the medical people. Constant resistance, executed by me. Life-affirming pain, caused by Shem's slow entrance into the world.

My mother, my husband, and I had viewed the climax of nine

months with some trepidation, a mixture of eagerness and anxiety. And now—with my water having broken 25 hours earlier—we are poised to discover what the fetus will look like—the shade of her hair, the color of her eyes. *Whom will she resemble? Will Shem look like me and start off with a blonde head of hair or will her genes follow Matt's and be brunette at birth? Will her eyes be hazel like mine or brown like Matt's?*

I steal naps in between the contractions. Each labor pain surprises me anew and thrusts me into consciousness. Each time—when my eyes pop open—I hear the word "push!" yelled frantically by everyone around the bed. Tired and lacking energy, my body begins to have problems processing the meaning of the word "push."

Awake, I focus on Dr. McGovern, sitting to my right, removed from the group calmly reading the birth plan. (He may be the only one besides the doula who has read what Matt and I wrote.) My right hand fiercely grips Matt's. Then: pain subsides and nap time resumes.

This satisfying routine continues for 21 minutes. I grab a cat nap until my eyes pop open. Then: focus on Dr. McGovern and squeeze Matt's hand.

Suddenly, my routine shifts without warning. My team seems a little over-excited and yells, "PUSH! I CAN SEE HER HEAD! PUSH!" I try to push with the contraction—as I am advised—but I cannot grasp the concept of pushing something out of my vagina. The information comes to me as belonging to a foreign and unfamiliar language. The lower half of my body is not unpacking the word, "PUSH!"

Nevertheless, I push—or try to—and then take a little nap again.

03:55. PAIN! I open my eyes. The setting has changed. Now, Dr. McGovern is standing in front of me (over six-feet tall, he dwarfs everyone else). The monitors indicate that my heart rate and blood pressure are rising dangerously while the fetus's heart rate drops.

Dr. McGovern speaks calmly. "This baby is going to be born now. Your friend, Dr. Rubin, advocates a birth process called the McRoberts Maneuver. We will place your feet in stirrups, and I will help you push the baby out. Agree?" *Agree.*

Dr. McGovern then massages the opening of my vagina and the

circumference of Shem's head with his right and left forefingers and middle fingers. The intensive-care medical team, dressed in sterile suits and donning hazmat-looking hats that cover their heads and faces, rush into the room and set up their equipment on my right. The time of delivery is now.

With the help of my doula, the registered nurse on the floor, Lynn Dryden, my husband, and my mother, I deliver Yetta Zipporah Krummel-Adkins, a mere 6 lbs., 5.2 oz., at 40 weeks, on her due date, July 8, 2005, before the nurse administers the second dose of amoxicillin. With the help of this team and, especially, with Dr. McGovern's supervision in the final moments, Yetta arrives without Pitocin, without an epidural, and without an episiotomy, at 4:11 a.m.

With the same fingers that had enticed Yetta to enter the world, Dr. McGovern unwraps the nuchal cord, which encircles Yetta's neck twice. Yetta is then brought to me.

Stunned by the little girl that is placed on my belly—a little girl who is neither macrosomic nor even the documented weight of the 38-week ultrasound—I welcome Yetta in a tremulous voice.
She is so small.
Unexpectedly, I greet my little girl with the words of a Cat Stevens song.

> *and if I ever lose my legs*
> *I won't moan and I won't beg,*
> *oh if I ever lose my legs,*
> *oh if ...*
> *I won't have to walk no more*
> *...*
> *I'm being followed by a moon shadow*
> *moon shadow — moon shadow*
> *leaping and hopping on a moon shadow*
> *moon shadow — moon shadow*
> *moon shadow — moon shadow.*

My first child and I are lost together in these lyrics, this dreamland, that rises up from my past to claim a new present belonging to me and to this small bit of life, dependent on me for protection and safety.

Yetta rests on my abdomen, at peace. I hold her wrinkled fingers.

Then the intensive-care medical team whisks her away to evaluate her. She cries. Matt follows her. I can't.

When Yetta is returned to me, I breastfeed her for the first time. My little girl. With no hair on her head and blue eyes.

[1] At the editors' suggestion, I have changed the names of the medical personnel. This piece is dedicated to two people who have taught me the most about strength and perseverance: Rifke Pomeranz and William Krummel.

[2] The notion of being only "spectrally present" is informed by the work of Steven F. Kruger.

[3] The full sentence reads "[d]on't present it [the Birth Plan] like a terrorist with a list of nonnegotiable demands" (*The Birth Book*, 233). While William and Martha Sears' point may seem reasonable, a woman who tries to possess her birth is viewed with both suspicion and doubt.

[4] When the bag of water breaks, there are three possible ways to move forward: "have the mother stay at home, with some precautions, come into the office for an examination, or go to the hospital" (Simkin 48).

[5] At this moment—when I am denied the right to choose and to speak—I occupy the space of the voiceless subaltern who follows the rituals without agency of action. In my mind, I liken my situation to the nonagentic Indian woman about whom Gayatri Spivak writes.

WORKS CITED

American Diabetes Foundation. *Exchange Lists for Meal Planning*. Chicago: American Dietetic Association, 2003. Print.

Balaskas, Janet. *Active Birth: The New Approach to Giving Birth Naturally*. Rev. ed. Boston: Harvard Common Press, 1992. Print.

Curtis, Glade B. and Judith Schuler. *Your Pregnancy Week by Week*. 5th ed. Cambridge, MA: Perseus Books Group, 2004. Print.

International Diabetes Center. "My Food Plan." Minneapolis: Park Nicollet Institute, 2004. Print.

Kettering Medical Center. "Labor Progress Report." 10 July 2005. 1-8. Print.

Kruger, Steven F. *The Spectral Jew: Conversion and Embodiment in Medieval Europe*. Medieval Cultures. Vol. 40. Minneapolis: University of Minnesota Press, 2006. Print.

Krummel, Miriamne Ara. "Am I MS?" *Embodied Rhetorics: Disability in Language and Culture*. Eds. James C. Wilson, and Cynthia Lewiecki-Wilson. Carbondale: Southern Illinois University Press, 2001. 61-77. Print.

Munves, R. Peter for Philips Music Group. *Mozart for Mommies and Daddies*. Universal Music Group, 1999. Print.

Radhakrishnan, R. "Postcoloniality and the Boundaries of Identity." *Identities: Race, Class, Gender, and Nationality*. Eds. Linda Martín Alcoff, and Eduardo Mendieta. Malden, MA: Blackwell Publishing, 2003. 312-29. Print.

Sears, William and Martha Sears. *The Birth Book: Everything You Need to Know to Have a Safe and Satisfying Birth*. New York: Little, Brown and Company, 1994. Print.

Simkin, Penny. *The Birth Partner: Everything You Need to Know to Help a Woman Through Childbirth*. 2nd ed. Boston: The Harvard Common Press, 2001. Print.

Sonek, Croom, and Ron Neiger, Drs. Perinatal Partners LLC. Obstetric Ultrasound Report. 27 June 2005. Print.

Sonek, Croom, and Ron Neiger, Drs. Perinatal Partners LLC. Obstetric Ultrasound Report. 18 Feb. 2005. Print.

Spivak, Gayatri Chakravorty. "Can the Subaltern Speak?" *Marxism and the Interpretation of Culture*. Eds. Cary Nelson, and Lawrence Grossberg. Chicago: University of Illinois Press, 1988. 271-313. Print.

Stevens, Cat. "Moon Shadow." *Teaser and the Firecat*. Island Music. 1971. CD.

2.
Loving Mothers

International Guatemalan Adoption and Digital Literacies

LAURA NEWHART

ON OCTOBER 12, 2007, we picked up my nine-month-old adopted son from Guatemala. On December 31, 2007, international adoptions from Guatemala closed in order for Guatemala to reform its adoption procedures to comply with the Hague Convention on Protection of Children and Co-operation in Respect of Intercountry Adoption. In the last year that Guatemala had international adoptions, fiscal year 2008, the rate of adoptions by the United States from Guatemala surpassed even that of China (Wheeler 4). There have not been any new international adoption cases in Guatemala since they closed. Three primary problems with international adoptions from Guatemala have been identified: (1) the potential and actual exploitation of Guatemalan birth mothers; (2) the imperialism inherent in the adoption of children from developing nations by citizens from developed nations like the United States; (3) the all too common alienation of the adopted child from his or her language and culture of origin (Larsen; Noonan; Wheeler). The purpose of this chapter is to propose the use of new digital literacies, supported by electronic social media, as a way to forge relationships among Guatemalan birth mothers, Guatemalan foster mothers, and U.S. adoptive mothers in order to minimize these kinds of problems. The assumption is that if birth mothers, foster mothers, and adoptive mothers are able to communicate with each other to the extent that each is comfortable and able, there will be more assurance that birth mothers are not being exploited but rather are acting on their own free will, adoptive mothers are not acting out of arrogance or ignorance but rather out of concern and understanding, and adopted children have a greater and more authentic connection to their language and culture of origin. After a brief review of the problems listed above, drawing on my own adoption experience, the theoretical work of Maria Lugones, and published interviews with Guatemalan foster parents, I propose ways in which digital literacies and the use of electronic social media might be used to foster loving relationships among birth, foster, and adoptive mothers involved in Guatemalan-U.S. adoptions.

PRIMARY ISSUES IN GUATEMALAN-U.S. INTERNATIONAL ADOPTIONS

The first, and probably most important, problem with Guatemalan-U.S. adoptions up until the time they were discontinued was the potential and actual coercion and exploitation of Guatemalan birth mothers in the efforts to meet the demands of adoptive parents in the United States for Guatemalan children available for adoption. Articles like "Did I Steal my Daughter?" (Larsen) and books like *Between Light and Shadow: A Guatemalan Girl's Journey through Adoption* (Wheeler) recount incidents of adoptive families in the U.S. who track down their adopted child's birth mother only to find that the mother felt coerced into and conflicted about giving the child up for adoption. Given that 60 percent of Guatemalans live in poverty and the same percentage or greater of indigenous Mayan women (where many adopted children come from in Guatemala) are illiterate, that birth control is not permitted, and that the machismo culture discourages men from raising children who are not their own, birth mothers in Guatemala are extremely vulnerable to such coercion and exploitation. In *Between Light and Shadow*, Wheeler describes the role of adoption intermediaries, also called *jaladoras* from the Spanish verb *jalar* meaning "to grab," which was to find desperate pregnant women and aggressively recruit them to give up their children for adoption (8).

The second problem identified with Guatemalan-U.S. adoptions is the inherent imperialism of adoptive parents from the United States traveling to Guatemala, which is a poverty-stricken, wartorn, developing nation, to adopt children and take them back to the United States to be raised as their own. In "Adoption and the Guatemalan Journey to American Parenthood," Emily J. Noonan recounts comments on the support listservs for adoptive parents that express this imperialism and arrogance. In one post, a woman states, "As our journey comes to [a] close in the next two weeks when we travel to bring our son home, much of my heart and future life experiences are now tied to a country I could hardly locate on a map two years ago" (308). While in Guatemala, adoptive parents from the United States often stay in commercial hotel chains, like the Marriott or the Radisson, and usually get little feel for authentic Guatemalan life. Moreover, in general, the people of Guatemala seem to resent the presence of adoptive parents and chafe at their reason for being in the country. When visiting Guatemala City to pick up my son, if the expressions on the faces of the people in the street weren't enough to convey their contempt for a White American couple with a nine-month-old Guatemalan baby, the graffiti on the wall of a city building, "Yankee, go home!" was.

The third major problem identified with Guatemalan-U.S. adoptions is that children who are adopted from Guatemala are often radically stripped of their language and culture of origin. Such children become North Americans in citizenship, language, and culture. They often do not learn Spanish much less the Mayan dialects from their places of birth. To be fair, education provided to adoptive parents in the U.S. throughout the adoption process stresses the importance of teaching children about the culture of their birth countries, and adoptive parents often try to comply; however, these attempts are often limited to Culture Camps in the U.S. that provide intense immersion in the culture of origin (Wide Horizons for Children) or locally accessible "international" festivals. These experiences are often forced and artificial or woefully incomplete.

While it's easy to see how all of these problems are inextricably related, together they create a picture of Guatemalan-U.S. adoption as a constellation of stereotypes involved in a business transaction, which can then be used to support opposition to international adoptions between Guatemala and the United States. These stereotypes include the three different mothers involved in the process: (1) the married, wealthy, privileged, arrogant, ignorant, self-serving adoptive mother from the United States who is buying what she can't have biologically; (2) the greedy, "grabbing," culturally traitorous, self-serving foster mother in Guatemala; and (3) the unwitting, unwilling Guatemalan birth mother victimized by poverty, illiteracy, fundamentalism, sexism, and imperialism. With little to no communication between the adoptive mother, the foster mother, and the birth mother, these may be the best composite personality profiles that can be put together based on the facts. Nevertheless, my personal experience does not support these stereotypes, and I would venture to say that if more were known about the individual mothers—birth, foster, and adoptive—most adoptive situations would not support these stereotypes. Even more importantly, if there were communication among these different mothers, the problems listed above, i.e., coercion and exploitation of the birth mother, imperialism on the part of the adoptive mother, and the loss to the child of his or her birth culture, could be minimized if not eliminated, thereby benefitting not only the mothers but even more importantly the child who has been the object of each mother's love and care.

ADOPTION AND DIGITAL LITERACIES: MY EXPERIENCE

At the time of the adoption of my son, I was 43 years old. I was not wealthy. I was unmarried, although I was in a committed relationship. I was no longer able to biologically reproduce but even when I was able I was indifferent concerning the choice of adopting children or having them biologically. I felt no social pressure to have a child. In fact, it was more the opposite. What I did feel was this inexpressible, unexplainable pull toward adopting internationally. I would search the internet for international adoption agencies. Then, I would dismiss the idea as too expensive, too much work, or too intimidating. The next day I would be back on the internet again figuring out how I could pull it off. Finally, in August of 2006, I applied to a particular adoption agency, Families Thru International Adoption (FTIA). After the most intense scrutiny I've ever experienced, reams of paperwork, and approval by two different nation's governments, I was able to pick up my son in Guatemala in October of 2007. Based on some of the descriptions in the articles and essays by opponents of Guatemalan-U.S. adoption, one might picture clumsy, arrogant Americans striding through the streets of Guatemala City with their camera equipment and baby supplies, oblivious or even rude to the Guatemalans who live there. This was not me. Although I was excited to meet my son, I was also terrified. The agency had given me his foster mother's phone number but I only called once the entire nine months she had him because I was shy and intimidated about meeting new people at all, not to mention one who was taking care of my as-of-yet unmet child.

When I met my son's foster mother, I realized that my shyness and intimidation were misplaced. She was as little like the stereotype of the intermediaries in Guatemalan adoptions as I was like the stereotype of the U.S. adoptive parent. She was crying when she dropped him off and asked if she could come back for breakfast our last day at the hotel. She had brought all of the clothes he had been wearing at that age even though she wasn't expected to as the agency said she might keep them for future foster children. She had hand-written a letter that was six pages long on both sides with all of the benchmarks of my son's development while he was with her, including turning over, standing with help, new teeth, when they received packages from us, etc. My son could not have been more loved or cared for. He was healthy and happy. His foster mother continues to call from Guatemala to the United States every year to wish him a happy birthday.

I know very little about my son's birth mother. I have one picture from one of the two DNA tests that the U.S. Embassy required in order to prove that she was in fact his biological mother. Other than that she is a mystery, a secret to my son that I may never know. She is the ghostly presence in the movement of his wrists and the shape of his ankles. She is the origin of the facial expressions that he shares with his biological half-brother who was adopted by another family in our state. She is the two seconds of silence when my four-year-old son asks where he came from or if he came out of my "belly." I began the process of searching for her through an agent recommended on the post-adoption Guatemalan listserv while writing this chapter; however, after his description of the delicacy of the situation for her and much deliberation, I decided not to go forward with the search. Instead, as a kind of subconscious substitute, I decided that my son and I would sponsor a little boy his age from his area of Guatemala to go to pre-school through a charitable organization called Mayan Families. Mayan Families also facilitates donations to the boy's family. That way my son would have a connection to his area of Guatemala and we would be able to help some people there even if they weren't my son's birth family.

The adoption agency that facilitated the adoption of my son was wonderful. The entire process took a little over a year. FTIA made great use of electronic interactive and social media throughout the process. As an adoptive parent I had password access to a webpage called "My FTIA." Every bureaucratic step in the process of our specific adoption was recorded here as it happened. Thus, it was very easy to track the process of the adoption and to tell where the process got delayed when it did and who to contact. When I received the referral of my son, FTIA sent me pictures of him via the internet, and they continued to send monthly pictures and measurement updates by email throughout the adoption process. They also sent an initial referral package by postal mail with pictures, contact information for his foster mother, a questionnaire completed by his birth mother, and his birth mother's identification information.

FTIA set up pre- and post-adoption listservs so that prospective and actual adoptive families could communicate with each other. In this way, we were able to identify and connect with the prospective adoptive parents of the little girl who was the only other child with my son in his foster home. My son's foster-sister and her adoptive family live in the state adjacent to ours. We have been able to get the two children together a number of times here in the United States, most recently for their birthdays. FTIA also maintains an electronic sibling registry with Yahoo, and through this we were able to identify and connect with my son's biological half-brother. Once you become a member of the sibling registry group, you must enter the first name and enough of the last name of your child's birth mother to be recognizable to those who would know it but not to those who wouldn't. Only having done this are you then able to search the registry for other adoptive parents whose child might have the same birth mother. We were lucky and found a match right here in our own state. My son's biological half-brother is a year older than him. Once we all met in person, we were able to verify the match through the answers on their birth mother's questionnaires. We try to get the boys together as often as possible. I like to joke that between my son's foster sister and half-brother he has more connections in the United States than I do, but I am exceedingly grateful that these aspects of his culture of origin have accompanied him to his new home in the U.S. as part of a uniquely blended but real and existing community.

THEORETICAL SOLUTIONS: LOVING MOTHERS

In "Playfulness, 'World'-Traveling, and Loving Perception," Maria Lugones distinguishes the arrogant eye from the loving eye. Basically, she claims that when someone perceives another arrogantly, they view that other in terms of how he or she meets their needs and they are unable to imagine a world in which that other person has dignity, value, and agency in their own right. Lugones claims that women of color are particularly adept at traveling between worlds where in one world they may have a great deal of value, dignity, and agency, and in the other, i.e., mainstream Anglo society, they may have very little. Lugones suggests as a social and political strategy that women of color use this talent to travel to each other's "worlds" in order to perceive each other with loving eyes, as opposed to arrogant ones (Lugones 77-100).

The impetus behind this chapter is the desire that the different mothers involved in Guatemalan-U.S. adoptions—birth, foster, and adoptive mothers—be able to travel to each other's "worlds" with love. Interviews, blogs, and listservs show that these different kinds of mothers are socially isolated in different ways, and each might benefit from interaction with the others. For example, Emily Noonan argues that, unlike birth mothers in the United States, the "baby project" for adoptive mothers in Guatemalan-U.S. adoptions, i.e., "the process of obtaining a child and becoming a mother," includes, "the bureaucratic process and paperwork, bonding with the child (as a non-specific person, or as a specific person through photos and videos), the discussions they engage in with family, friends, and other adoptive parents, and all experiences of travel to Guatemala" (305).

Likewise, in a study based on interviews with 16 Guatemalan foster mothers and 1 foster father, Gibbons et al., note, "Little is known about this group of caregivers. Guatemalan foster parents keep a low profile due to rumors of baby stealing that fuel negative perceptions of international adoption within the general population of Guatemala" (63). Guatemalan foster parents reported feeling stigmatized for their role as foster parents and being disparaged for it when it was discovered (67). These interviews also reflect the investment that foster mothers make in the children that they foster. One foster mother claimed that she saw herself as a "third mother," and many expressed grief at giving up the child to the adoptive parent(s) once the adoption process was complete. Others, when asked how to improve the international adoption process, suggested "to increase communication between the foster and adoptive parents, to insist that the adoptive parents visit the child during the process, and to provide emotional support for the adoptive parents, child, and foster parents" (68).

Finally, when asked about whether birth mothers would try to hide the adoption from their families and the father of the child, 79 percent of the foster parents stated that "mothers would hide or lie about the pregnancy and/or adoption. 'They lie ... they say that the baby died. In some cases they say they were stolen.'... A reason that participants gave for the mother hiding the birth from her own parents was that they would prevent the adoption and would raise the child themselves" (67). Foster parents also expressed mixed views on birth mothers. While some claimed that birth mothers' decisions to relinquish their children are selfless and based on the good of the child, they also described birth mothers as "irresponsible, deceitful, detached" (70) and believed that the birth mothers often saw the adoption as a business transaction. When asked if they thought birth mothers would want to maintain contact with the child after the adoption, 82 percent said that some mothers would not want contact with the child, 31 percent said contact would be desired but that the birth mothers wouldn't know how to connect with the child, and 25 percent reported that the birth mothers would expect that the child would return to them (67).

It is important to note, however, that these last statistics are based on Guatemalan foster parents' perceptions of Guatemalan birth mothers and might be influenced more by stereotypes than actual knowledge of the birth mothers' backgrounds and motivations. It seems that birth, foster, and adoptive mothers would benefit from having the option to understand one another better through travelling to each other's "worlds," and that loving relationships between them would be much more possible than within the current system. Even more importantly, the adopted child would benefit from this "world"-traveling among loving birth, foster, and adoptive mothers. The issue of the internationally adopted Guatemalan child being stripped of his or her language and culture of origin is motivated by a concern for the healthy formation of the child's subjective identity. Maria Lugones suggests that fragmented social groups create fragmented individuals. The various social groups which comprise mainstream culture in Guatemala and the United States that would characterize the birth, foster, and adoptive mothers in a Guatemalan-U.S. adoption according to the stereotypes above are bound to construct the adopted child's subjective identity as split, i.e., fragmented, between his or her culture of origin in Guatemala and mainstream American culture. Quoting Renato Rosaldo, Lugones claims that in the dominant mainstream American view, culture is "something that happens to other people," and "if it's moving it isn't cultural" (125). Thus, as an American, the child will be expected to have no culture; and, as a Guatemalan, the child will be expected to embody a reified, static, and dying "authentic" Guatemalan culture filtered through the mainstream American perception. Referring to Mexican/Americans, Lugones describes this "authentic" culture:

> The mythical portrait, therefore, has acquired a degree of reality that both justifies and obscures Anglo dominance. It makes one feel proud to be *Raza* because the portrait is heroic. It also makes one stilted, stiff, a cultural personage not quite sure of oneself, a pose, pure style, not quite at ease in one's own cultural skin, as if one did not know one's own culture, precisely because it is not one's own but a stereotype and because this authentic culture is not

quite a live culture: it is conceived by the Anglo as both static and dying. (136)

In contrast to the fragmentation of social groups and individuals, Lugones suggests a social strategy of resistance to oppression that she calls curdling-splitting or *mestizaje*. Curdling-splitting or *mestizaje* is the occupation of an "in-between" rather than an "either/or" position for both social groups and individuals. More specifically, Lugones calls for bringing the different intersecting aspects of one's social groups and oneself into the public discourse as a strategy of resistance against those social powers that strive to divide and conquer groups and individuals through fragmentation. Moreover, Lugones recommends that oppressed and/or marginalized social groups and individuals recognize the in-between or *mestizaje* in each other and form coalitions and connections. This could be a very effective strategy for birth mothers, foster mothers, and adoptive mothers in Guatemalan-U.S. adoptions against social powers and influences that keep them separated and fragmented. Lugones explains:

> A more solid ground (for thinking of others as "our own") because it is a more positive ground is the one that affirms the lack of constraint of our creativity that is at the center of curdling; that holds on to our own lack of script, to our being beings in the making; that might contain each other in the creative path, who don't discount but look forward to that possibility. (144)

Out of such creative affiliations among birth mothers, foster mothers, and adoptive mothers might come interpretations of the Guatemalan-U.S. adoptive process that are more conducive to the healthy development of the adopted child's subjective identity. For example, as opposed to the mainstream view that adoptive parents from the U.S. "settle" for Guatemalan children in exchange for the convenience and efficiency of the adoption process, the foster mothers interviewed by Gibbons et al. suggest that American adoptive parents actually prefer Guatemalan children because of their "'lineage,' noting a desire for dark-skinned children or reflecting that Guatemalan people are 'kinder,' 'stronger,' or 'smarter' people" (67). This view of U.S. adoptive parents was at times compared to local racial attitudes toward the indigenous people in Guatemala. One foster mother stated, "' [Adoptive parents] aren't prejudiced against skin color; here many people are prejudiced'" (69). Likewise, in contrast to the mainstream view that Guatemalan birth mothers are coerced or exploited into *relinquishing* their children for U.S. adoptions, most Guatemalan mothers use the verb *regular* meaning "to gift," thereby reflecting generosity on the part of the birth mothers both toward U.S. adoptive parents and toward their children who they believe will have a better future in terms of material wealth and improved education (Gibbons et al. 74, 67).

In describing the efficacy of curdling-splitting for social groups and individuals, Lugones also describes the development of a healthy, culturally hybridized, subjective identity on the part of a child adopted from Guatemala by U.S. parents:

> Ambiguous, neither this nor that, unrestrained by the logic of this and the logic of that, and thus its course not mapped, traced already in movements, words, relations, structures, institutions; not rehearsed over and over into submission, containment, subordination, asceticism—we can affirm the positive side of our being threatening as ambiguous. If it is ambiguous it is threatening because it is creative, changing, defiant of norms meant to subdue it. (144)

PRACTICAL SOLUTIONS: DIGITAL LITERACIES

I have argued that rich, dynamic relationships among birth mothers, foster mothers, and adoptive mothers in Guatemalan-U.S. adoptions are beneficial for the mothers, both in terms of assuaging the loneliness and social isolation of individual women in each of these groups and in terms of minimizing coercion/exploitation and imperialism within the adoption process. I've also argued that rich, dynamic relationships among birth, foster, and adoptive mothers are good for the adopted child in terms of contributing to the development of a healthy subjective identity. In what follows, I suggest ways in which digital literacies supported by electronic social and interactive media might serve as means for establishing and maintaining such relationships. Technologically speaking, we have far surpassed the days when the only hope birth mothers and their adoptive children had of reuniting was by means of hand-written or typed letters left in a file cabinet at the adopting institution. With the current state of digital literacies and the electronic media that support them, it seems feasible to develop a more efficient and effective system whereby birth mothers, foster mothers, and adoptive mothers could find each other and build the kinds of rich, dynamic, loving relationships that would diminish opportunities for exploitation, minimize the arrogance of imperialism, and foster a healthy subjective identity, culturally and otherwise, on the part of the child.

Such a system might combine certain aspects of the Yahoo Guatemalan Sibling Registry, Facebook, and the Mayan Families website into an accessible, secure, centrally moderated and maintained, electronic database and social network. In order to log on to the system, each mother would have to use the *cédula* number of either the Guatemalan birth mother or the Guatemalan foster mother. The *cédula* is the official identification card issued by the Guatemalan government; and, at least in my experience, the *cédula* numbers of both my son's birth mother and his foster mother were given to me in the packet of information I received with his referral. Once in the system, each mother would be required to enter enough of the birth name of the child that the other two mothers would recognize it but not so much that anyone else would. Once each mother has entered the birth name of the adopted child, she would be assigned an ID number that would be listed with the name of the child. This ID number would be linked to a personal webpage where she could put as much or as little information as she chose. Only after this linked information was entered into the database would she be able to search the database for the other two mothers' information. When a potential match was discovered, the mother would send a "friend" request to the other possible mother, which that mother could accept or decline upon having viewed the first mother's personal webpage. Once the "friend" request has been accepted, the mothers can begin to build and nurture a rich, dynamic, and loving relationship, sharing photographs of their families (including the adopted child), developmental landmarks, and personal updates. For each adopted child's birth name, additional precautions would need to be taken to verify the identities of the three mothers and anyone else authorized to access the web pages for that child.

The website of Mayan Families, a small non-profit organization serving indigenous and poor people in Guatemala for the past 25 years, might provide a model for the proposed system. Mayan Families is a charitable organization that was started by Patricia Mort, Sharon Smart-Pogue, and Dwight Pogue, all of whom live and work in the Highlands of Guatemala in the Lake Atitlan region. The mission of Mayan Families is to provide "opportunities and assistance to the indigenous and impoverished people of Guatemala, through education and community development programs" (Mayan Families). Mayan Families operates a wide variety of programs for the families in their service region including providing egg-laying hens, water filters, holiday food baskets, and family and student sponsorships. Concerning the student sponsorships, each student has a personal webpage that their sponsor can access with a user name, password, and student ID number. These student web pages are regularly updated by Mayan Families staff with the students' photographs and news. The Mayan Families website allows sponsors to donate money and gifts electronically to their students and their families. Sponsors are also able to send letters by email or postal service to their students, which are translated and read by Mayan Families staff, and to visit their sponsored students and their families by previous arrangement.

Many adoptive parents of Guatemalan children in the United States would like to donate money and provide support for their adopted children's birth families in Guatemala. With the incorporation of the security measures described above, a system and website similar to that of Mayan Families could be developed for birth mothers, foster mothers, and adoptive mothers of Guatemalan-U.S. adoptions. Such a system would provide translation services, security and technical support to moderate and maintain the website, and opportunities for adoptive mothers/families to contribute financial and material resources to the birth mothers/families of their adopted Guatemalan children. Moreover, in some cases emails, letters, and visits to their birth families in Guatemala might provide a way for adopted Guatemalan children to maintain contact with their families and cultures of origin. Of course, participation at every level would be voluntary for all of the mothers involved.

DISCUSSION

This is not to suggest that such a system will create a seamless literacy between the three mothers. Such a multicultural, multilingual, multi-media, multi-modal context fraught with power relations will challenge and encourage each woman to stretch beyond her current literacy competencies, always taking into account the underlying question of "'whose literacies' are dominant and whose are marginalized or resistant" (Street 77).

First, computers and the internet might be seen as a context for literacies that originated outside of the rural Guatemalan birth mothers' local cultural context and, hence, risk assimilating them into a field of power relations characterized by multiple conflicting interests and distant, more "global," agendas. In spite of this, and in spite of the consolidating nature of the technologies themselves, it is still possible, and in fact necessary, that rural Guatemalans "take hold of these new practices and adapt them to local circumstances" for their own empowerment (Street 80). Between 2000 and 2010, internet usage in Guatemala increased steadily and dramatically from 0.6 percent of the population to 16.8 percent (Internet World Stats). According to *AntiguaDailyPhoto.com*, 67 percent of the population has access to the internet through work, restaurants with Wi-Fi, public Wi-Fi areas, cellular telephones and Internet cafes; and by 2012, it is predicted that 90 percent of the population will have access (Giron 7). Commentators on the article containing these statistics expressed the desire that internet access in public places in the U.S. be as common and effective as it is in Guatemala. Moreover, organizations such as Roots and Wings, International are working to provide computer literacy skills to impoverished youth in rural Guatemala (Roots and Wings).

Rudy Giron cites *el Periodico: La Guerra digital contra la pobreza*: "Extreme poverty is almost synonym of extreme isolation, especially in rural areas. But cellular telephones and wireless Internet access finally put an end to isolation and, therefore, these will end up being the transforming technologies of economic development in our time" (7).

Second, the fact that there will be several languages at play within the proposed system—Mayan dialects, Spanish, and English—will require each woman to take extra steps to understand the languages of the other mothers in certain situations, whether through consulting a human or software translator or picking up the rudiments of the other languages oneself. It is hoped that this dynamic, multilingual, social process will mirror and nurture the child's comfort and familiarity with multiple languages, and hence, contribute to his or her healthy subjective development. As Gloria Anzaldúa states in "How to Tame a Wild Tongue":

> [I]f you really want to hurt me, talk badly about my language. Ethnic identity is twin skin to linguistic identity—I am my language. Until I can take pride in my language, I cannot take pride in myself. Until I can accept as legitimate Chicano Texas Spanish, Tex-Mex and all the other languages I speak, I cannot accept the legitimacy of myself. Until I am free to write bilingually and to switch codes without having to translate, while I still have to speak English or Spanish when I would rather speak Spanglish, and as long as I have to accommodate the English speakers rather than having them accommodate me, my tongue will be illegitimate. (81)

Finally, such a multimodal, multi-media system will challenge and encourage each woman to develop her visual literacy competencies. Photographs, by their very nature, raise questions of meaning and interpretation, including questions concerning what is happening outside of the frame. These questions will be compounded and complicated for the mothers involved by their relative lack of familiarity with the cultural contexts and languages of the others. Such questions might include: 1) How are the people in the photo feeling? 2) What are the people around them doing? 3) What does the photo indicate about the characteristics and conditions of the individuals' lives? 4) Where was the photo taken? 5) Is the person who sent the photo (or took it) trying directly or indirectly to express something to me by its means?

In spite of, and in fact because of, the discontinuities and glitches, i.e., the lack of seamlessness and transparency in the literacies involved in the proposed system, it is meant to be a context in which the three mothers involved in a Guatemalan-United States adoption can form loving relationships based on understanding which resist the power relations which have kept all of the mothers isolated from each other, exploited Guatemalan birth mothers, and subjected U.S. adoptive mothers to an arrogance based on ignorance and stereotypes. Echoing Lugones, Brian Street cites Lesley Bartlett and Dorothy Holland's proposal of the notion of "figured worlds." Bartlett and Holland define a figured world as "a socially produced and culturally constructed realm of interpretation" (Bartlett and Holland cited in Street 82). The system proposed in this chapter is meant to be a space where the figured "worlds" of experiences and literacies of birth mothers, foster mothers, and adoptive mothers can interact dynamically with one another in order to empower the participating mothers and contribute to the healthy subjective development of the adopted child.

Also echoing Lugones' advocacy of the political efficacy of the *mestizaje,* Street explains, "The result of local-global encounters around literacy is always a new hybrid rather than a single essentialized version of either." The focus of literacy studies should be on these "hybrid literacy practices" rather than "either romanticizing the local or conceding the dominant privileging of the supposed global" (Street 80). While there is not space to pursue this topic in any detail in this chapter, should the proposed system actually be implemented a potentially productive means to measure its effectiveness would be Nancy Hornberger's continua model of biliteracy. The continua model of biliteracy is a theoretical framework consisting of four nested sets of three intersecting continua each, where the sets represent the contexts (continua include micro/macro, oral/literate, bi- or multi-lingual/monolingual); development (reception/production, oral/written, first language/second language); content (minority/majority, vernacular/literary, contextualized/decontextualized); and media (simultaneous /successive exposure, dissimilar/similar structures, divergent/convergent scripts) of biliteracy. The advantages of this model are its ability to capture the fluidity and infiniteness of movement along each continuum; its recognition of the interrelationships and intersections among the different continua within and among the individual sets; and its challenge to the "power weighting" or privileging of one end or the other of the continua (e.g., written over oral, literary over vernacular, majority over minority, etc.) by the traditional hierarchical binary models that have historically informed policies and practices surrounding biliteracy (Hornberger 156-159).

CONCLUSION

Rich, dynamic, loving relationships among birth mothers, foster mothers, and adoptive mothers in Guatemalan-U.S. adoptions, and the digital literacies that could support them, require openness within international adoptions. The United Nations Hague Convention on Protection of Children and Co-operation in Respect of Intercountry Adoption of 1993 contains mixed messages concerning openness in international adoptions. Article 30 states that competent authorities in a contracting state will maintain records of the identity of the adoptive child's birth parents and medical history and will ensure that the child or his or her representative has access to them to the extent allowed by state law. Article 31, however, states that without prejudice to Article 30, personal information gathered for the purposes of the adoption process, e.g., "information about his or her identity, adoptability, background, social environment, family history, medical history including that of the child's family, and any special needs of the child" will be used "only for the purposes for which they were gathered or transmitted" (Hague Convention). In spite of the mixed messages, one of the most prominent international adoption agencies in the U.S., Children's Home Society and Family Services of Minnesota, has shifted to advocating for openness in international adoption and has begun offering services in birth family searches (Larsen 3). In allowing the creation of relationships among the mothers who love the adopted child, such openness contains the potential for minimizing the risks of exploitation, discouraging the arrogance of imperialism, and contributing to the development of a healthy subjective sense of identity on the part of the child, all of which are primary goals of the Hague Convention.

WORKS CITED

Anzaldúa, Gloria. *Borderlands=La Frontera: The New Mestiza.* San Francisco: Aunt Lute Books, 1999. Print.
Bartlett, Lesley, and Dorothy Holland. "Theorizing the Space of Literacy Practices." *Ways of Knowing.* 2.1 (2002): 10-22.
Families Thru International Adoption. Web. 26 Oct. 2011.
Gibbons, Judith L., Samantha L. Wilson, and Alicia M. Schnell. "Foster Parents as a Critical Link and Resource in International Adoptions from Guatemala." *Adoption Quarterly* 12 (2009): 59-77. Print.
Giron, Rudy. "Internet Access in Every Corner of Guatemala." AntiguaDailyPhoto.com. 17 Feb 2009: 6-12. Web. 22 May. 2012.
Guatemala Adopt Sibling Registry. Web. 26 Oct. 2011.
"Guatemala." *Internet World Stats: Usage and Population Statistics.* Web. 21 May 2012.
Hague Conference. Hague Conference on International Law: Final Act of the 17th Session, including the Convention on Protection of Children and Co-operation in Respect of Intercountry Adoption. *International Legal Materials* 32 (1993): 1134-1146. Print.
Hornberger, Nancy H. "The Continua of Biliteracy and the Bilingual Educator: Educational Linguistics in Practice." *Bilingual Education and Bilingualism.* 7.2&3 (2004): 155-171. Web. 23 May 2012.
Larsen, Elizabeth. "Did I Steal My Daughter?" *Mother Jones* 32.6 (2007): 52-59. Web. 23 Feb. 2011.
Lugones, Maria. *Pilgrimages/Peregrinajes: Theorizing Coalition against Multiple Oppressions.* Lanham: Roman & Littlefield, 2003. Print.
Mayan Families. Web. 26 Oct. 2011.
Noonan, Emily J. "Adoption and the Guatemalan Journey to

American Parenthood." *Childhood* 14.3 (2007): 301-319. Web. 7 February 2011.

Roots and Wings, International. Web. 21 May 2012.

Street, Brian. "What's 'New' in New Literacy Studies? Critical Approaches to Literacy in Theory and Practice." *Current Issues in Comparative Education.* 5.2 (2003): 77-91. Web. 21 May 2012.

Wheeler, Jacob. *Between Light and Shadow: A Guatemalan Girl's Journey through Adoption.* Lincoln: University of Nebraska Press, 2011. Print.

Wide Horizons for Children: Post Adoption Support and Education. Web. 21 May 2012.

3.
"We Can Get Old or We Can Get Dead"

Celebrating Fifteen Years of the Midwifery Coalition of Nova Scotia's Newsletter

ERIN HEMMENS

Strewn over my kitchen table were papers, rulers, scissors, glue-sticks, photos and pens. I had just put the kids to bed and now it was time to pull the newsletter together. I liked this part. People in the community would send me stories of births, baby health articles, pregnancy tips and updates on the progress of midwifery as a regulated profession within our health system. I would type the articles at work during slow times having convinced my boss that it was his contribution to the Coalition. Now, it was time to piece them together on an 18 x 11 paper. Cut, copy, paste: old style. (Holwerda)[1]

FROM 1986 TO 2001, the Midwifery Coalition of Nova Scotia (MCNS) published a quarterly newsletter that served as the glue for a small but determined group of midwives and midwifery advocates. The newsletter explored and reported on the political climate surrounding midwifery in Nova Scotia and abroad, while providing a key forum for mothers from around the province to connect, share stories, and learn from one another's experiences of accessing this particular type of care.

> *This was the time before email and Google and we wanted to share our message. We wanted midwifery to be accepted as a profession and we needed midwives beside us as we birthed our babies. We were a group of people, women mostly, who wanted to give birth in non-hospital settings with support to honour the process of birth in warm and caring environments. It was a time when midwives were scarce, illegal and considered very counter culture. We decided to start an organization called the Midwifery Coalition of Nova Scotia to help bring these dreams to fruition. The MCNS felt by writing a newsletter that we could familiarize our community and make them more comfortable with the possibility of midwives and consequently bring more support to our cause.* (Holwerda)

The first edition of the newsletter in the winter of 1986 was mailed to MCNS members across the province. It featured hand-drawn bubble-lettered headings, a roughly sketched logo of two women, typed articles, and a picture of the newly-elected inaugural board of directors of the MCNS. The articles were written largely by the women featured in that lone photograph and covered topics ranging from long-distance studying to become a midwife, to how to avoid an episiotomy, to an update on the criminal trial of two Vancouver midwives. In and amongst the articles were inspiring quotes on being a mother, being an activist, and the consequences of not standing up for what you believe in.

Over the years, the newsletter changed; it became more polished and less homespun. It began to focus more on the political side of getting midwifery recognized and integrated into the health system and left fewer spaces for the rabble-rousing quotes that marked the early editions. The newsletter mirrored the evolution of midwifery in Nova Scotia as it inched closer every year to becoming a regulated and funded health profession. Along the way it transitioned from reporting on events in Vancouver to reporting on meetings with Ministers of Health and government committees tasked with looking at maternity care in the province. Midwifery was moving along in Nova Scotia, and the newsletter was there to report on its progress to the broader community.

> *Being a part of this movement for change was exciting and empowering for many of us. Alongside our new roles of mothering we discovered skills of leadership and social networking, newsletter creating and policy making.* (Holwerda)

The newsletter functioned as a rallying point for the community—a place to celebrate midwifery, talk politics, and connect with others who shared the vision of midwives working within the health system. Amidst the reporting, the sharing of stories, and the community organizing, the creators of the MCNS newsletter transformed into writers, editors, political pundits, artists, activists, and experts, ultimately recognizing and honoring the deep connection between motherhood and social change.

This chapter sets out to explore the content, context, and evolution of the MCNS newsletter throughout the fifteen years that it was in print. It will reflect on the role the publication played in bringing women's thoughts, ideas, and stories into the public and political arena and how, through that medium, a small group of women in Nova Scotia challenged dominant discourses around childbirth and mothering and engaged a province in dialogue around an agenda set by women and families.

EDUCATE, INSPIRE, ORGANIZE, AND POLITICIZE

Within the pages of the MCNS newsletter, women used words and stories to challenge the maternity system that did not serve them, and to celebrate the ways in which midwifery did. Specifically, they used the content of the newsletter to educate, inspire, organize, and politicize midwifery.

One of the key ways that the newsletter served to educate the public was through the "Ask the Midwife" column. In this section, women from the community were encouraged to write in with their questions and have them answered, in print, by a local midwife. Through this column, women learned of anemia in pregnancy, delayed umbilical cord clamping, group B strep, turning posterior babies, planning for an intervention-free birth, hypertension in pregnancy, weight loss in newborns, birth plans, and miscarriage from a midwifery perspective. Similarly, "The Nursery," a column devoted to answering breastfeeding questions, provided mothers with expert advice from local midwives on issues such as cracked nipples, milk supply, birth control methods, and safe herbs. By providing answers from a midwifery perspective, "Ask the Midwife" and "The Nursery" went deeper than simply answering questions about childbearing—they served to highlight the midwifery model of care and reinforce the unique skill set of midwives in Nova Scotia.

Aside from the regular columns, each edition of the MCNS newsletter featured editorials and thought-provoking articles that further served to educate: "Avoiding Episiotomy" (Winter 1986), "Protecting the Normal Birth" (Spring 1988), "Visualization, What Is It?" (Spring 1990), "Mother, Baby and Fibroid–All Doing Well" (Spring 1992), "Women and AIDS" (Autumn 1992), "Women's Spirit Rising with Hopes of Province's Newest Midwife" (Spring 1993), "Following the Mother to Her Choice of Birthplace" (Autumn 1993), "Midwifery and Health Reform" (Winter 1995), "Ten Reasons Why We Need Midwifery in Nova Scotia" (June 1996), "Community Health Boards and the MCNS" (Winter 1997), "The Diaper Debate" (Winter 1998), "Is Homebirth Safe?" (December 1999), and "Katsi Cook, Aboriginal Midwife" (Winter 2001), among many others.

News articles related to midwifery from other Canadian provinces were also featured, as were reports and updates on any movement around midwifery in Nova Scotia. In all, the MCNS newsletter acted as an educational tool for both midwifery supporters and those with just a passing interest. It collated all relevant information on midwifery in Nova Scotia while providing personal connections to the practicing midwives and the families who supported them.

Alongside the educational/informational pieces, the MCNS newsletter served to inspire and organize the community. Feel-good pieces, small (and occasionally large) political victories, and wisdom from the ages were written up and shared as a way to reinforce the good, and necessary, work of the MCNS. Inspiring quotes figured prominently, particularly in the earlier editions. Given the uphill battles that faced the Coalition, perhaps Polly Spence Richardson's quote, published in the very first edition of the newsletter, best describes the philosophy that underlined the work of the MCNS: "We have two alternatives: we can get old or we can get dead. Sometimes fate intervenes and the choice is made for us. But the choice to live until we die is ours" (Richardson).

The newsletter served as a crucial organizational tool for the community throughout the years. Members of the Coalition were spread across Nova Scotia, from Yarmouth to Cape Breton, and the newsletter provided a rallying point and a place of connection for the geographically diverse group. Fundraising dinners, raffles, dances, auctions, and MCNS yard sales were all announced and reported on, and larger initiatives, such as political lobbying campaigns, were often managed through the newsletter. The newsletter also functioned as an educational and inspirational tool for those on the periphery of the community, devoting regular print space to outlining the objectives of the Coalition and explaining how interested individuals could get involved.

Embedded within all of the articles, announcements, editorials, and educational pieces was the understanding that midwifery is, at heart, a political issue. Recognizing it as such, the writers of the MCNS newsletter embraced and explored the political nature of the push to regulate midwifery and devoted regular print space to political discussions. The earlier editions did this primarily by reporting on the political climate surrounding midwifery in other provinces and countries, while the later editions focused almost exclusively on the evolution of midwifery in Nova Scotia. Across the spectrum of fifteen years, through birth stories, editorials on current issues, and detailed instructions on how to lobby governments, the MCNS newsletter politicized midwifery in a way that kept women and families at the centre of the movement.

THE POWER OF STORY

To experience the birth of a child is to participate in the drama of creation. Having experienced it we will never be the same. No child, no universe, no mountain, sea or poem

> *was ever born without great labour, yet when that labour's done there exists a thing of beauty with a life all its own. To experience the birth of a child is to witness the promise of tomorrow. Our hopes and dreams are all renewed by the child who rests peacefully, safe within our arms.* (Duda)

Serving as a counterpoint to the political aspects of pushing for regulated midwifery, the newsletter featured birth stories of women who had used midwives in Nova Scotia.

> *To me, the birth stories were the most important thing to share—each was unique and very personal, yet also universal. They were engaging, and also instructive. They showed people that we can each make choices and create birth experiences that reflect who we are and what we believe in.* (Hammett Vaughan)

The birth stories gave voice to many of the ideals that united the mothers/writers while illuminating the deeply personal nature of their involvement with the midwifery movement. Homebirth, embracing birth as a family and sometimes community event, and the trusting, caring relationship between mother and midwife punctuated the birth stories and demonstrated some of the reasons why the mothers/writers chose to become involved in fighting for midwifery.

> *Then the baby's head—a little hand there, too, and Charlene working it out. "Now reach down, reach down and get your baby." My hands brushing under his arms, his little chest so wet and warm as I lifted him and he slithered out of me and Charlene's hands guiding him to my belly. Let me never forget those precious moments. The feelings of love, pride, joy ... the wonder of it all.* ("Asher's Birth Story")

Story is also shared through images in the MCNS newsletter. Photographs of birth, moms and midwives, and families gathered around the newborn baby and mother figure prominently in nearly every edition. The cover image of Fall 1994 features a newborn family immersed in a deep tub of water, the mother gazing adoringly at the babe, the father peering over the mom's shoulder, and the midwife's hands helping to support the baby's head. Reprinted images, block prints, and hand-drawn sketches of birth are also featured as representations of the story(ies) of birth.

HISTORY, CONTEXT, AND EVOLUTION

The 1990s saw great strides in the movement to regulate midwifery across Canada. In 1991, both Quebec, with Bill 4, the law that authorized the evaluation of the practice of midwifery through a pilot project, and Ontario, with the Midwifery Act, which legalized the profession, led the country in recognizing and regulating midwifery, followed by Alberta and British Columbia in 1994 and 1995 respectively.

At home in Nova Scotia, 1995 marked a major victory for the MCNS and other midwifery supporters with the decision to exclude the phrase "the management of pregnancy and parturition" in the provincial *Medical Act*. This decision protected midwives from charges of practicing medicine without a license while providing midwifery services, but perhaps more importantly, it recognized the expert care of pregnancy, birth, and postpartum that lay outside of the formal medical establishment. The victory was a major milestone for midwives and the women who employed them. However, it may have been particularly sweet for the women of the Midwifery Coalition, an organization that was founded on the public and financial support of two local midwives who were charged with criminal negligence causing bodily harm following the homebirth of a baby in Halifax in 1983. The charges were dismissed following a preliminary hearing that lasted three days; however, the vulnerability of midwives to litigation while supporting families lit the fire of resistance in the community and arguably birthed the modern midwifery movement in Nova Scotia.

Invigorated by success, spring 1995 saw the MCNS newsletter renamed *Midwifery Now!*, and as the new title suggested, was focused primarily on the political push to have midwifery recognized within the Nova Scotia health system. The articles reflected less on the feel-good aspects of midwifery care and more on the work to be done to make midwifery available to more families. The appearance of the newsletter also changed at this time, shifting from a homespun look to a polished, professional one, complete with a brand-new logo of a mother holding a babe in one arm and flexing the other in a show of strength.

As perceptions of midwifery began to shift across the country and within Nova Scotia, the women behind the MCNS and *Midwifery Now!* were undergoing their own evolution. MCNS board members went from publishing birth stories and organizing fundraisers (although these were still important parts of their work) to becoming major political players in the push to regulate midwifery in Nova Scotia. In 1997, the MCNS lobbied and succeeded in placing a consumer representative on a committee tasked with reviewing midwifery in the province. Following the release of the committee's report, "The Potential for Midwifery in Nova Scotia," the MCNS presented, in *Midwifery Now!*, in the mainstream media, and to the Minister of Health, a detailed critique of its findings. When another committee was struck a year later, this one to look at the details of implementing midwifery in Nova Scotia, the MCNS once again lobbied for and succeeded in attaining a seat at the table. After over a decade of being on the fringes, the women of the Midwifery Coalition were finally gaining recognition as significant political voices. As Jan Catano, co-founder of the MCNS, often reflects, "for a small group of women, mostly young mothers, who volunteered their time and skills to fight for midwifery, we punched way, way above our weight" (Catano).

Along with the greater interest and deeper involvement in midwifery across the country, new issues emerged that complicated the objectives of the Midwifery Coalition. An article, "Dissent from Ontario," reprinted from *Special Delivery* and featured in the Spring 1995 issue, outlined the disappointment that many women and families were feeling following regulation of midwifery in that province: "In the midwifery movement itself, cracks were appearing long before the cheering stopped. My small misgivings, about the rigidity of the law, its criminal applications, and the academic exclusivity of the school, became a deep sense of betrayal and dismay as time went on" (Terpstra 4). In Nova Scotia, the MCNS response to "The Potential for Midwifery in Nova Scotia," printed in the Fall 1997 edition of *Midwifery Now!*, outlined the board's disappointment with both the process and the findings of the report. Despite having a seat at the table and a voice in the discussions, the MCNS felt increasingly marginalized as their concerns with the direction of the report were repeatedly dismissed. Eventually, those involved were forced to question whether they had indeed succeeded in gaining credibility with the powers that be, or whether the MCNS presence in the discussions were merely a political tactic to allow the government to claim that women and families were consulted on the issue. Amidst these difficult questions and situations, the MCNS used the pages of *Midwifery Now!* to critically engage with the complex issues and openly share their perspectives.

Reflecting the major changes in the practice and politics of midwifery throughout the 1990s, *Midwifery Now!* shifted both its look and its reporting style to mirror the broader shifts happening in the cultural perception of midwives and midwifery. The newsletter devoted more print space to political debates, reporting on and responding to government decisions on midwifery in the province, and engaging more and more families in the push to regulate the profession. At the same time as the newsletter underwent changes, the voice of the MCNS grew louder: Women's perspectives were moving from the pages of *Midwifery Now!* and into the political arena that would eventually decide on the value of midwifery in the provincial health care system.

REFLECTION

The MCNS newsletter provided its creators with an outlet for expression on a topic that was at once deeply personal and highly political. The content of the newsletter mirrored this fine balance with intimate images and stories of birth cast alongside critical analyses of current practices and policies around maternal health.

> *Choosing to birth at home or having the care of midwives is a fundamental right and it was time to fight for it. We were taking back our bodies and bringing our innate intelligence to birthing. It felt like the medical model had*

veered off course over the years and we wanted to bring it back to serve us. We hoped the newsletter would help awaken people to that wisdom. (Holwerda)

Arguably the greatest achievement of the MCNS newsletter was that it brought women's voices into the mix. It challenged the dominant paradigm of birth as a medical event with stories, pictures, and poems that showed birth as empowering, raw, beautiful, gritty, and, above all else, a transformative event in the lives of mothers and families. Further, it created a forum through which discussions surrounding what was quickly becoming a hot topic in the landscape of Canadian health care remained entrenched in the thoughts, ideas, and experiences of the women who were most affected.

The newsletter became a rallying point for the community, propelling its creators and supporters into the political arena. As more and more women became involved, and the collective voice of the MCNS grew, the organization gained political momentum and its members gained access into the world of policy-makers and politicians. This resulted in a remarkable revolution in which a small group of women from diverse backgrounds were meaningfully contributing to political agendas and policies. This coup did not take place overnight, however, and throughout the years that the MCNS fought to include women in the process of regulating midwifery, the creators and supporters of the newsletter gained political insight and skills; practical experience with community organizing, reporting, and writing; and lifelong relationships with women from all walks of life.

Ultimately, much scholarly analysis could be applied to what the creators of the MCNS newsletter accomplished throughout the fifteen years that it was in print. Theories of resistance to dominant discourses, authoritative knowledge, patriarchal medical practices, and embodied wisdom could all be woven throughout how and why the women fought for their vision of maternity care in Nova Scotia. In the end though, theory does not hold the same weight, or resonate as deeply, as the personal stories, intimate images, and concise, inspired political engagement that the newsletter became known for. What does resonate deeply is that women engaged in a fight for their right to birth how, where and with whomever they chose in attendance used the written word, *their* written words, to challenge the system that oppressed them. They wrote and shared stories and poetry, created art, and editorialized on an agenda that affected them deeply, and in doing so, they created change within the lives of individual women and influenced both the practical and political landscape of health care in Nova Scotia.

From 1986 to 2001, a small group of women, determined to see midwifery integrated into the Nova Scotia health care system, wrote, shared, inspired, and educated through the pages of a community newsletter. In doing so, the women not only transformed themselves into a significant political force, but they did it in a way that kept women and families at the centre of the story of regulated midwifery in Nova Scotia.

EPILOGUE

In 2009, Nova Scotia became the first Atlantic Canadian province to regulate and fund the profession of midwifery. This much celebrated event came a full twenty-five years after the Midwifery Coalition of Nova Scotia first began lobbying the government and rallying for change. The MCNS remains a significant political force, punching way above their weight, by lending their voice, and often their critique, to midwifery-related policy across the province. Their goal of keeping women and families at the forefront of any discussions surrounding midwifery in Nova Scotia holds true today, and as such, they often represent the lone consumer voice on multiple complex and bureaucratic committees tasked with overseeing maternity care. Given their history of fighting through when all others have left the field, they will likely continue to meet, on the third Sunday of every month, until midwifery as they know it is available to all women in Nova Scotia.

The author wishes to thank all of the women who have lent their time and creative energy to the Midwifery Coalition of Nova Scotia throughout the years, for the inspiration to carry the midwifery agenda forward and the foundation upon which to do it. Partic-

ular thanks to past editors of the MCNS *newsletter, Lisa Hammett Vaughan and Donnalee Holwerda, for their input and encouragement, and to Jan Catano and Charlene McLellan for sharing their memories of the early days of fighting for midwifery in Nova Scotia, along with their insights into where it's headed. Last but not least, thanks go to the midwives who helped birth this story and this mother: Karen Robb, Leslie Niblett, and Maren Dietze. Efforts to revive the* MCNS *newsletter are currently underway.*

[1]The italicized quotes found throughout the chapter have been provided by women involved with the MCNS throughout the years. The quotes were collected by the author from the newsletter, through email correspondence and during personal conversations. Much like the aims of the newsletter, the quotes are meant to provide context and connection, through story, to the broader topic of midwifery in general.

WORKS CITED

"Asher's Birth Story." *Midwifery Coalition of Nova Scotia Newsletter* (Spring 1989): 4-5. Print.
Catano, Jan. Message to the author. 18 Nov. 2010. Email.
Duda, Diane. "A Birth That Had to Be." *Midwifery Coalition of Nova Scotia Newsletter* (Summer 1989): 5. Print.
Hammett Vaughan, Lisa. Message to the author. 26 Oct. 2011. E-mail.
Holwerda, Donnalee. Message to the author. 31 Jan. 2011. E-mail.
Richardson, Polly Spencer. *Midwifery Coalition of Nova Scotia Newsletter* (Winter 1986): 2. Print.
Terpstra, Aliss. "Dissent from Ontario." *Special Delivery* 18 1994. Reprinted in *Midwifery Now!* Spring 1995: 4. Print.

II.
Literacies and Schooling

4.
Advising for Inequity

Literacy Advice to Mothers

SUZANNE SMYTHE

ON A RAINY November evening in a coastal North American city, a "panel of experts" has been organized at the central library by the local teachers' association. The topic of discussion is how educators can encourage parents' involvement in young children's literacy development. The panel includes university educators, school district administrators, teachers and children's librarians. The fifty or so audience members include parents, teachers and community groups working with young families. The panel members lament the latest wave of funding cuts to schools, express concern about growing poverty among families with young children, and the increasing inequality in family income and access to resources to support child development. In fact, the audience is informed that at least 34 percent of children under six in the city are vulnerable in areas associated with school readiness such as social, emotional, behavioural and cognitive development (Human Early Learning Partnership 7).

The theme running through the discussion is that parental involvement in children's early learning is a key to addressing these inequalities in children's education outcomes. The challenge for educators is to reach the "hard to reach" parents with that important message. One panelist advocates face-to-face parent recruitment: visiting parents in their homes, accompanying mothers to the library, reading with them and their children in the Laundromat, or wherever young children and their families happen to spend their time. The thing to keep in mind, shares this educator, is that poor families care about their children and can and should support their learning, but the added burden of poverty means that it takes much longer to get everyday things done. The solution is to help these parents find time to integrate reading into their everyday lives, and share the value of reading with their children.

A woman in the audience speaks up: She wants to be honest. As a part-time kindergarten teacher with an infant and a three-year old daughter, she just doesn't find time to go to the library or read to her children as often as she knows she should. She wants to know how others find the time to do all the things she knows she is supposed to be doing for her children's literacy and brain development, because she is simply overwhelmed. Her question is received with a brief silence. Then members of the panel begin to offer advice and encouragement: "It doesn't take much—just 15 minutes a day"; "make learning part of your daily life, when you're shopping, doing laundry, riding in the car and pointing out signs, you know...." "Try to have fun, don't worry, just make it part of your life."

This family literacy forum is one of many parent education initiatives that have taken place in communities across North America in the early twenty-first century, organized around what Jill Blackmore and Kirsten Hutchison (501) identify as conflicting discourses of deficit and agency surrounding parents' roles as "children's first and most important educators" (Government of Alberta 19; ReadNow BC 1). Parents are told they are natural teachers, and have the strongest influence on their child's development (McCain and Mustard 118; Willms 22), but they cannot carry out their "natural" role effectively without the advice of experts. This parent's question represented a "discursive break" (Foucault, *Archaeology* 31) in the panel proceedings, in which her lived experience came up against the ideals about mothering and children's literacy swirling around the room. Within this "moment in the practice of the discourse of mothering" (Griffith and Smith "What Did You Do in School" 23) was an opportunity to re-think literacy advice in light of parents' actual lives. Yet the panelists were unable to respond to her problem, to suggest that others in the family or community could share in supporting children's literacy, that schools could be responsive to the literacies her children bring to school rather than expecting them to arrive already "equipped," or even that the expectations for children's literacy knowledge in Kindergarten may be unreasonable. There was little discursive space in the context of this event to consider the factors that underpin the time crunch this mother experienced in a Canadian society that expects parents to contribute to the economy through work outside the home (without access to affordable, quality childcare outside Quebec), and while meeting the increasing expectations for their children's literacy development in the early years (Hays 23). Feeling overwhelmed? "Try harder" is the inevitable answer.

RELATED LITERATURE AND STUDY GOALS

In the study discussed in this chapter, my goal is to trace the discursive landscape of literacy advice to mothers, creating a "history of the present" (Foucault, *Discipline and Punish* 31) to understand how the moment in the central library unfolded as it did, and how the work of mothering is discursively implicated in ideals surrounding children's literacy acquisition; ideals that are regenerated within waves of education reform, such as that surrounding parental involvement in schools (Blackmore and Hutchison 503). Indeed, even as contemporary advice uses the term "parent," closer analysis suggests that mothers are the intended audience. In their study of child development, Anne Woolett and Ann Phoenix pointed out that, "the apparent gender blindness in the use of the word 'parent' appears to be disingenuous, as it serves to maintain traditional gendered divisions of labour between mothers and fathers" (82).

The concerns of this inquiry intersect with a growing body of feminist sociological and literacy scholarship concerned with the deeply gendered institutional arrangements that produce North American family life, and indeed, valued mothering and literacy practices. N. P. Weiss (520) observed that advice on any aspect of childraising implicitly and explicitly involves the regulation of mothering practices, a point illustrated by Mace in her account of social reform movements that seek to "educate mothers to educate their children":

> The evidence of the literacy problem in industrialized countries with mass schooling systems has revealed that schools

cannot alone meet this need. Families must therefore be recruited to do their bit, too. This is where the spotlight falls on the mother. She it is who must ensure that the young child arrives at school ready for school literacy, and preferably already literate. (5)

Critical ethnographies and case studies of families and schools suggest the important role of advice texts in organizing family literacy practices and mothering work. Alison Griffith and Dorothy Smith employed analytic strategies associated with Smith's Institutional Ethnography (IE) to explore the problematic of mothers' relations with education institutions "from the standpoint of those who are active within it, however indirectly" (2005: 4). They traced "the hidden gendered labour that stands behind school success and failure" (2005: vii), and linked this labour back to the texts and practices of educational reforms ostensibly designed to create more equality in children's educational outcomes. Just as we observed in the central library event, Griffith and Smith (2005) found that such reforms often look to parental involvement in children's early learning and schooling (and by extension, predominantly women's unpaid labour) as a social lever to address educational equity.

In Australia, Blackmore and Hutchison interviewed parents, teachers and administration in affluent and low-income schools about the workings of parental involvement. They found that the invisibility of women's literacy and education work also renders invisible the material circumstances that drive educational advantage (508). Similarly, from the "kitchen table" standpoint of Californian families, Griffith and Lois Andre-Bechely mapped the ways in which that State's education accountability and standardized testing regimes reach into the home, organizing women's domestic literacy work around the standardizing practices of the *Open Court Reading* curricula and test-preparation booklets (49-50).

Taken together, this scholarship documents the inner workings of inequality within a "one-size-fits-all" approach to educational reform. Interestingly, the similarity in the reforms and their supporting discourses across settings draw attention to how texts travel, how the "global is instantiated in the local" (Hamilton 222), and, as the analysis presented below suggests, how the past is instantiated in the present. Indeed, as researchers attend to the effects of gendered parental involvement policies in various jurisdictions, a social-historical perspective can illuminate the cultural models and discursive resources surrounding mothering and literacy that are so readily adopted in this education reform project.

The focus of the analysis presented in this chapter is nineteenth and early twentieth century British and North American domestic literature, through which I cut a broad swath as space allows. It was during the early nineteenth century that the Industrial Revolution and the rise of the factory system in Europe generated the first wave of domestic advice to mothers. New forms of social organization made literacy advice to mothers possible, and seemingly necessary: the rise of social reform movements (particularly suffrage, child labour laws, and abolitionism), new gendered divisions of labour linked to the factory model and the growth of an upper-middle class, and role of Christian moral values in structuring Victorian life. Sarah Robbins illuminated nineteenth-century narratives about domestic literacy as a source of power for middle class women readers and writers, an "indirect but influential route into political culture from which they were legally excluded" (2). My goal here is to build upon her recognition of the importance of this archive, and to generate insights into how this domestic literature has continued to shape contemporary parenting and literacy advice.

There are constraints in the interpretations and conclusions that can be drawn from advice literature. Jay Mechling argued that there is evidence of large discrepancies between mothering practices and the advice they receive (44), and indeed "no persuasive evidence to suggest that official advice affects the parents' actual behaviour" (45). Advice to parents says much more about the people and institutions that generate advice than about the people who may read it. While this creates difficulties for historians wishing to reconstruct parenting practices of the past through child-raising advice texts, it does not impede an investigation of child-raising advice as discourses of dominance that shape "what counts" as literacy and mothering in particular historical and social contexts. The challenge in this study was to capture continuities and discontinuities and to sample historical shifts, while managing vast volumes of text. I settled on a sample of ten magazine articles and books per decade (according to subscription rates and best selling rates), privileging multiple edition texts (and best-selling/popular texts) that allowed for comparison over time. The data is organized and reported in two distinct periods: early Victorian society, from 1821 to 1860s, and later Victorian society, from the 1870s to the turn of the century, distinguished by the consolidation of public education in North America.

DANGEROUS AND POWERFUL PRACTICES: LITERACY ADVICE TO MOTHERS AND THEIR CHILDREN IN THE EARLY VICTORIAN ERA

"Parents wonder to taste the streams bitter, when they themselves have poisoned the fountain" (John Locke). So Mrs. Louisa Hoare quotes the philosopher in the epigram to her 1821 London edition of *Hints for the Improvement of Early Education and Nursery Discipline*. The fifth edition was published in the United States in 1826, and re-published again in 1905 as *Mrs. Hoare's Hints on Early Education*, so creating a text that circulated in public discourse for almost eighty years (and indeed remains available in its digitized form). Louisa Hoare joins Lydia Maria Child's (1831) *The Mother's Book*, Lydia Sigourney's (1838) *Letters to Mothers* and *Household Education* (1848) by Harriet Martineau, as prolific and popular writers of their time, each of their work enjoying several editions, reaching across several generations and two continents.

Early Victorians valued reading as a powerful cultural performance embedded in morality and soul salvation. As Kate Flint observed, "reading as an activity was as natural, as essential, as eating, supplying the food of the mind" (50). There was considerable debate, however, about how children should best be socialized into this culture, falling roughly along the lines of a Lockeian preference for direct instruction, and Rousseauian values for the "natural" unfolding of children's faculties under the guidance of sensible mothers. Louisa Hoare, calling to mind the rigidity of California's lock-step domestic curricula described by Griffith and

Andre-Bechely, adopts an austere tone, recommending that reading in the home be structured as "lessons," within finite boundaries of time and space "from which there is no escape":

> Let it be an object to give them employments which they cannot evade—from which there are no means of escaping; something to be done, and not merely to be learnt. For instance, it will be better to set them so many lines to write, rather than to learn by heart ... children will also learn more readily when their lessons are regulated by established rules. If a child is uncertain how much to read, he will probably murmur when the portion is shewn to him. Rather let it be fixed, that, to read so much, to spell so many words, so many times, &c. is to be the regular business of every day. (Hoare 98)

Here, the goal to read and "spell" (not write) is above all to appear to cultivate "regular" habits. The importance of this is considered paramount, but mothers are extolled not to force their children to learn. This, argues Hoare, is a reflection of the "self love" of mothers and teachers, who "do not like that other children should read and write better than ours" (100). Similarly, Lydia Child advises: "In all that is related to developing the intellect, very young children should not be hurried or made to attend unwillingly.... Do not try to force his attention to his letters, when he is weary, fretful and sleepy, or impatient to be doing something else" (53). Child describes an ideal literacy moment in which mothers "take pains" but "do not urge," outlining quite a detailed lesson in decoding:

> When they are playing with their letters, and you are at leisure, take pains to tell them the name of each as often as they ask; but do not urge them. When the large letters are learned, give them the small ones. When both are mastered, place the letters together in a small word like CAT; point to the letters, name them and pronounce cat distinctly. After a few lessons, the child will know what letters to place together in order to spell CAT. (53)

Mothers must walk the tightrope between providing the appropriate instruction but not to coerce (or be seen to be coercing) the child to read. Tracing a similar conflict between deficit and agency in twenty-first century parent involvement advice, Victorian women's literacy practices were considered potentially dangerous, invested as they were with power and influence derived from religious canon, but also with mistrust that they could damage their children without the guidance of domestic literature. In *Letters to Mothers*, Lydia Sigourney (1838) evoked Locke's *Tabula Rasa* to outline the problem for mothers, and for social reformers: "who can refrain from trembling at the thought, that every action, every word, even every modification of voice or feature, may impress on the mental tablet of the pupil, traces that shall exist forever" (34). Referring to children's habit to ask many questions, Child (1836) admonished mothers who may become impatient or exhausted in their powerful role:

> I am aware that these habits of inquiry are at times very troublesome; for no one, however patient, can be always ready to answer the multitude of questions a child is disposed to ask. But it must be remembered that all good things are accompanied by inconveniences. The care of children requires a great many sacrifices, and a great deal of self-denial; but the woman who is not willing to sacrifice a good deal in such a cause, does not deserve to be a mother. (15-16)

Harriet Martineau, an abolitionist, scholar of American democracy, and prolific social commentator, adopted a different tack. She argued that in many homes "both mother and father work very hard, particularly in American homes where there were no nurses, servants and the like, formal instruction in letters cannot be possible" (Martineau 193). Her point was that these parents were effective educators in spite of the absence of books and toys, because they were less distracted than their upper middle-class counterparts by "societal visiting," and did not have nurses or governesses to whom literacy work could be delegated. Moreover, the spatial constraints of a small cottage made it a necessity for "old and young to learn together" (Martineau 193). Martineau developed the idea that what counts as "educated" varied from circumstance to setting, and must necessarily be broader than "book learning." She told the story of children who did not have access to schooling and whose parents could not read, nor had the time to teach them letters and numbers, but who were, nevertheless, very "educated":

> They knew every tree in the forest, and every bird, and every weed. They knew the habits of domestic animals. They could tell at a glance how many scores of pigeons there were in a flock, when clouds of these birds came sailing towards them ... they could give their minds earnestly to what they were about; and ponder and plan, and imagine, and contrive. Their faculties were awake. (127)

Given that literacy rates in Britain in the 1840s and 1850s hovered between 40 percent and 50 percent (Vincent 45), it was indeed necessary to promote domestic learning that was not print based, reflecting the somewhat tangential place literacy occupied in social life in early nineteenth-century Britain and North America. David Vincent argued that although literacy would become more widespread as the nineteenth century progressed, it also "had to compete for the child's limited time with a wide range of skills which had equal or greater priority" (56). He cited social commentator and Rousseauian educator William Cobbett, who in 1830 observed that it was possible to "earn a great deal of money, and bring up families very well, without ever knowing how to read" (Cobbett cited in Vincent 59). For others, however, reading practices were emblematic of middle class moral and cultural supremacy. That most commentators felt it necessary to warn against "urging" children to read, suggests the social pressures that may have been attached to children's reading. Domestic literature in the first half of the nineteenth century thus reflected considerable diversity in the pathways open to children's learning, along with much contestation over the timing, purposes, and methods for literacy instruction that should shape these pathways.

The Victorian connection between "good" reading practices and the achievement of moral ideals often took precedence over any benefits reading may have for children's learning or education. In a 1848 article titled "Family and Social Reading" in *Mothers' Magazine*, "social reading" at the hearth among family and friends was presented as a practice of social and cultural distinction:

> The benefits of social reading are manifold. Pleasures shared with others are increased by the partnership. A book is tenfold a book, when read in the company of beloved friends by the ruddy fire, on a wintry evening: and when our domestic pleasures are bathed in domestic affection.... Among a thousand means of making home attractive— What is more pleasing? What more rational? What more tributary to the fund of daily talk? What more exclusive of scandal and chatter? He would be a benefactor indeed, who should devise a plan for redeeming our evenings, and rallying the young men who scatter to clubs and taverns, and brawling assemblies... Families which are in a state of mutual repulsion have no evening together over books or music. (77-78)

Inhabitants of "the house of the poor man" were advised that they could attain middle class social status by adopting such practices:

> I beg leave to add, this is a pleasure for *the poor man's house*, and for this I love it. The poor man, if educated, is one day placed almost on a level with the prince, in respect to the best part of literary wealth. Let him ponder the suggestion, and enjoy the privilege. ("Family and Social Reading" 78; emphases in original)

In this way, the gendered ideals of literacy and pedagogic roles in the home were predicated on a long standing belief that the performance of such practices could address social inequality: "The children of rich and poor have, or may have, about equal advantages under the care of sensible parents" (Martineau 189). While advice may well have been intended to create a perception that poor and wealthy mothers alike were capable of appropriately educating their children, the discursive effect was also to mask the important material differences that structured women's mothering roles and families' time and uses for literacy. In fact, the content of literacy advice can be traced along rigid class divisions. For while artisan or "cottage" mothers could be "good enough" teachers if they were sensible, this sensibility was defined and embodied in the literacy habitus of upper classes that was normalized throughout the advice (indeed, those writing the advice were firmly located in this class, and their audiences of course, were literate, upper class women).

In the second half of the nineteenth century, the effects of the factory system and the incremental rise in public schooling had a significant impact on recommended domestic literacy practices, predicated on the categorization of differently situated mothers. *Mothers' Magazine* began to offer "hints to parents" and "hints to mothers" ("Hints to Parents") who could not teach their children at home themselves. Such texts recognized the increasing number of women who worked outside the home, and the growing number of children who attended formal schooling on a regular basis (Flint 68-75; Vincent 30-44). This advice emphasized the importance of punctual and regular attendance at infant and normal school, the mothers' role in monitoring of homework and inquiring of children what they learned at school, as well as the importance of reinforcing at home the lessons learned in school ("The School in the House" 215). Advice to middle-class mothers who stayed at home with their children extolled the virtue of their presence in the home, and used strategies embedded in guilt and Christian imagery to underline the opportunities for pedagogy that this constant interaction afforded:

> How many times, when the inward teacher has called us to our closet, where a spiritual table was spread a rich feast provided for us have we replied, 'When I have finished what I am doing' but the feast is removed, our High Priest is left the sacred chamber ... and we return to our worldly occupations unblest-unfed. ("The Lovely Family" 157)

DOMESTIC LITERACY WORK FOR SCHOOLING AND NATION BUILDING: LATER VICTORIAN DOMESTIC LITERATURE

In the 1870s and 1880s we observe a continuation of these themes but also, interestingly, an intensification of expectations as children's reading practices emerge as a tool for new forms of moral regulation attached to nation building and schooling in the North American context (Graff 84; Comacchio 1999: 48). Charlotte Mason (1878), an icon of the contemporary Christian home schooling movement in North America, articulated growing concern for the abilities of mothers to adequately teach their children: "The children are the property of the nation, to be brought up for the nation as is best for the nation, and not according to some whim of the individual parent" (35). As Cynthia Comacchio (1993) noted, "the developing view was that 'society' should decide the standards for effective parenting and a proper home life" (53).

Ideal domestic literacy management roles for this "new nation" and "new century" emerged most strongly in the image of the fictitious Gertrude, a creation of early nineteenth-century Italian philosopher Johann H. Pestalozzi. His *Leonard and Gertrude* (1781) and *How Gertrude Teaches Her Children* (1801) were popularized and reprinted and circulated in 1885 and 1894 respectively. Pestalozzi evoked Madonna-like reverence for the power of mothers, such as that expressed by Hoare (1826) and Sigourney (1838), with domestic and political ideals of "race development" and nationhood that appealed to Darwinist race theorists and social reformers of the time. Pestalozzi's ideas held important implications for evolving ideals of mothering and literacy. Children required much more "hands on" attention and instruction, and like the twenty-first century counterparts (ReadNow BC 5), were advised to be constantly on the look out for learning opportunities in the "natural" settings of everyday life. From Pestalozzi's perspective, this domestic literacy work was important not only for the development of the individual child, but for resolving the problems of an unjust and exploitative world. When he wrote *Leonard and Gertrude* in 1781, it was to illustrate "how the world might be regenerated through education; the mother, Gertrude, being the chief teacher" (xviii). Pestalozzi's painstakingly detailed directions to mothers emerged from his concern for the "gap that has arisen in the maze we call human culture," through the inability of the "lowest classes" to speak, which he understood as the ability to make oneself understood to (and understood by) the ruling classes (Pestalozzi 112-113). For example, according to Pestalozzi, "[the Indians'] lack of 'proper' speech ... breed[s] a degraded race of men as sacrifices to their idols" (112). In this way, beyond the promotion of reading, domestic literacy advice served as a bridge between the sanctity of the domestic sphere and the legitimization of class and race supremacy.

Pestalozzi's ideas found new life and purpose in the work of his student, Friedrich Froebel. Froebel's influence upon the creation of the contemporary kindergarten movement is well documented (Dehli 198; Griffith and Smith). His ideas about children's learning were, like Pestalozzi's, embedded in the normalization of traditional gendered divisions of labour as well as intensive mothering and domestic pedagogy (Walkerdine and Lucey). A leader in the popularization of Froebel's ideas was Andrea Hofer Proudfoot, the American editor of the *Kindergarten Magazine* and author of *A Mother's Ideals* (1897), an advice manual for mothers that popularized the work of Froebel within the context of the burgeoning maternal feminist movement. Proudfoot called for Froebel's ideals of the "new family" and the Kindergarten to become part of mothering practices and the everyday routines and relationships in homes:

> [In his work] we get a glimpse of ideal family life in the Kindergarten, and if we have nothing better to build up to in our homes, we can make no mistake in aiming at that. Let us visit the kindergarten and learn its simplest lessons and emulate them in our homes. (Proudfoot 135)

These "lessons" included modeling and monitoring children's literacy and learning in the home, in ways that were largely dependent on the resources and consumer practices of the middle-class culture and household organization. This included "airy playrooms full of well chosen and durable toys that are close to the library, large kitchens, carefully selected domestic help and lots of windows" (Proudfoot 32). Ellen Key's *Century of the Child* similarly evokes the sanctity of the domestic realm in the wake of rapid industrialization and its social dislocation. In her imagined new century, "the children will be taken from the school, the street, the factory and restored to the home. The mother will be given back from work outside, or from social life, to the children" (164). Kindergartens would be available only to children from unfortunate circumstances and whose mothers, for reasons of "weak will or depression" (234), could not educate her children herself. These "new homes" for the "new century" required mothers well versed in the latest pedagogical theories and child raising tenets, such as "an understanding of heredity, race hygiene, child hygiene and child psychology" to ensure appropriate child raising for the aspirations of the century (Key 67). Indeed, the view of public child care as a preserve of "weak willed" mothers and their children persists in contemporary debates that demonstrate suspicion that "non-maternal" care is damaging to children and should be targeted to families who are "at risk."

CONCLUSIONS

The rise of public schooling in the late nineteenth century, a key project in the goal of nation building, heralded a power struggle between homes and schools surrounding the responsibility and regulation of children's literacy practices. In public schools, rather than learning literacy through living, children would learn literacy to live (Vincent 23-26) and mothers would support, but not supplant, that project. Mothers' responsibilities entered an ambiguous space: providing a home context that facilitated children's learning in school, rather than, in the image of the "cottage mother and father," teaching their children the literacies of their material survival and cultural continuity. Indeed, schools came to educate the ideal child, supported by the ideal mother. The cultural and pedagogic reference point for the mother as literacy teacher was rooted in the image of *Gertrude,* a woman who never actually existed. This is a telling example of the ways in which power/knowledge works in these discourses to "form the objects of which they speak" (Foucault, *Archaeology* 49). Interpreting literacy advice to mothers as a gendered practice of power, rather than as scientific truth, makes visible advice to mothers in the twentieth and twenty-first centuries as variations on nineteenth century discursive themes. The content of literacy advice has indeed shifted according to various moral panics along the way: Sputnik and the Cold War; a nation "at risk" from poor teachers, reading and homework practices (1-20); and "new brain research" (Canadian Institute of Child Health 18).

The discursive structures that underpin this advice remain entrenched in the irreconcilable contradiction between deficit and agency, expressing an unrealized social vision of women's domestic literacy work as a lever for contemporary nation-building visions: educational equality, economic prosperity and global competitiveness. A significant difference however, is that the nineteenth-century mother was invested with considerable power and agency (Robbins 5-10); domestic reading could be a source of pleasure as well as political and social influence. Literacy as a source of maternal power and pleasure is undermined for many contemporary mothers in an "age of anxiety" (Warner 118), in which the spiraling expectations of attachment parenting, expressed in increasingly vague terms of "success" (Sears and Sears 34), persist in a context of scarce and unevenly distributed resources.

This ambiguity persists today, manifest in the pull women feel to meet the spiraling expectations of attachment parenting within a context of scarce material resources. As Glenda Wall found, even expressions or manifestations of this anxiety are the basis for new scientific worry that "hyper parents" are "creating problems that will last a lifetime" (Bartlett and LeRose qtd. in Wall). It is indeed, a short discursive jump between Child's (1836) admonition that "the care of children requires a great many sacrifices, and a great deal of self-denial" and the library panel's response to the mother who was "doing the best she could" to "try harder." However, as Tamara Hareven reminds us, families are active agents in the production of social change rather than the objects of it. It is within the discursive breaks that a broader cultural struggle over what it means to be a mother, to be literate, to be "successful" are challenged and recreated.

WORKS CITED

Blackmore, Jill, and Kirsten Hutchison. "Ambivalent Relations: The 'Tricky Footwork' of Parental Involvement in School Communities." *International Journal of Inclusive Education* 14.5 (2010): 499-515. Web.

Canadian Institute of Child Health. *The Early Years Last Forever: I Am Your Child*. Ottawa: Canadian Institute of Child Health, 1997. Print.

Child, L. M. *The Mother's Book*. 2nd ed. Boston: Carter and Hendee, 1836. Print.

Comacchio, C. *The Infinite Bonds of Family: Domesticity in Canada, 1850-1940*. Toronto: University of Toronto Press, 1999. Print.

Comacchio, C. *Nations are Built of Babies: Saving Ontario's Mothers and Children*. Montreal: McGill-Queen's University Press, 1993. Print.

Dehli, K. "They Rule by Sympathy: The Feminization of Pedagogy." *Canadian Journal of Sociology* 19.2 (1994): 195. Print.

"Family and Social Reading." *Mothers' Magazine* 1848: 78. Print.

Flint, Kate. *The Woman Reader, 1937-1914*. London: Oxford, 1993. Print.

Foucault, M. *Discipline and Punish: The Birth of the Prison*. Trans. Alan Sheridan. New York: Pantheon, 1977. Print.

Foucault, M. *The Archaeology of Knowledge and the Discourse on Language*. New York: Pantheon Books, 1972. Print.

Government of Alberta. *Kindergarten Curriculum: A Handbook for Parents*. Edmonton: Government of Alberta, 2011. Web. October 25, 2011.

Graff, H. J. *The Literacy Myth: Literacy and Social Structure in the Nineteenth Century City*. New York: Academic Press, 1979. Print.

Griffith, A. and D. E. Smith. *Mothering for Schooling*. Toronto: University of Toronto Press, 2005. Print.

Griffith, A. and D. E. Smith. "What Did You Do in School Today? Mothering, Schooling and Social Class." *Perspectives on Social Problems*. Eds. G. Miller and J. Holstein. Greenwich, CT: JAI, 1990. 3-24. Print.

Griffith, A. and L. Andre-Bechely. "Institutional Technologies:

Coordinating Families and Schools, Bodies and Texts. "*People at Work: Life, Power, and Social Inclusion in the New Economy.* Ed. M. E. DeVault. New York: New York University Press, 2008. 40. Print.

Hamilton, M. "Putting Words in their Mouth: The Alignment of Identities with System Goals through the use of Independent Learning Plans." *British Educational Research Journal* 35.2 (2009): 221-242. Print.

Hareven, T. *Families, History and Change: Life-Course and Cross-Cultural Perspectives.* Boulder: Westview Press, 2000. Print.

Hays, S. *The Cultural Contradictions of Motherhood.* New Haven: Yale University Press, 1996. Print.

"Hints to Parents." *Mothers' Magazine* 1859: 212. Print.

Hoare, L. *Hints for the Improvement of Early Education and Nursery Discipline.* 5th ed. Salem, MA: James. R. Buffum, 1826. Print.

Human Early Learning Partnership (HELP). *EDI Mapping Package 2008 - 2009: All School Districts.* Vancouver, BC: HELP, 2009. Web. October 26, 2011.

Key, E. *The Century of the Child.* New York: The Knickerbocker Press, 1909. Print.

Mace, J. *Playing with Time: Mothers and the Meaning of Literacy.* London: Routledge, 1998. Print.

Martineau, H. *Household Education.* London: E. Moxon, 1848. Print.

Mason, C. Unknown, 1878. Print.

McCain, M. N. and F. J. Mustard. *The Early Years Study: Reversing the Real Brain Drain.* Toronto, Ontario: Canadian Institute for Advanced Research, 1999. Print.

Mechling, J. "Advice to Historians on Advice to Mothers." *Journal of Social History* 9.1 (1975): 44-63. Print.

Pestalozzi, J. H. *Leonard and Gertrude.* Third ed. Boston: D.C. Heath & Co., Publishers., 1885. Print.

Pestalozzi, J. H. *How Gertrude Teaches Her Children: An Attempt to Help Mothers Teach Their Own Children and an Account of the Method.* London: George Allen and Unwin Ltd., 1894. [1801].

Proudfoot, A. H. *A Mother's Ideals.* New York: A. Flanagan Co., 1897. Print.

ReadNowBC. *Helping Your Preschooler Get Ready for School.* Victoria, BC: Government of British Columbia, 2008. Web. June 8, 2009.

Robbins, S. *Managing Literacy, Mothering America: Women's Narratives of Reading and Writing in the 19th Century.* Pittsburgh: University of Pittsburgh Press, 2004. Print.

Sears, W. and M. Sears. *The Successful Child: What Parents can do to Help Kids Turn Out Well.* Boston: Little Brown and Company. Print.

Sigourney, L. H. *Letters to Mother.* Hartford: Hudson and Skinner, Printers, 1838. Print.

"The Lovely Family." *Mothers' Magazine* 1860: 157. Print.

"The School in the House." *Mothers' Magazine* February 1858: 215. Print.

Vincent, D. *The Rise of Mass Literacy: Reading and Writing in Modern Europe.* Cambridge: Polity Press, 2000. Print.

Walkerdine, Valerie and Helen Lucey. *Democracy in the Kitchen: Regulating Mothers and Socialising Daughters.* London: Virago, 1989. Print.

Warner, J. *Perfect Madness: Motherhood in the Age of Anxiety.* New York: Riverhead Books, 2005. Print.

Weiss, N. P. "Mother: The Invention of Necessity." *American Quarterly* (Winter 1977): 519. Print.

Willms, D., ed. *Vulnerable Children.* Edmonton: University of Alberta Press, 2002. Print.

Woolett, A. and A. Phoenix. "Motherhood as Pedagogy: Developmental Psychology and the Accounts of Mothers of Young Children." *Feminisms and Pedagogies in Everyday Life.* Ed. C. Luke. New York: State University of New York Press, 1996. 81-102. Print.

5.
Reclaiming Literacy

A Kindergartner Teaches Her Mom to Read

JILL BRYANT

THE DRIVE FROM Seattle to Portland can be a struggle. A two hundred mile drive takes between two-and-a-half to four hours depending on traffic. Being trapped in the car with a bored five year old while sitting in crawling traffic can be intolerable. The mini-DVD player has always saved us in these situations. Today's drive was going just fine until the DVD player ran out of battery power.

"Didn't you plug it in last night?" I ask my partner.

"I thought you were going to," she snaps back at me. We pause, not knowing what to do next.

I plunge in: "Maya, you are going to have to read to yourself for a while."

"No. I want you to read to me!"

"Maya, your moms just need to relax for a while. You can do it." Maya is an only child and lacks the ability to entertain herself. Silence and pouting from both the front and back seat.

"Mommy, I can read this book to myself! See ... one berry two berry make me a shoe berry...." Giant smile takes over her face—she can hardly breathe she is so excited.

"Maya you can read!" Elizabeth and I say in unison.

For the next hour, Maya reads the Jamberry book over and over until we get home. The drive is saved and so is my career.

Being a former middle-school language arts teacher and currently a literacy teacher educator at a small, private liberal arts university, I have thought and read extensively about the literacy process for nearly twenty years. I graduated from a progressive teacher preparation program with an undergraduate degree in English education and some strongly held convictions about how I planned to approach literacy in my middle school language arts classroom. I maintained those beliefs throughout my public school teaching and have built my career as a teacher educator on those theoretical foundations as well as the instructional practices that emerged from my teaching philosophy.

As a teacher educator, I have always emphasized to my preservice and inservice teachers the importance of creating and facilitating a reading curriculum that keeps language whole and authentic (Goodman and Wilde). I have believed that focusing learners solely on the smallest parts of language, i.e. phonics, can actually inhibit the comprehension process (Goodman and Goodman; Smith). Kenneth Goodman and Yetta Goodman put it this way, "…preoccupation with language itself detracts from meaning and produces inefficient and ineffective language use" (24). Phonics is only one element of the reading process, not *the* reading process (Reutzel and Cooter). Privileging the teaching of skills in isolation can also give learners the impression that reading is about getting the "right" answers, not about exploring, inferring, predicting, and comprehending (Goodman, Watson and Burke). Because of my philosophical stance, I have assigned my preservice and inservice teachers to read the authors referenced above to help them understand and integrate into their teaching pedagogies that reading is the construction of meaning and that meaning is constructed in context—not by practicing skills in isolation. Thus, I have spent my career advocating that "…optimum learning occurs when learners are engaged in functional, relevant, and meaningful experiences" (Goodman, Watson and Burke 192).

Needless to say, when I became a parent, I was determined to implement what I had believed all these years about language acquisition with my daughter, Maya. I was determined to avoid any language experiences that were inauthentic. Throughout Maya's preschool years, we took many trips to the library and brought home armfuls of picture books, had fun with language through songs and rhymes, and interacted with environmental print as the focus of our literacy instruction for Maya. We intentionally did not teach Maya the alphabet, except when she showed an interest; did not sing the "ABC" song (though she learned it from friends and it was one of her early favorites); and did not teach her the sound-symbol relationship unless she asked—which was very little. Additionally, we selected preschools that emphasized play and inquiry—not "academics."

Up until the summer before Maya began kindergarten in 2009, I had little to no doubt about our approach to her literacy development. The following is a journal entry I wrote the winter before she started kindergarten—she was six.

> ...[Maya has had] a wide range of experiences, has multiple family members with multiple graduate degrees, a mom who teaches reading methods, a[nother] mother who is a librarian, and is addicted to books ...how could you go wrong? But, we're not teaching her [the alphabet]. And she has absolutely NO CLUE about the sounds of letters. I'm so eager to see this play out. I don't think that her kindergarten pushes phonics at all. I can't wait to get in there and see what they do. (Journal 2/27/09)

It is evident from this journal entry that the winter before Maya started kindergarten I was interested in her language development and was excited to see what I would find out about the effects of our "whole language parenting" (Goodman, Watson and Burke 188) once Maya started school.

IDEOLOGICAL UNCERTAINTIES

As the start of kindergarten got closer, I found myself involved in a number of conversations with other parents whose children were going to start kindergarten in the fall as well. During these conversations parents described their phonics practice regimen, the success they have had with teaching their children shapes, colors, and numbers, and they shared their children's stick figure drawings—which seemed far more anatomically accurate than anything Maya had been drawing. These conversations led to an irresistible impulse to compare Maya to her peers. This unexpected inability to avoid comparing my child to other children her age caused a completely unexpected internal conflict about my parenting and my college teaching. Because of my holistic ideological stance, I have grown used to being the dissenting voice against the dominant literacy message ignited by NCLB (Meier and Wood). Rarely have I faltered from my message of meaning first, teaching skills in context, and the social construction of knowledge (Vygotsky; McLaughlin). I was surprised by my sudden uncertainties about my ideological and practical stance. Perhaps it was the other parents, the pressure of raising a child, or the fact that I have always been fighting against the traditionalists and reductionists throughout my teaching career that I began to experience a professional identity crisis. Questions emerged for me: Why couldn't Maya identify the letters of the alphabet? Why didn't she show much, if any, interest in reading words? Why couldn't she draw her stick figures anatomically correct when some of her peers were able to? I could not help but also wonder if all this meant that I had been espousing inaccurate and unrealistic information to my teacher candidates all these years.

I have always demanded of myself that I practice what I preach in my teacher preparation classes. Designing all my classes using a constructivist and critical theorist (McLaren; Wink) approach, I put writing, student questions, and issues of social justice at the center of my curriculum. Now, I questioned even that. Maybe I should have been preparing my K-12 preservice and inservice teachers to better implement the skills-based, production-oriented demands of standardized teaching elicited from NCLB legislation. Elizabeth began to doubt our approach to Maya's literacy development as well. She wanted to trust me and she intuitively agreed with my philosophy, but she too, saw the other children's language development and compared their language skills to Maya's and felt that Maya was not as far along as her peers.

When September came around and it was time for Maya to join her neighborhood peers in kindergarten, I decided to take on this job of parenting an emergent reader as my own case study. I wanted to draw everything I could from this experience, so I became intentional and thorough with my data collection: I journaled regularly about my observations as well as my reflections and reactions to Maya's language development; I asked her kindergarten teacher to give to me all of the writing that Maya produced during Writing Workshop (Atwell); I interviewed Maya's teacher at the end of the school year after the last day of classes; I recorded a few interviews with Maya (only when she was interested and thought it would be fun); and I periodically recorded her reading her writing to me when she brought her writing home (again, only when she showed interest in this.) Sometimes I would ask her if I could record something and she would say, "No." I did not insist because I wanted to respect her comfort level with participation in the study. I also expanded my reading on early childhood literacy as well as connected with my doctoral advisor, Dorothy Watson from the University of Missouri—Columbia. Last, I volunteered in Maya's classroom during writing workshop time once a week during most of the school year.

The week before school started, Maya's teacher scheduled a meeting with each family. We were to bring our child for an "assessment." Needless to say, I was leery and skeptical of any formal assessment done in kindergarten, while at the same time, I was nervous about how Maya might do when tested by her soon-to-be kindergarten teacher. Aside from the assessment, I was very excited about the meeting and Maya starting school. I suspect I was more excited than Maya. I knew that participating in the K-12 schools as a parent and not as an educator could be a tremendous learning experience for me—both as a mother and a literacy teacher educator.

During our brief meeting with the teacher, I managed to "out" myself to her as a teacher educator. I had anticipated not telling her what I did for a living because I did not want to create any distance between the teacher and me. I could not resist, though, because I was so eager to get a glimpse of how she was going to teach reading and writing. I asked her, as neutrally as I could, about her approach to teaching reading. Since the school is not a Title One school, I anticipated she would not use Dynamic Indicators of Basic Early Literacy Skills (or DIBELS, a set of procedures and measures for assessing early literacy skills), but I did not know how much skills-based instruction Maya would be receiving. The teacher gave me a politically savvy and equally vague response about how she teaches some phonics, but also tries to get the students interested in reading. What I found encouraging was that she told me she had missed the DIBELS training as a teacher in a different school because she was out of teaching with her young children for a few years. I then blurted out that I was a teacher educator and that I was not fond of DIBELS (so much for holding my cards close!) and was glad to hear that her focus was not going to be on phonics (Goodman "The Truth about DIBELS").

After our ten-minute talk with the teacher about what to expect in her classroom, Elizabeth and I were left with our knees crammed under the kindergarten-sized table to fill out paper work while her teacher took Maya to a table across the room for her first assessment. I, of course, did not care about the paperwork. I watched, with great curiosity, out of the corner of my eye what the teacher was doing with Maya. I noticed that she first pointed to the letters of the alphabet so Maya could name the ones she knew. I remember thinking, "Oh no ... I'm caught now—the university professor's kid does not even know her letters!" And, of course, Maya only knew a few of them. Maya could identify even fewer sounds of the letters (later, her teacher told me that Maya did not know any of the sounds associated with the letters). Then, she asked Maya to count rocks out of a jar. I was less worried about this assessment because I knew Maya was a pretty good counter—in spite of our lack of formal "math" instruction.

RETHINKING LITERACY

I took my growing concerns about whether I was an effective literacy instructor and parent head on by volunteering in Maya's kindergarten classroom during writing workshop. As a middle school teacher, I had conducted my own action research project on the implementation of writing workshop and its impact on student voice and was transformed by the process (Weisner). I felt that the best way for me to determine what was right for Maya and if I needed to adjust my theoretical foundation as a literacy educator was to get into her classroom and interact with children engaged with what I have always loved and believed in for decades—writing workshop.

The evening before my first day to volunteer in her classroom,

I wanted to find out from Maya what she thought my role would be when I helped the children with their writing. I thought hearing her words about how grown ups should help children with their writing would give me insight into how her teacher facilitates writing workshops as well as be a useful way for me to learn more about Maya's conceptualization of what it means to be a writer. In other words, I wanted to know what Maya's focus was on when writing in the classroom (this would give me insight into how she viewed reading as well). Our conversation was as follows:

Jill: "...what should I do, what kind of things do the teachers and parents [do in writing workshop]?"
Maya: "You usually sound out words."
Jill: "Ok, so a kid will raise their hand and say, "How do I spell 'famous?'"
Maya: "Yeah."
Jill: "Is that what they'll ask me?"
Maya: "...People ask you how do you spell 'flowers' cause there are lots of kids [who] are writing books about flowers."
Jill: "Right now they are?"
Maya: "So yeah. So and then pretend that I was a student and you [be the teacher]?"
Jill: "How 'bout I be the student and you be the teacher?"
Maya: "Okay."
Jill: [pretending to be a student in Maya's class] "How do you spell flowers? And what do I do?"
Maya: "Oh, and then, and then you'll say, 'FF ... FF' because that's the first letter of flowers...."
Jill: "The teacher says 'FF ... FF'?"
Maya: "You say, 'FF ... FF' if they [are] spell[ing] flowers because 'F' is the first letter of flowers."
Jill: "Okay. So do I like help them sound it out or do I tell them how to spell it?"
Maya: "Sound it out."
Jill: "Do I make them go 'FF ... FF' or do I go 'FF ... FF'?"
Maya: "...Um you 'FF' like sound it out."
Jill: "Okay."
Maya: "Like 'OH' ... 'AH' ...'AHH' ... and 'FF' and...."

Jill: "Do the kids ever get frustrated and just want me to tell them how to spell it?"
Maya: "No."
Jill: "...How do *you* figure out how to spell words... during writing workshop?"
Maya: "I usually don't have help. I just usually do words I know how to spell."
Jill: "Oh, I see...." (Interview 12/18/09)

I was keeping a close eye on the role of phonics instruction in Maya's kindergarten classroom. Phonics has played such a powerful role in the reading debate (Pearson). This is where I believed I had the most to learn as well as the most emerging uncertainties about its role in early literacy development. During the 12/18/09 interview, listening to Maya describe that my primary teaching task would be to help her classmates sound out words immediately disappointed me. I asked her if peers got frustrated when the teacher would not just tell them how to spell a word. I had imagined myself interrupting their fluency by making them struggle through sounding out each rather than just telling them to how to spell it or to give it their best shot (Ouellette and Sénéchal). The way Maya articulated the role of spelling in her own writing process also concerned me: "I usually don't have help. I just usually do words I know how to spell." I did not want her early writing experiences to be inhibited by concerns about spelling. Was she really avoiding words that she did not know how to spell? If so, where was she getting the notion that writing was about spelling, not the exploration and communication of ideas?

Working with 31 kindergartners during writing workshop was key to the evolution of my thinking about literacy during that year. The first-hand experience I had with those five- and six-year-olds offered me a site where I could work through my cognitive disequilibrium around literacy education. Note the following journal entry I wrote in January of 2010:

> Something that I thought about is how the focus on the sounds of the letters interrupts fluency. I wonder how to get kids to just write and not worry about how to write it?

Wondering if that is the right approach or not. I could see how one student [during writing workshop] was not able to write because she didn't appear to have much sound-letter connection. Just wondering about the timing of pushing kids to sound out words before they write them? Should they just draw? How can you help them to begin to make the connection and keep their fluency? (Journal 1/19/10)

"How can you help them to begin to make the connection and keep their fluency?" was a question at the heart of the issue for me. As is evident from my writing above, attention to timing, individual student needs, sounding out letters/words, and fluency were teaching strategies that were all in question for me.

Early in the second semester, I became increasingly agitated about Maya's lack of interest in reading independently and felt like she had an inability to write using invented spelling (Bissex) that illustrated an understanding of sound-symbol relationship (see Fig. 1 & 2).

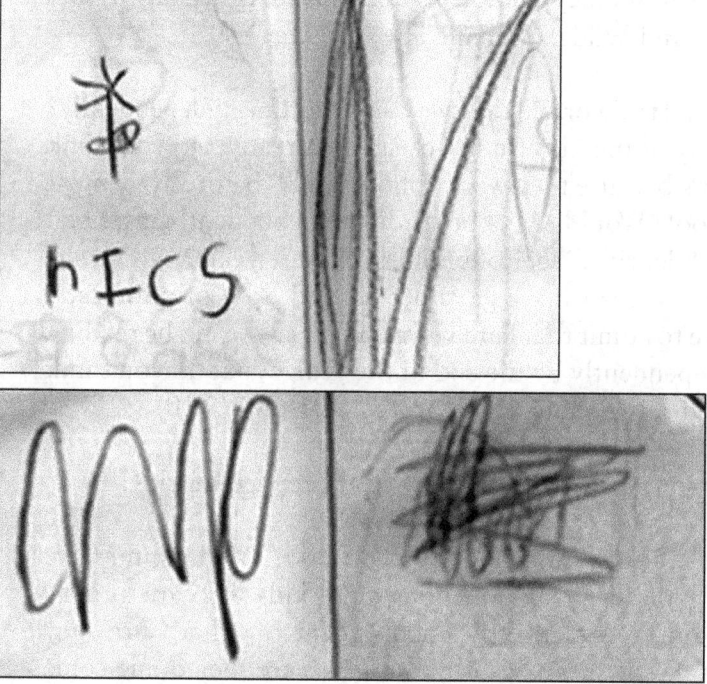

Top: Fig. 1, Bottom: Fig. 2

I was surprised by my agitation. Throughout my teaching career I had grown used to being the minority voice—pushing the pedagogical edges. As a middle school teacher I was the only one in my rural Illinois school who did not use textbooks, positioned desks in groups rather than rows, and encouraged student dialogue as opposed to stifling talk in the name of good classroom management. As a teacher educator I have encouraged my students to be activists as progressive literacy instructors rather than blind recipients of standardized curriculum and assessment. The unexpected pressure of being a parent and feeling responsible for the growth and development of my own child made the stakes seem much higher—thus challenging the core of who I was as an educator. Note the following journal entry: "It is just that it feels like a lot is riding on this for me. All the things that I believe in and have been espousing for 20 years feel like they are riding on Maya's ability to make meaning from print" (Journal 1/27/10).

In order to sort through my uncertainties, I decided that I should return to my literacy mentor, my doctoral advisor, Dorothy Watson (Watson and Wilde). I emailed her my worries:

> Should I be worried that Maya isn't reading independently? Many of the kids [in her class] do already. Do you think that's because they were "phonicated" before arriving at school? Would Maya be reading independently if we had not "deprived" her of phonics all these years? Would she learn to read if we gave her a good dose of phonics? I have to admit that I am worried that she won't be reading independently by the end of the year. What do you think of all this?" (Email to Dorothy Watson 2/5/10)

Dr. Watson, who rarely minces words, replied quickly:

> So she's not reading independently. 6 1/2? Hmmmm? Give the kiddo a break! ...About those kids who are already reading independently. Independent of what? Are they getting the meaning of the story, or are they doing some barking at print? I'll bet Maya knows that a story is sup-

posed to make sense, not just sounds. Remember phonics is a part (small part) of whole language." (Email from Dorothy Watson 2/5/10)

The email left me with the sting of a ball hitting my bare skin. Dr. Watson, who I had looked up to all these years had given me the academic equivalent of a spanking. "She's right," I thought. When she says, "Give the kiddo a break!" I realized I needed to give myself a break.

RECLAIMING LITERACY

> *Riding bikes together on our 12 block ride to school pedaling in and out of every driveway testing her expertise and my tolerance as she moves from driveway to street, driveway to street. Pink lunchbox hanging over the pink handlebar grip. The pink polka-dotted poncho drawing attention to her as she mindlessly sings, "A aa apple, B bb bear, Ccc Cat, Ddd dog...."*

Slowly over the next two months, I was able to put less pressure on myself. In some way, Dr. Watson's email gave me permission to trust the process and not feel so attached to an outcome, i.e. reading independently, and performing at a certain rate or ability level. I was beginning to grow back into my whole language, constructivist skin. In addition to getting a "talking to" by Dr. Watson, Maya's increasing skill with language also renewed my confidence in a holistic, meaning-centered literacy approach. The following entry from my journal entry in March, 2010:

> This was a huge week for Maya's literacy development. I guess I should say that it is a huge week for my literacy development. I feel like I should have known better, but I didn't. I was caught up in the two-decade-long argument I have had with others about literacy development. I have spent so much time defending myself and my beliefs about teaching, that I seriously doubted what I had been teach-

ing about learning to read. I know that if I had worked with early language learners before then I would have not doubted myself so much. But I hadn't. I didn't have any experience with little kids." (Journal 3/29/10)

As I point out in the journal entry above, my understanding of language developed right along with Maya's. With each step she took, I took one. Relief settled in each time I noticed a developmental shift in her literacy. My confidence re-emerged only after returning to my roots as an educator as well as witnessing emergent language users learning to read and write in a whole language context. I noted this in the following statement: "I know that if I had worked with early language learners before, then I would not have doubted myself so much."

In the spring it became clear that Maya was making connections between print and meaning. One day she brought home a "Family Traditions" book. This was the first of her writings that most resembled standard spelling. For this writing task, the teacher gave the children the sentence frames that provided Maya with the opportunity to write about her family's traditions. The invented spelling in Maya's writing is not necessarily easily deciphered, but in conjunction with her illustrations, meaning can be derived from the text. For example, "In the fall we LKT [rake] leaves" (see Fig. 3); "In the fall we go to the pog [pumkin] ppch [patch]" (see Fig. 4); "In the winter we cut down KRESMS [Christmas] tree" (see Fig. 5); and "In the winter we hangup strkng [hang up stockings]" (see Fig. 6). What encouraged me about her writing was that her pictures related to her text and that there were sounds represented in her spelling that could help the reader decode what she was writing. This book felt like a much-needed sign of progress for me. (It is important to note that I did not voice any concerns about her progress to Maya.)

This brings me back to the beginning of this chapter—the vignette of Maya reading independently for the first time in the back of the car on the way home from Seattle. When she began reading *Jamberry* (Degen) out loud, she was giddy with excitement—Elizabeth and I were too. Her reading and our celebration took us the remaining hour home from Seattle with smiles

From left to right: Fig. 3, Fig. 4

on our faces. How exhilarating it was for her to finally be able to decode the book and make sense of the print on the page! How moving for her moms to get to witness this moment. How energizing for me to observe the fruits of our commitment to a whole language family literacy approach and whole language kindergarten classroom.

RENEWED IDENTITY

When I began my inquiry into Maya's literacy development, I had set out to learn about literacy instruction. Though I did learn about the literacy process, the study ended up helping me to reclaim my early theoretical foundations and inspirations as an educator. As stated by Richard Meyer and Kathryn Whitmore, "Reclaiming …includes regaining access to prior and important work done by teachers and researchers. It also involves a dramatic change in the current perception of reading being perpetrated by special interest groups, such as corporations, right-wing organizations, and some legislators who are convinced that schools are chronically failing" (2). What amazes me now as I write this chapter is how, in spite my years of observing how middle and high schoolers benefit from a whole language approach as well as the strong mentoring I had over the years, I still struggled to parent my emergent reader in a way that was consistent with my beliefs about teaching and learning. In order to "reclaim" what I knew about teaching young children to read, I had to return to my mentors and my mentor texts. Just as Meyer's points out about the importance of returning to work done by teachers and researchers, my process of re-reading the likes of Glenda Bissex, Kenneth and Yetta Goodman, Dorothy Watson and Frank Smith re-acquainted me with my theoretical roots—it reignited my convictions to provide enriching literacy experiences for my child, preservice and inservice teachers. Reading back through my mentor texts and reading the margin notes that I had written back in the 1990s has provided me with the opportunity to literally go back in time and observe my thinking when I was encountering these ideas for the first time.

Reclaiming reading is just what I have done. I continue to have conversations with family members, my partner, and preservice and inservice teachers about our whole language approach to Maya's literacy development. The difference is that now, after parenting a kindergartner, I have *experienced* the developmental process of acquiring a first language—not just read about it. I now trust the process even more than I had before being a parent. I will continue to question and explore new ideas, but I will not allow the loud voices of the current standardized-testing culture to influence my understanding of it.

I have learned a great deal during Maya's kindergarten year. I have learned that anticipating a pre-determined outcome for my child is unproductive and sometimes painful. Holding on to expectations based on comparisons of other children is unrealistic and unproductive. As a parent and as a literacy educator, it is my obligation to provide an environment where exploration, risk taking, and curiosity can flourish. This is just what I intend to do.

WORKS CITED

Atwell, Nanci. *In the Middle: Reading and Writing in the Middle School*. 2nd ed. New Hampshire: Heinemann, 1998. Print.

Bissex, Glenda. *GYNS at Wrk: A Child Learns to Read and Write*. Cambridge: Harvard University Press, 1980. Print.

Degen, Bruce. *Jamberry*. New York: Harper & Row, 1983.

Goodman, Kenneth. "I Didn't Found Whole Language." *The Reading Teacher* 46.3 (1992): 188-199. Print.

Goodman, Kenneth S. *The Truth about DIBELS: What it is, what it does*. Portsmouth, NH: Heinemann, 2006. Print.

Goodman, Kenneth, and Yetta Goodman. "Learning to Read: A Comprehensive Model." *Reclaiming Reading: Teachers, Students, and Researchers Regaining Spaces for Thinking and Action*. Eds. Richard J. Meyer and Kathryn Whitmore. New York: Routledge, 2011. 19-41. Print.

Goodman, Yetta M., and Sandra Wilde. *Notes from a Kidwatcher: Selected Writings of Yetta M. Goodman*, 1996. Print.

Goodman, Yetta M., Dorothy Watson and Carolyn Burke. *Reading Strategies: Focus on Comprehension*. 2nd ed. New York: Richard C Owen Publishers. Print.

McLaren, Peter. *Life in Schools: An Introduction to Critical Pedagogy in the Foundations of Education*. 5th ed. New York: Longman, 2006. Print.

McLaughlin, Maureen. *Guided Comprehension in the Primary Grades*. Newark, DE: International Reading Association, 2010.

Meier, Deborah, and George H. Wood. *Many Children Left Behind: How the no Child Left Behind Act is Damaging our Children and our Schools*. Boston: Beacon Press, 2004. Print.

Meyer, Richard J. and Kathryn Whitmore. "Reclaiming Reading is a Political Act." *Reclaiming Reading: Teachers, Students, and Researchers Regaining Spaces for Thinking and Action*. Eds. Richard J. Meyer and Kathryn Whitmore. New York: Routledge, 2011. 1-16. Print.

Ouellette, Gene and Monique Sénéchal. "Pathways to Literacy: A Study of Invented Spelling and its Role in Learning to Read." *Child Development* 79.4 (2008): 899-913. Print.

Pearson, David. "The Reading Wars." *Educational Policy* 18.1 (2004): 216-252. Print.

Reutzel, D. Ray, and Robert B. Cooter. *Teaching Children to Read: Putting the Pieces Together*. Upper Saddle River, NJ: Merrill/Prentice Hall, 2004. Print.

Smith, Frank. *Reading without Nonsense*. 4th ed. New York: Teachers College Press, 2005. Print.

Vygotsky, Lev. *Thought and Language*. Cambridge: MIT Press, 1962. Print.

Watson, Dorothy, and Sandra Wilde. *Making a Difference: Selected Writings of Dorothy Watson*, 1996. Print.

Weisner, Jill. "When Someone in Us Awakens: Emerging Teacher Voice and Student Voice." Ph.D. University of Missouri-Columbia, 1999. Print.

Wink, Joan. *Critical Pedagogy: Notes from the Real World*. 4th ed. Upper Saddle River, NJ: Prentice Hall, 2010. Print.

6.
"You Are Your Child's First Teacher"

The Construction of Maternal Subjectivity in Family Literacy Programs

STACEY CROOKS

AS A LITERACY PRACTITIONER, I see family literacy programs as potentially supportive and empowering spaces for mothers; yet, at the same time, I see that programs sometimes emphasize outcomes for children at the expense of mothers' needs. This contradiction points to the persistent presence of a regulatory discourse in family literacy that blames mothers for their children's literacy problems while also denying that women have literacy needs and desires of their own (Auerbach "Deconstructing the Discourse" 651; Caspe; Cuban and Hayes 5-8).

This chapter explores the contradiction cited above by engaging with the iconic family literacy mantra, "You are your child's first teacher." The phrase—and the narrative it represents—appears repeatedly in family literacy promotional literature, training documents and research texts. I wish to open up this usually incontestable idea to contestation. Informed by critical understandings of gender, literacy and diversity, I will consider how the narrative discursively constructs the subjectivities available to mothers in family literacy programs and what alternatives it may work to silence (Gambles 704). To begin, I offer two stories.

A STORY FROM PRACTICE

Several years ago I helped design a family literacy program for immigrant families who were learning English as an additional language. At the time, I was working in a one-to-one tutoring program that also offered part-time English for employment classes. Program staff noted that many of the participants in these classes were stay-at-home moms who came to learn English and make social connections but who were not looking for immediate employment. We thought a family literacy program that included English classes for mothers and an early childhood component for children might better meet the women's needs.

The women we thought might attend the program came from diverse language and cultural backgrounds and had different levels of comfort with English. Some had attended almost no schooling in their first language and some had university degrees and had worked as professionals before coming to Canada. All of them faced the challenges of raising children in a new country far away from family. We wanted to support the women with the diverse literacy and English language demands they encountered in their daily lives as mothers and we wanted to do so in an empowering and welcoming environment. Drawing on the participatory model of Elsa Auerbach (*Making Meaning* 5-22), we envisioned a community-based, learner-centered and strengths-focused program in which participants co-created the curriculum.

We needed funding to cover food, transportation and early childhood staff. We drafted a proposal to apply for provincial funding and contacted literacy organizations to request letters of support to include with our application. One request went to an influential provincial literacy organization that was seen as the leader in family literacy work in the province. After a few days, we received a response from the executive director of that organization explaining that the group's family literacy coordinator did not feel comfortable with the proposal and, therefore, the organization would not provide us with a letter of support.

I contacted the director for more information and then spoke directly to the family literacy coordinator. After a series of e-mails and conversations, I felt that I understood her position. She was concerned our program lacked an explicit component intended to teach parents to support the development of their children's pre-literacy skills. Her example was teaching parents to read to their children.

I consulted with the others involved in developing the program proposal. We all felt puzzled as to why an intergenerational program centered on the literacy and English language needs that women face as mothers was not worthy of support. We made some revisions to the proposal and I contacted the family literacy coordinator again. I explained to her that we were not ruling out the kind of activities she was asking us to include; however, we wanted to work with the mothers to develop a program that would address their literacy needs as family members and individuals. In the end, she did not write us a letter of support. She suggested that while the program might be valuable and needed, it was not, in her eyes, family literacy.

We submitted the funding application to the provincial government and included letters of support from other organizations in the community. A while later, the funding program manager at the province contacted me with concerns similar to the ones expressed by the family literacy coordinator who had refused to support the program. I once again explained our rationale. My organization had a good relationship with the department and this may be why, in the end, we did receive the funding. The program has now been running for several years and, in terms of participation and learner satisfaction, is a success.

THE STORY OF "YOU ARE YOUR CHILD'S FIRST TEACHER"

If you look at a family literacy website or the cover of a family literacy brochure, you will often see the iconic image of an adult reading to a small child (Anderson, Streelasky and Anderson 147-148). The adult and child are likely cuddled up together; the child is sitting on the adult's lap and the adult is holding the book so they can both look at it. The adult's face is animated as she (or sometimes he) reads and the child is thoroughly engaged with the story, staring intently at the page. The scene is one of pure contentment and family bliss: a moment of parenting perfection.

This image is the visual representation of the ubiquitous family literacy slogan, "you are your child's first teacher." And if, as they say, a picture is worth a thousand words, we might guess that there is much more to this story. The slogan "you are your child's first teacher" and the image that often accompanies it reflect the way that many people think of family literacy, both as a type of program and as something that families do. Furthermore, this representation tells a story about the ideal family, particularly about the ideal mother.

The story told in family literacy discourse and titled "you are your child's first teacher" goes something like this: Once upon a time a mother gave birth to a child. In that moment of pure blissful bonding, her life was forever changed. The mother, being a good mother, sang lullabies, read books, and played games with her child from the moment of birth or (according to recent ideals), even before that. Changing diapers was a chance to count toes. Breastfeeding was a time to look deeply into the child's eyes and sing nursery rhymes. As the child grew, the mother found more "teachable moments" every day. Going for a walk, making lunch, or brushing teeth were moments of literacy learning and bonding.

As a baby, the child learned to love books and as the child learned to speak she or he developed a large vocabulary. The child learned to recite the alphabet, rhyme words, and count to ten. At age three, the child attended a quality pre-school for a few hours a week. Although the mother was nervous about being separated, she never let the child know. The transition was easy, partly because the child was "preschool ready" and partly because the teachers were competent and compassionate professionals. The child easily met the expected benchmarks at the expected times, learning to write his or her name before entering kindergarten, recognizing letter sounds (phonemes) and some sight words before grade one, and reading age appropriate material independently before entering grade two.

Throughout these early school years, the mother has gradually stepped back, recognizing the greater expertise of her child's classroom teachers in matters to do with literacy (and other things). As her job as "first teacher" ends, the mother's role changes. Now she is always ready to support her child's classroom teacher and the school in any way that she can (or any way that is requested). She fills out forms and returns them on time, volunteers in the classroom, attends parent teacher nights, bakes cookies (peanut free) for snack times, joins the parent council, checks homework, sells magazines and teaches her child to respect the teachers and the school. Outside of school, she continues to take her child to the library, provides supplies for writing and drawing, keeps good quality reading materials in the home and reads with her child. She also visibly engages in her own literacy activities daily so that her child has a role model. And they live happily ever after; the child's literacy learning (and future schooling) is a success.

CONNECTING THE STORIES

This chapter explores how this "first teacher" narrative works to create the disconnect that I witnessed in developing a family literacy program for immigrant families. This disconnect occurs between the understanding of family literacy programs as empowering spaces for families and mothers and the role that family literacy programs serve in regulating mothers and prescribing a narrow set of idealized behaviors (Luttrell 347; Prins and Toso, 557, 585; Smythe and Isserlis 30-38; Smythe 16; Toso 8). The first teacher narrative ignores "the cultural contradictions between the high social expectations for appropriate child-raising and literacy achievement on one hand, and the everyday lives and material conditions that shape mothering on the other" (Smythe 5). It also ignores that the "everyday lives and material conditions" of many families (mine included) tell a slightly (or sometimes very) different story.

> Within the iconic image of a mother-figure reading to a child, we can see the outlines of common discourses of mothering and literacy that rarely take into account women's lived experiences of mothering, the role of fathers in children's literacy learning, or the diversity of family structures and child-raising practices which give meaning and context to the literacies of everyday life. (Smythe 6)

The recognition that "real" families and "real" mothers often do not reflect the image presented as ideal in family literacy discourse is an important step in acknowledging that these ideals can sometimes serve to marginalize the families with whom we work. Literacy practitioners who wish to challenge deficit thinking need to recognize that there are many different, and equally valid, ways of doing literacy and of being a family. As Joan Scott observes, "making visible the experience of a different group exposes the existence of repressive mechanisms" (778). However, this recognition of difference does not help us understand *how* oppressive images appear in our work and how they function to regulate mothers.

In order to better understand these mechanisms, I am examining the first teacher narrative as a "historical process" that "through discourse, position(s) subjects and produce(s) their experience" (Scott 778). By drawing on examples of the narrative as presented in texts produced by organizations promoting family literacy programs and practices, I try to better understand the "conditions of possibility" (Davies 426) that are created and maintained for mothers and for family literacy practitioners in and through the first teacher narrative.

GENDER

Many writers have discussed the gendered nature of family literacy discourse (Cuban and Hayes 7; Luttrell 342; Smythe and Isserlis 30-38; Toso 24-33) and the prescribed role of mothers in the literacy development and education of children (Griffith and Smith 33). One interesting aspect of the "you are your child's first teacher" narrative is the way in which the narrative is gendered. In my version of the narrative above, I have presented the mother as the subject "you." No father appears. This is not true in every version of the narrative. In fact, Jim Anderson, Jodi Streelasky and Terri Anderson (148) have pointed to an increase in images of fathers on family literacy websites. However, despite these representations, the narrative continues to be implicitly gendered and the job of the child's first teacher is generally seen to be a woman's job, specifically that of the mother.

Reflective of the "silent gendered discourse" in family literacy (Caspe), particular examples of the first teacher narrative rarely refer directly to mothers; instead texts use the pronoun "you" or refer to the first teacher as the "parent" or "caregiver" (e.g. Saskatchewan Literacy Network; Toronto District School Board;

Whitehurst). Yet, family literacy programs still tend to be created with mothers in mind. This may be because mothers are more often the primary caregivers of young children and more likely to attend family literacy programs. However, it is also reflective of the way in which family literacy practice is embedded in mothering discourses that emphasize the mothers' role as critical to their children's (literacy) development. And, although family literacy programs work with female caregivers other than mothers (Anderson and Morrison 70), the investment in the notion of the "Standard North American Family" (Smith 159) puts the focus on mothers specifically.

As constituted by family literacy discourse, the narrative, "you are your child's first teacher" is gendered in that it specifically addresses mothers; conversely, the narrative also works to constitute family literacy discourse as gendered. In other words, the narrative promotes gendered assumptions regarding the roles of mothers and fathers in families. A closer look at the ways in which the first teacher narrative appears in texts produced by family literacy organizations confirms that the narrative constructs literacy work as mothers' work. Thus, it is embedded in the "gendered discourse" but it also reinscribes it.

For example, the Saskatchewan Literacy Network links the role of the child's first teacher with the "basics of life" and with the "bond" that develops between parent and child. Similarly, the Toronto District School Board states, "your bond is the greatest influence on your child's success at school." Despite the fact that many fathers' bond with their children and provide them with the basics of life, these tasks are still more often associated with and taken up by mothers in caring for babies and young children. As Amanda Richey observes, "gender and literacy are constitutive of one another" (168) with "both tied up in the knot of motherhood" (169). In addition, the use of the word teacher itself suggests that the "you" is a woman. After all, "to imagine a teacher is to conjure the image of a woman" (Cammack and Phillips 124). Furthermore, since more than 95 percent of early childhood educators in Canada are women (*Early Childhood Educators and Assistants* n. pag.), this observation is particularly relevant in regards to teachers of young children.

THE SUBJECTIVITY OF MOTHERS IN THE
FIRST TEACHER NARRATIVE

The first teacher narrative shapes the way that practitioners and others view family literacy programs by contributing to the creation of a "hegemony of the normal" (Davis 149) in which an ideal is constructed as normal and all mothers are expected to live up to it. The role of family literacy programs from this perspective is to support mothers to become this ideal, so that they can fulfill their roles as good mothers. The model for this ideal mother is constructed from the perspective of the school, rather than from the diverse families in which children grow and learn to read. Thus, instead of expanding our notions of what it means to "teach," the narrative narrows our notion of what it is to "mother."

Citing Bronwyn Davies and Sue Saltmarsh, Amanda Bethel Richey notes that subjectivities are formed partly in the intersection of discourses of literacy and gender. "That is, literacy learning—from early childhood—has reproduced and exercised the gender order in our society such that we are simultaneously produced as gendered and literate" (42). The first teacher narrative, as a gendered narrative, contributes to this process. In laying out the "terms of submission" for mothers, it describes what mothers "are to become" (Davies 429). The first teacher narrative constitutes mothers as subjects in particular ways. In doing so, the narrative can be seen to "govern" mothers to the extent that it "structure(s) the possible field of action" of mothers (Foucault qtd. in Davies 430).

Beyond the ways that mothers are constituted in the narrative, the ways that these subjectivities are resisted and reproduced in the experience of mothers are also intertwined/embedded in the performances of maternal subjects in family literacy; that is, women "perform" motherhood in relation to the first teacher narrative. We must be conscious of the agency of mothers as subjects and how mothers "take up" the subjectivity that is constituted for them by the narrative. This is a complex question but understandings of how mothers enact agency in the context of family literacy discourse are always present in our discussions of how that discourse constitutes mothers as subjects.

"YOU ARE YOUR CHILD'S FIRST TEACHER"

CHARACTERISTICS OF THE MATERNAL SUBJECT IN THE FIRST TEACHER NARRATIVE

The mother is constituted as a subject in contradictory ways in the first teacher narrative. Similarly, Sharon Rosenberg explains one of the contradictions of the way we perform gender:

> ...for gendering to work really well, gendered subjects must occupy a particularly intense paradox: On the one hand, we are told that gender is just who we are, and on the other hand, we are told that gender is an (almost impossible) achievement that takes enormous effort, resources, and labour (our own as well as others). (45)

In the first teacher narrative, the mother is her children's natural teacher, but she needs to be taught by experts to perform appropriate, sometimes contrived ways to support her children's literacy. She is isolated and solely responsible for her children's literacy (and therefore their academic and economic futures) but she is also in need of close supervision. She is a nurturing mother motivated by love, but she is professional and efficient in directing her children's literacy progress. She always makes learning fun, but she is also seriously committed to her children's success.

The natural teacher/mother

At the core of the contradictory nature of maternal subjectivity in the narrative is the presentation of mothers as natural, but flawed, teachers of their children. Mothers in this narrative are naturally caring and supportive of their children's literacy. They are also natural teachers who fulfill this role without being aware that they are doing so. But this is not enough. Mothers need to expand what they do naturally in order to truly be their child's first teacher. The following example from a family literacy "tool kit" suggests this relationship:

> Since parents are the first adults in a child's life to pass on information, they are essentially the child's first teacher. It is from a parent or caregiver that a child learns the basics

of life, such as how to walk, talk, hold a spoon, etc. This develops through a nurturing process that *comes naturally* without much thought by the caregiver towards structured learning. As a child learns these basics, a bond develops and creates a foundation for extended learning. If the caregiver *decides to build on* this foundation through reading out loud, asking questions, building vocabulary, etc. they have already developed their own family literacy initiative. (Saskatchewan Literacy Network; emphasis added)

Here mothers are portrayed as "essentially" and "naturally" their child's first teacher. However, it is only through particular kinds of effort and work that mothers can perform in the way that family literacy discourse demands. Other examples of the narrative emphasize that this performance requires the help of "experts" (e.g. Toronto District School Board).

A further example of the paradox is the emphasis that the narrative places on the kind of activity that Suzanne Smythe describes as "a contrived pedagogical experience" (2). This is evident in tools such as the "Home Literacy Environment Checklist" (Whitehurst). The checklist purports to measure the literacy-friendliness of the home and asks about the parent's actions, but also about what children have (e.g. "My child has magnetized alphabet letters to play with") and what the child sees adults doing (e.g. "My child sees me or another adult in the house reading books"). Another category of question is titled "what I am" and asks parents questions about their own vocabulary and their pleasure in reading. Here it is not enough for a mother to support her child's literacy learning; she also must *become* a particular kind of person in order to perform her role as first teacher appropriately.

The isolated/independent mother

The mother in the first teacher narrative appears alone. Family or community members who might support her (as she supports her children) are largely absent. Children in this narrative do not appear to be nurtured or taught by extended family and community members. Since ultimate responsibility for children's success lies firmly on the shoulders of the mother, the contributions of others are not relevant to the story. This is evident in that pictures of the child's first teacher most often show one adult, although they may show more than one child (Anderson, Streelasky and Anderson 148).

At times the narrative acknowledges that being a parent of young children can be isolating (e.g. Toronto District School Board). However, the solution described is not for the parent (mother) to find employment outside the home, pursue a personal project, or get together with friends. Nor does the solution involve addressing the structural realties that may create her isolation. Instead, the solution is to attend a program where she can learn to be a better parent and teacher: "Visit your local Parenting and Family Centre and relax with other parents and our friendly experts. Share ideas and discover new activities for at-home fun" (Toronto District School Board). The focus of this interaction is on improving the mother's ability to perform her role. The first teacher/mother will then return to her home, alone (but always with her child), re-dedicated to helping her child succeed.

The responsible/untrustworthy mother

The first teacher narrative places responsibility for the literacy "success" of children solely with parents, particularly mothers. Mothers, as their children's first teachers, are ultimately responsible for their children's success or failure in school. This narrative ignores the "toxic literacies" (Taylor 2) and structural inequalities in women's lives (Richey 149) that construct women in ways that may make it difficult for them to fulfill their "role" as their child's "teacher." It also ignores the structural factors that make it difficult for children to succeed in school. Ultimately, by placing responsibility with the family, the narrative works to absolve schools and society for literacy (and economic) inequalities that, according to the narrative, have their origins in the home and in the inadequacy of mothers.

As they are solely responsible for the literacy success of their children, mothers in the narrative are under a great deal of pressure. According to the first teacher narrative, the "early years" (before six years of age) are critical in a child's development and if children miss particular opportunities in this stage, their future success is in jeopardy. Mothers are not only expected to provide these opportunities, but they also are expected to want to give their children "every advantage" (Toronto District School Board). Here, the narrative refers to the presence of a hierarchical social and economic system and suggests that mothers are in competition with each other to ensure their children's place in the hierarchy.

The emphasis on the early years may also be why family literacy programs tend to be developed for mothers of preschool-aged children. Mothers of older children are not seen as needing the same support. When our children enter school, our role as our child's first teacher is complete. At that point in the narrative, if the mother has been successful, the school takes over as teacher. A new story begins in which the school and teacher are in the lead role and the mother is shifted to a supporting character who fulfils her new role by coordinating her life, and the lives of her family members, in response to the organizational and educational demands of the school (Griffith and Smith 10).

WHAT ISN'T THERE

When the first teacher narrative informs family literacy work, it erases mothers as subjects outside of their roles as mothers and literacy teachers. Furthermore, the ways that mothers are constructed as subjects in this narrative are narrow and prescriptive. In focusing on mothers as teachers, it ignores all the other things that mothers do and the different ways they do them. In the first teacher narrative, "there is nothing more important than being a parent" (Toronto District School Board). The mother who is her child's first teacher does not seem to have needs or interests outside her need to support her children. She is her child's first teacher but also first, before all else, she is her child's teacher. The only literacy or learning that she practices is with her child or in order to set an example for her child. Furthermore, she is not a complex human being who feels stressed out and ambivalent about things. She is not frustrated or tired in her role as mother/teacher. She doesn't want a break from her children—she only wants to know better how to fulfill her role as first teacher. In this sense, she is a non-subject: a "conduit" through which the child is reached (Richey 25).

Furthermore, mothers as subjects in this narrative are not even complete as mothers. The representation of the mother as the child's first teacher erases most of the day-to-day work that mothers do. Focusing on the mother as "teacher" without acknowledging the never-ending tasks and complex realities of "motherwork" (Collins 47) creates a picture of mothering that denies the challenges of this work, including the structural inequalities that characterize mothering in our society. It assumes there is one right way to do literacy, one right one way to mother, and one right way to be a family. By holding up one type of literacy practice as ideal, the narrative works to erase cultural models of literacy outside the mainstream (Auerbach "Deconstructing the Discourse" 647). Families with other language or cultural backgrounds are constructed as "at-risk," "disadvantaged" (Auerbach "Deconstructing the Discourse" 646).

The narrative also denies economic realities other than middle class ones and obscures the presence of structural inequalities (such as racism) that marginalize many mothers and families. For example, the narrative never addresses the power imbalances that exist between non-mainstream families and schools (Reyes and Torres 74). Instead it focuses on the behaviors of individual mothers and programs constructed based on this narrative focus on "fixing" families by changing these behaviors. In the end, by labeling non-mainstream families as "deficient" and by failing to address systemic barriers to their participation in schools, such programs may further marginalize them (Reyes and Torres 75).

In the narrative of "you are your child's first teacher," it is evident both what constitutes the ideal mother as well as what constitutes the abject mother. The ideal mother is never attainable, yet mothers are expected to aim towards it and in doing so some who most closely resemble the ideal may be "recognized and accepted" (Davies 434) as good mothers. Mothers who do not strive for this ideal, or mothers whose subjectivities are for some other reason seen as incompatible with it, are at risk of being seeing as abject, as not "viable" (Davies 434) as maternal subjects.

As Bronwyn Davies notes, "freedom does not vanish when power is exercised. The relation is much more complex" (430). Similarly mothers' subjectivities are not wholly determined by family literacy discourse or by the first teacher narrative. However it also true that "the available meaning structures are deeply inscribed in our bodies, in our emotions and in desire" (435).

LOOKING BACK AND LOOKING FORWARD

As Michel Foucault argues, "the fundamental point of anchorage ... is to be found outside the institution" (791). In this case, the discourse of family literacy that I am locating in the utterance, "you are your child's first teacher" is itself located in larger regulating discourses. Family literacy as a "discipline" or "institution" did not originate these regulating discourses but is formed by them (and, in turn, reforms them).

The link between the first teacher narrative and practice is an important one. When the family literacy coordinator I spoke of earlier refused to support our program, I think it was partly because of the way this narrative constitutes mothers as subjects. If mothers in family literacy programs are subjects who do not have needs (or who do not use literacy) outside supporting their children's literacy development, then programs that do not focus explicitly on the ways they do this cannot be family literacy programs. And if mothers in family literacy programs are natural teachers, but ones who need experts to support them in fulfilling this role, then it should be the experts and not the mothers themselves who determine the curriculum of programs.

The idea of "you are your child's first teacher" does not have to be a negative one or one that primarily works to discipline mothers. In contrast, I can imagine a way of understanding this narrative as a recognition of the important role that parents play in their children's literacy development. In this interpretation, schools might see their role as supporting families in their literacy practices and teachers might view parents as sources of expert information about the children in their classrooms. This proposes the creation of a rather different relationship between mothers and families, and programs.

If family literacy programs are to foster such a relationship, practitioners need to be critically aware of the way that they position mothers in their narratives. Conscious attention to mothers as knowledgeable subjects may contribute to the development of an alternative version of the first teacher narrative and the creation of programs to which mothers can bring their whole complex and contradictory subjectivities.

WORKS CITED

Anderson, Jim, Jodi Streelasky and Terri Anderson. "Representing and Promoting Family Literacy on the World Wide Web: A Critical analysis." *Alberta Journal of Educational Research* 53.2 (2007): 143-156.

Anderson, Jim, and Fiona Morrison. "'A Great Program ... For Me as a Gramma': Caregivers Evaluate a Family Literacy Initiative." *Canadian Journal of Education* 30.1 (2007): 68-89. Print.

Auerbach, Elsa. "Deconstructing the Discourse of Strengths in Family Literacy." *Journal of Literacy Research* 27.4 (1995): 643-61. Print.

Auerbach, Elsa. *Making Meaning, Making Change: Participatory Curriculum Development*. McHenry, IL: Center for Applied Linguistics & Delta Systems, 1992. Print.

Cammack, J. Camille, and Donna Phillips. "Discourses and Subjectivities of the Gendered Teacher." *Gender and Education* 14.2 (2002): 123-33. Print.

Caspe, Margaret. "Family Literacy: A Review of Programs and Critical Perspectives." Cambridge, MA, 2003. Harvard Family Research Project. Harvard Graduate School of Education. Web. Oct. 31, 2011.

Collins, Patricia Hill. "Shifting the Center: Race, Class, and Feminist Theorizing About Motherhood." *Mothering: Ideology, Experience, and Agency*. Eds. E. N. Glenn, G. Chang and R. Forcey. New York: Routledge, 1994. 45-66. Print.

Cuban, Sondra and Elisabeth Hayes. "Women in Family Literacy Programs: A Gendered Perspective." *New Directions for Adult and Continuing Education* 70 (1996): 5-16. Print.

Davies, Bronwyn. "Subjectification: The Relevance of Butler's Analysis for Education." *British Journal of Sociology of Education* 27.4 (2006): 425-38. Print.

Davis, Lennard J. *Enforcing Normalcy: Disability, Deafness and the Body*. London, England: Verso Press, 1995. Print.

Early Childhood Educators and Assistants. Service Canada, 2012. Web. 2 Apr. 2012.

Foucault, Michel. "The Subject and Power." *Critical Inquiry* 8 (1982): 777-795. Print.

Gambles, Richenda. "Supernanny, Parenting and a Pedagogical State." *Citizenship Studies* 14.6 (2010): 697-709. Print.

Griffith, Alison and Dorothy Smith. *Mothering for Schooling*. New York: Routledge Falmer, 2005. Print.

Luttrell, Wendy. "Taking Care of Literacy: One Feminist's Critique." *Educational Policy* 10.3 (1996): 342-65. Print.

Prins, Esther, and Blaire Wilson Toso. "Defining and Measuring Parenting for Educational Success: A Critical Discourse Analysis of the Parent Education Profile." *American Educational Research Journal* 45.3 (2008): 555-96. Print.

Reyes, Loui V. and Myriam N. Torres. "Decolonizing Family Literacy in a Culture Circle: Reinventing the Family Literacy Educator's Role." *Journal of Early Childhood Literacy* 7.1 (2007): 73-94. Print.

Richey, Amanda Bethel. *(M)Other Literacies: Transgressive Identity and Education in Women's Narratives*. Diss. Tennessee Technological University, 2011. Print.

Rosenberg, Sharon. "An Introduction to Feminist Poststructural Theorizing." *Feminist Issues: Race, Class and Sexuality*. Ed. Mendell, Nancy. 4th ed. Toronto: Pearson/Prentice Hall Inc., 2004. 35-57. Print.

Saskatchewan Literacy Network. "Principles and Philosophies of Family Literacy." Saskatoon, SK, n.d. *Family Literacy Tool Kit*. Saskatchewan Literacy Network. Web. April 24 2011.

Scott, Joan. "The Evidence of Experience." *Critical Inquiry* 17.4 (1991): 773-97. Print.

Smith, D. E. *Writing the Social: Critique, Theory and Investigations*. Toronto: University of Toronto Press, 1999. Print.

Smythe, Suzanne. *The Good Mother: A Critical Discourse Analysis of Literacy Advice to Mothers in the Twentieth Century*. Diss. University of British Columbia, 2006. Print.

Smythe, Suzanne, and Janet Isserlis. "Regulating Women and Families: Mothering Discourses in Family Literacy Texts." *English*

Quarterly 34.3/4 (2002): 30-38. Print.

Taylor, Denny. *Toxic Literacies: Exposing the Injustice of Bureaucratic Texts*. Portsmouth, NH: Heinemann, 1996. Print.

Toronto District School Board. "Welcome to Our Parenting and Family Literacy Centres." Toronto, 2010. *Parenting and Family Litracy Centre Fact Sheet*. Toronto District School Board. Web. July 2011.

Toso, Blaire Willson. *Latina Mothers' Enactments of Agency: Achieving Desires through Discourses in Family Literacy*. Diss. Pennsylvania State University, 2010. Print.

Whitehurst, G. "Get Ready to Read: Home Literacy Environment Checklist." National Centre for Learning Disabilities, 2004. Print.

III.
Mothering and Visual Literacies

7.
Social Representations of Motherhood Through the Practice of Art Journaling

JESSICA SMARTT GULLION AND ARIEL COOKSEY

THE PRACTICE of keeping a journal is a mainstay of popular culture. Oprah Winfrey advocates daily "gratitude journaling." Bookstores carry shelves of blank books, journals with daily prompts, wedding journals, pregnancy journals, journals for grandparents to write to their grandchildren, and diaries complete with lock and key. The popularity of journaling as an exploratory activity, an academic exercise, and a tool for therapy has increased in recent years as the perks behind the practice become more evident through research and literature. Indeed, part of being human is the ability to tell stories that draw meaning to our experiences (Murray 653). Journaling allows for both personal contemplation as well as giving the author a creative, private space to document life. The function of journaling does not merely extend to the pragmatic, but also lends itself to personal growth and development. Sheri Klein found evidence that journaling as a reflective or meditative act can foster creativity, self-reflection, and personal development, and can draw the writer's attention to details that may have been lost in the chaos of daily living. "If we think about development as a spiral process rather than a linear process," writes Klein "it is then possible at any time to revisit knowledge, experience, and memories with new insights and greater self-awareness and understanding" (49). This potential for self-awareness and attention to detail often heightens one's creative impulses. Many artists have found Julia Cameron's "morning pages" technique—rapid freeflow writing of three pages upon waking—helpful for removing creative blocks and unlocking creative potential (9-18).

This form of contemplative inquiry can also benefit academic and professional study. By linking the practice of keeping a journal to assignments, educators promote reflexivity in their students and thereby improve learning outcomes. With this type of explicit use, journaling helps students gain understanding of discrete events, develop their critical thinking skills, improve their writing and literacy, and make connections between classroom-based knowledge and life experiences. The development of these competencies is effective in bridging a gap between the academic, the personal, and ultimately the professional.

A form of journaling underrepresented in academic work is the art or visual journal. In this chapter we explore the practice of art journaling and examine its use as a tool for both reading and writing motherhood.

ART JOURNALING AND MOTHERHOOD

"I started using a small set of watercolors that I could stash in my bag when we went to the park. It had to be easy when my kids were small, or I wouldn't get to it" (Berry 113).

Art journaling is a creative outlet for processing experience and emotion with a visual component. Rather than being bound by lined paper to write pages of text, art journalers use a variety of expressive tools. Art journals are typically mixed-media projects. Painted pages are affixed with ephemera—the flotsam and jetsam of daily life. Patterned papers, photographs, images and text cut from magazines and other printed materials, memorabilia, inks, rubber stamps, markers, special pens, pastels, chalk...anything that can used to make a mark may be found within. The book itself may have begun as a blank book, a handmade book, or an altered book repurposed for art journaling. Writing is integrated into the visual components and often becomes a point of visual interest. It is typically free form, illustrating public or private moments, the grand or every day. A page may have no words, but rather allow expression of emotion through imagery. A word or phrase may dominate the page, or the page may spill with text. Key to the practice of art journaling is this interface between the creative act of artistic expression, and the functional act of writing (Dunn 2).

Many mothers engage in the practice of documenting family life, and this documentation may take many forms. Combining visual and written elements, the art journal functions as a chronicle and also as a space for introspection. Art journaling is an effective way to creatively express meaningful events, offering the journal creator the opportunity to understand, analyze, deconstruct, and express feelings they are experiencing. Images and words coalesce to create a visual narrative of mothers' struggles, joys, and lived experience, improving intra-personal communication and strengthening literacy in both traditional and unconventional ways.

> Each day I rose very early, making coffee, and settled into my big couch in my dark houseful of my sleeping family, to watch the sun come over the Rocky Mountains. I noticed the colors of the sky, how the alpenglow cast pink on the hills, and what shapes the blue shadows made. I would look around my house to see things I loved and I drew maps of my rooms and walls. When the kids got up, I would leave my journal with one pen on the table, so I could jot down the funny things they did and said. (Berry 113)

Through the process of developing art journals, mothers have the opportunity to synthesize important or note-worthy events, and create a visual text that tells the reader their story, using images to depict ideas, vignettes, and emotions in a manner that deviated from the usual practice of daily written diary entries. As texts, these journals give the viewer a nontraditional outlet for reading motherhood and provide an interaction that plays to a multitude of response and understanding.

Social representation theory guides our discussion, and we focus on the creative process as a means of dissemination through symbols to further communicative skills. Our research highlights the continued need to expand definitions of literacy to encompass ways in which individuals may demonstrate expression in addition to written text. We have peppered our chapter with quotes from mothers who practice art journaling as a means to voice their personal experiences.

> I love to [art] journal. I have to journal. I have to feed my journal, and my journal returns the favor by always being right there to hear me. My journals are subject to ranting, venting, gushing, crying, praising, praying, questioning, and accepting. And I love them for it. (Todd 74)

The practice of art journaling can be iterative. Amanda Mercer et al. described this phenomenon by noting that "the visual journal successfully combines written and visual interventions allowing for the experience of both emotional satisfaction and cognitive awareness" (144). It is in this dimension beyond the scope of pragmatism that visual journaling transcends the mere use as a record of events, allowing art journalers to enter into the sphere of the therapeutic. Women use images and words in aesthetically chosen ways to symbolically release tension, distress, and joy. The journals serve as a meditation, as a means to process emotion, and ultimately as a catharsis for many women.

> "I am an artist because I create. I create daily—one step closer to healing with every layer of paint." (Phillips 11)

In 1998, Pam England and Rob Horowitz introduced a revolutionary approach to labor management within the pages of the book, *Birthing From Within*. The book focused on the nature of pregnancy and childbirth from more than a medical standpoint; it tackled the topics from emotional and creative standpoints. The central premise is advocacy of art making to understand and process what is happening in the life, the mind, and the body of the pregnant woman. Creation of art validates the mother's innate, intuitive knowledge. By recognizing this, the authors advocate a series of creative prompts and interactive exercises to "help them discover and validate their own knowledge, rather than directing a stream of information at them" (ix). In the chapter "Discovery Through Drawing and Painting," the authors guide pregnant women through several soul-searching exercises to illuminate and conquer fears. Through visual representation, these mothers are asked to explore their perceptions of self-image, what meanings they associate with pregnancy, and the fantasies they hold of labor and birth. In the first section, expectant mothers are guided to "draw, paint or sculpt your image of Pregnant Woman. This image could be an abstraction or a human form, a self-portrait...or how you see pregnant women in general." Through this activity, women create images that mirror their emotions and perspectives as they apply to pregnancy. They are encouraged to caption or verbally express their thoughts on creating and living the picture (41-55).

This approach to pregnancy and preparation for childbirth and even child rearing has certainly caught on. Bookstore shelves carry fabricated pregnancy journals with fill-in-the-blank style prompts for similar self-expression. Other pregnancy information books have mimicked the *Birthing From Within* approach with inclusion of interactive ideas to drive points home, often commemorating "firsts"—first OB visit, first time the mother heard the baby's heartbeat, the first time she saw her baby in a sonogram—to detailed accounts of what women see, feel, think, smell, touch, and taste that is unique to them during pregnancy. This type of sensory exploration is also used in counseling and therapy as prompts for self-discovery.

Expectant mothers have a unique relationship to embark upon; mothers must reconcile their emotions with their unborn child. Many women use this as a time for introspection, and art journaling allows a forum for emotional exploration without judgment. A two-page spread from artist L. K. Ludwig's journals shows a pregnant woman, drawn and cut out of a page of sheet music, attached to a black background. Colorful birds are glued over the image, the words "perching birds" written over the woman's shoulder. On the facing page, stamped in white letters are the words "I am mama bird egg nest." A note below the pages indicates that the pages were created during the course of a difficult pregnancy. She writes that, "often, we are able to broach childhood in our art journaling after becoming parents ourselves. Suddenly, we find that having children leads us to understand our own parents more and, at the same time, understand them less. Libraries and galleries could be filled with art journals that examined childhood" (Ludwig 42).

A few years ago on a trip to Arizona, I went on an outing

with my son. We were headed to a spacious park where he could skateboard. I loaded up a favorite bark cloth backpack with my journal and some supplies. I settled in; writing, doodling, and I listened to the birdsong while my son happily practiced skateboarding. I love the pages from that time. (Bunsen 84)

The ameliorative qualities of art journaling do not only come from tackling dark fears and sorrows. Ludwig encourages art journaling about relationships. "The examination of relationships has provided inspiration for artwork through history—art journaling is no exception" (Ludwig 33). Art journaling may be a celebration of life and of living. Striking design and emotional imagery fill Donna Dugon-Ahami's journal of living nine years cancer-free (73). On one page, painted in muted blues and browns, Dugon-Ahami includes photo-booth pictures of herself and her granddaughter making silly faces at the camera. A picture of a lion decorates the bottom of the page, and the number 9 is stenciled in the center. Faded words are stamped across the paper: "destination, unknown, JOURNEY, explore, now." Hand-written words read, "Cassie was born during chemo. This year I'm 9 years cancer free and my beautiful grand-daughter is 9. Here's to survival!!!!"

> We'll overthrow the old notions of a journal as either a plain-papered home for safe thoughts, or a "pretty" book created from premade project kits. (Woods and Dinino 7)

Ultimately, through the ups and downs, art journaling provides a means to process and understand the changes and emotions that go hand in hand with pregnancy and mother-child relationships. The pages do not have to be happy or sad; there are no rules and no arbiters. It is a means of a discovery that is wholly personal. As Shannon Sinclair, a mother of four children and a 911 operator, observes,

> For me, art journaling happens in the precious and few moments of the in-between: in the five minutes before leav-

ing for work, at the kitchen counter before picking up the kids from schools, or on a lunch break, sandwich in one hand, [paint] brush in the other... The many long hours I spend handling life or death emergencies and nurturing my family exacts a toll. It is easy to become overwhelmed by the incredible amount of stress and pressure. Art journaling reconnects me back to myself. It grounds, fills, sustains, and ultimately saves me. (101)

ART JOURNALING AND THE SOCIAL REPRESENTATION OF MOTHERHOOD

While art journaling in itself is generally a solitary practice, the mass of artwork produced by mothers seizes and creates a unique literacy. The symbolic, cathartic pages create a vibrant representation of motherhood that may be read by viewers. The process of creating meaning from experience is also the process of creating a collective consciousness about that experience. Deconstructing her life through artistic pages centers the mother in a collective experience of motherhood. Her expression both extends and refines meaning. In this manner motherhood is both mediated by and recreated through the larger conceptualizations and texts of motherhood. Social representation theory is a useful framework for exploring the role of art journaling among mothers as it connects the micro and the macro by linking individual values and beliefs with those of the collective. Through collective evaluation and integration of individual stances social reality is shaped.

When considering a representation of motherhood, we must examine the social mediation of that construct. Emile Durkheim viewed collective representations as the embodiment of knowledge a society holds over a given social object. The interplay between the individual act of creating a work of art flows both from and to a collective consciousness, a social design of motherhood. Durkheim wrote,

> Solely because society exists, there also exists beyond sensations and images a whole system of representations that possess marvelous properties. By means of them, men

understand one another, and minds gain access to one another. They have a kind of force and moral authority by virtue of which they impose themselves upon individual minds. From then on, the individual realizes, at least dimly, that above his private representations there is a world of type-ideas according to which he had to regulate his own; he glimpses a whole intellectual world in which he participates but which is greater than he. (438)

Thus through the creation of a private, individual page, the art journal is nonetheless ensconced in a larger social force, that of creating and maintaining the said social construct. Durkheim wrote that collective representations "add to what our personal experience can teach us all the wisdom and science that has collectively massed over the centuries.... Logical thought is possible only when man has managed to go beyond the fleeting representations he owes to sense experience and in the end to conceive a whole world of stable ideas, the common ground of intelligences" (437). Building off Durkheim's notion of collective representation, Serge Moscovici proposed social representation theory to understand common sense, or everyday knowledge. He sought to explain how people create social reality in their day-to-day lives. He conceptualized social representations as dynamic; that is, created and recreated in the course of social interaction. Areas of concern include the values, ideas, and practices that individuals draw upon both to establish social order and to facilitate communication. Through interaction of group members, representations are constructed and refined. New information is merged into a pre-existing framework. If the new information fits the framework, it is integrated and may serve to shape to the social representation. In the case that information is not compatible with existing frameworks, or when it is in conflict with existing frameworks, a new representation may be created. This involves a collective processing of information.

Michael Murray notes that social representations are "considered the defining characteristic of communities" (668). The mother art journaler is embedded in multi-layered communities. She is a part of the construction of the family, of motherhood, of artists, and so forth, intersectionalities of a myriad of social constructs. The level of involvement in a community per se may vary from person to person, from the mother who actively engages in artist retreats, to those that share their pages with others, to those who prefer a purely solitary practice. All are engaged, however, in an iterative process of creating and recreating a social representation of motherhood.

Wilhelm Wundt wrote that collective representations are "those mental products which are created by a community of human life and are, therefore, inexplicable in terms merely of individual consciousness, since they presuppose the reciprocal action of the many" (35). Art journals are both visual expressions of these mental products and are a continuing conversation in reciprocity.

Social representations are the means in which a social group influences individuals within the group. Social representations are guideposts for interpreting reality. They guide behavior and values. The lived experience of motherhood is not static. Rather, the mother herself is actively engaged in refining both meaning and being. Stages are demarcated often based on the age of her offspring: pregnancy, infant, toddler, preschooler, elementary-age, tween, teen, the bird who has flown.... Yet each moment of this process involves change, insight, and growth for the mother. This process is fodder for introspection and refinement not only of the individual conceptualization of Mother, but also lends itself to the collective.

Ludwig showcases a number of journal pages created by mothers depicting their thoughts and wishes, and fears and promises for their children. A page by Melanie Komisarski shows a backlit photo of Komisarski's children playing, glued on a blue and red background, the word "love" in small cursive at the bottom corner of the page (43).

> I want other women to know that we all struggle, we deal with similar hurts and crises. Maybe it's a bit of a reaction to the 'scrapbook happy' pages, the ones that highlight the trips to Disneyland, where everyone is happy all the time. Don't misunderstand, I love happy family scrapbooks, but I think it shields part of the picture. I hope that, through

sharing my pages, other women might feel more whole and less alone in the world. (qtd. in Ludwig 115)

A social representation has two components: a core and a periphery. The core is relatively stable. It creates meaning and places normative constraints on the individuals in the social group. The periphery is more malleable. While serving to protect the core, the periphery shifts with the accumulation of new information; however it functions to maintain the stability of the core. At its core, motherhood as a social representation carries certain socially constructed meanings, assumptions, and values. Thus we have the image of the mother as a caring figure, protective of her offspring, and, above all, loving. The periphery is mutable. Here we find an amalgam of variation, single mothers by choice, teen moms, lesbian mothers, punk mothers, welfare moms, hip mamas. Bad moms. Good moms. Every derivation from the core social construct exists on and enriches this periphery.

Social representations are driven by discourse (Potter and Edwards 447). Change is not a simple process. This is a process of debate and counter-debate. The creation of social knowledge is a permeable, dialectic process, a dialog between individuals and their environments. Ultimately, social knowledge is that which is important to the community.

ART JOURNALING AND LITERACY

Art journals may be read several different ways (Williams and Taylor 51). They serve as secondary texts for emotional expression. They tell stories. They creatively disseminate the social representation of motherhood. They are often symbolic in nature with mutable meaning. The traditional definition of literacy focuses on the ability to read and understand written language: books, signs, articles, quotes, and so forth, make up the media by which we measure literacy. Art journaling presents the opportunity to use written and visual language in order to deepen understanding of concepts and expand the writer's ability to self-express. In the conventional sense, art journaling contributes to the literacy of the practitioners.

In the ever more complex world in which we live, our definitions of literacy as well as our personal growth in alternate literacies have begun to necessarily broaden. In many ways, verbiage is limited in its expression. As Bonnie Thomas put it, "There are times when people need something more to express their deepest most vulnerable thoughts and feelings. This is where art and creative expression comes in ... it can say what words cannot" (9). Connie Fong observes,

> My kids often ask me about the times when they were younger, and I regret that I didn't write down my thoughts and memories back then. Now that I've discovered an artful way to write down these memories, I hope to write more often. I'm so happy to have found art journaling—it's a great way to express my thoughts, record great memories, and have something creative to work on. (121)

Art journaling provides a canvas, in some ways literally, for taking a more multi-faceted approach to literacy. Through art journaling, individuals learn to use materials and images to convey meaning in the way one would traditionally use words. This development of expression can be "facilitated through art, whether by clarifying themes, bringing forth dominant stories, or performing new stories for an audience" (Keeling and Bermudez 407). Each of these speaks to a new or unconventional understanding of cultural or social literacy.

For mothers, art journaling can be a way of storytelling without words, a way of reading motherhood without the constraints of language. Art, as an ultimately personal reflection, expands understanding of lived realities in a way that verbiage simply cannot. As Linda Woods and Karen Dinino noted, "Art journals are visual expressions of the true noise, colors, clutter, emotions and people around us" (7). They are telling us that truth is not always cleanly delineated by the black and white lines of text on a page, but may be more clearly or accurately interpreted in the images, the colors, the clash and composition of an emotional artistic display.

When recording these emotional realities in non-traditional ways becomes a form of literacy, a way of reading life, women may read pregnancy and motherhood through this visual storytelling. Lived events are blended with the inner experiences of the journal's creator to construct a fluid narrative of image and word. It is ultimately this marriage of traditional and non-traditional literacies, the practical with the emotional, that frame art journaling.

Mother and artist Kate Crane shared pages constructed around images of her children in *Art Journaling* magazine. Titled "reason for being #1" and "reason for being #2," the pages were painted pink and blue and stamped with patterns. Each contained a brief story about each child, with descriptions of them: "Eleanore is a whirlwind of love," "My little boy is never too busy for a cuddle." Of these images, Crane wrote, "My journals have ... become a record of the events in my day-to-day life and the lives of my family, just small events that would otherwise be forgotten in the mist of time" (9). What is worth recording is what one stands to lose—the story that lends a deeper understanding of the daily existence of women as mothers.

WORKS CITED

Berry, Jill K. "Lettering Away." *Art Journaling* 2.1 (2010): 112-117. Print.

Bunsen, Elizabeth. 2010. "Packed for a Creative Journey." *Art Journaling* 2.2 (2010): 84-91.

Cameron, Julia. *The Artist's Way*. New York: Tarcher/Putnam, 2002. Print.

Crane, Kate. "Achieving Balance." *Art Journaling* 2.1 (2010): 6-11. Print.

England, Pam and Rob Horowitz. *Birthing From Within*. Albuquerque, NM: Patera Press, 1998. Print.

Fong, Connie. "Ready, Set, Journal!" *Art Journaling* 3.1 (2011): 118-121. Print.

Durkheim, Emile. *The Elementary Forms of Religious Life*. Trans. by Karen E. Fields. New York: The Free Press, 1912/1995. Print.

Dugon-Ahami, Donna. "Nine Years of Living." Art Journaling 2.1 (2010): 68-73. Print.

Dunn, K.E. "Exploring Visual Journaling in a Graduate Art

Therapy Program." MS Thesis. Eastern Virginia Medical School, 2004. Print.

Fong, Connie. "Ready, Set, Journal!" *Art Journaling* 3.1 (2011): 118-121. Print.

Keeling, Margaret. L. and Maria Bermudez. "Externalizing Problems Through Art and Writing: Experiences of Process and Helpfulness." *Journal of Marital and Family Therapy* 32.4 (2006): 405-419. Print.

Klein, Sheri R. "Exploring Hope and the Inner Life Through Journaling." *Encounter,* 23.2 (2010): 49-52. Print.

Ludwig, L. K. *True Vision: Authentic Art Journaling.* Beverly, MA: Quarry Books, 2007. Print.

Mercer, Amanda, Elizabeth Warson and Jenny Zhao. "Visual Journaling: An Intervention to Influence Stress, Anxiety and Affect Levels in Medical Students." *Arts in Psychotherapy* 37.2 (2010): 143-148. Print.

Moscovici, Serge. "Attitudes and Opinions." *Annual Review of Psychology* 14 (1963): 231-260. Print.

Murray, Michael. "Connecting Narrative and Social Representation Theory in Health Research." *Social Science Information* 41.4 (2002): 653-673. Print.

Phillips, Paula. "Escaping with Layers." *Art Journaling* 3.1 (2011): 10-17. Print.

Potter, Jonathan and Derek Edwards. "Social Representations and Discursive Psychology: From Cognition to Action." *Culture and Psychology* 5 (1999): 447-458. Print.

Riley, Gerard A. and Dinah Baah-Odoom. "Do Stigma, Blame, and Stereotyping Contribute to Unsafe Sexual Behaviour? A Test of Claims About the Spread of HIV/AIDS Arising from Social Representation Theory and the AIDS Risk Reduction Model." *Social Science and Medicine* 71.3 (2010): 600-607. Print.

Sinclair, Shannon. "Reconnecting with Me." *Art Journaling* 3.1 (2011): 100-104. Print.

Thomas, Bonnie. *Creative Expression Activities for Teens: Exploring Identity Through Art, Craft and Journaling.* London: Jessica Kingsley Publishers, 2010. Print.

Todd, Carrie. "With the Eyes and the Heart: Artistic, Heartfelt Journaling." *Art Journaling* 2.1 (2010): 74-81. Print.

Williams, Rachel and J. Y. Taylor. "Narrative Art and Incarcerated Abused Women." *Art Education* 57.2 (2004): 46-52. Print.

Woods, Linda and Karen Dinino. *Journal Revolution: Rise Up and Create Art Journals, Personal Manifestos, and Other Artistic Insurrections.* Cincinnati, OH: F+W Publications, 2007. Print.

Wundt, Wilhelm. "Elements of Folk Psychology." *Classics in the History of Psychology* Web. Accessed 2/15/2013.

8.
Visual Literacies of Mothering

RACHEL EPP BULLER

WHAT IS VISUAL LITERACY, and what does it have to do with mothering? Just as children learn to read words, so, too, do they learn from an early age how to read images and visual symbols. This can begin with simple brand-name identification, such as a preschooler recognizing that the "Golden Arches" stand for McDonald's and fast food, but it also operates in relation to a more complex visual language. In an image-saturated society, marketers and other image-producers in popular culture often draw upon what is perceived to be a common visual language. The Mona Lisa, the Eiffel Tower, the Campbell's soup cans of Andy Warhol—references to all of these appear with frequency in commercials and advertisements, in films and on television, with the expectation that educated viewers partake in this shared body of knowledge. Visual literacy intersects with mothering on a variety of levels. Parenting magazines and popular media outlets offer a narrow range of images visualizing what motherhood looks like. Gretchen Papazian argues that many children's picture books address both children and parents, their words and images supporting conventional gender roles and supplying advice on how to mother through a White, middle-class sensibility (120). Art history offers all manner of maternal imagery, from Roman matriarchs to endless representations of that übermutter, the Virgin Mary. And yet, these images most often fall into a realm that Andrea Liss and others term "patriarchal" motherhood (25). Not only are many of the historical representations of mothers produced by male artists, they also picture the *institution* of motherhood, "the myth of the all-loving, all-forgiving and all-sacrificing mother" (Liss 26). These historical images advance a narrow and essentialist definition of motherhood and contribute to hegemonic constructions of maternity, but in recent years, contemporary artists have taken up the mantle of mothering in order to picture the diversities of maternal experience. Such alternative imagings of maternity offer viewers a new strand of visual literacy, one that not only brings a new attention to maternal identity but also actively *produces* a maternal literacy, encompassing socioeconomically, ethnically, and geographically diverse mothering.

This essay reflects upon the visual literacies of mothering produced and promoted through my own artwork. Since bearing children, maternal identity has galvanized both my art and my scholarship, providing a connection between my personal and professional worlds. In much of my art historical writing, I have shifted my focus to cast a critical gaze on cultural constructions of motherhood, gender, and domesticity. I also returned to printmaking after a ten-year hiatus, newly motivated by themes of maternal identities and family transformations. My recent prints and handmade books explore concepts of shared knowledge and shifting identity. Like other feminist artists who give worth to the unpaid, unseen work of domesticity, this work serves as an implicit valuation of women's labor. Grounded in the larger contexts of matrilineage and memory work, my essay will examine the ways in which I bring the maternal to the visual fore.

HER/STORIES

As I strive to develop a visual literacy of mothering in my work, I draw on a lengthy history of women's artistic creativity. Some of my work takes inspiration from the "feminine craft" traditions of quilting and sewing (Parker; Auther), addressing these specialized types of information that historically were shared between women and passed on through children. Family histories and fairy tales are disseminated between generations and within cultures, while practical skills are often taught from parent to child. In a series of monoprints from 2010-11, I explore maternal histories and creativity. Using cut paper shapes to block and layer colors, I create prints full of narrative, which I acknowledge through the series title, *Stories*. For me, the *Stories* prints underscore both process and content. They hold up such traditions of family knowledge as hand-made snowflakes and cut paper dolls amid visual references to storytelling and oral histories.

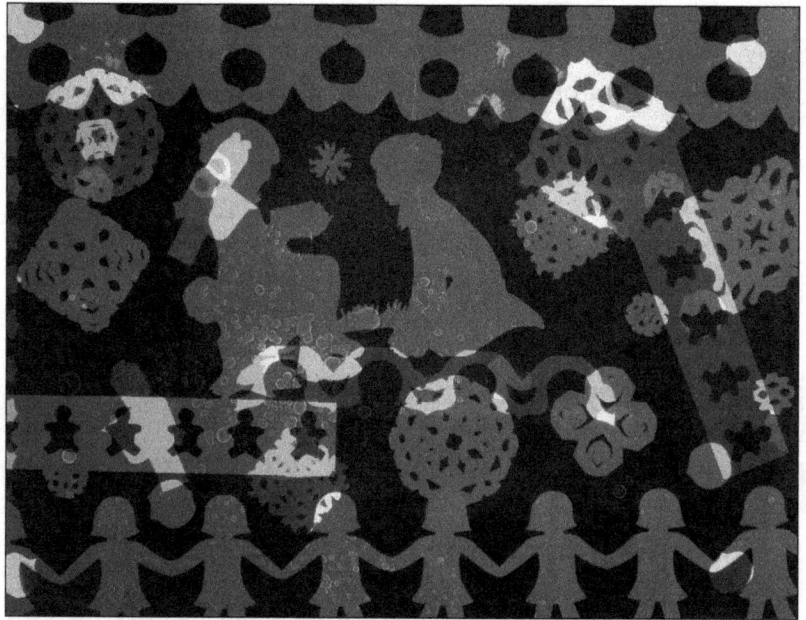

Fig. 1. Rachel Epp Buller, *First Paper Dolls*, 2010. Monoprint. Collection of the artist.

A motif that I repeat in several of the prints is that of the storytelling pair. Clearly distinguished in silhouette, an older girl sits on a tree stump, reading a book to a small child, presumably her younger sibling. The girl's action evokes the layers of childhood learning: the received learning and creativity gained from books, the modeled behavior learned from siblings and other children, and the familial and cultural knowledge gained from re-telling. The prints make reference to these varied layers, but particularly to the acquisition of shared family knowledge. In *First Paper Dolls* (2010), the two children occupy a central placement, the younger sibling leaning forward in eager anticipation (see Fig. 1). Simple cut paper shapes and more complex patterns encircle the pair, each marking the rites of childhood and passing on of traditions. Other prints in the series, such as *Along the Path* (2010), layer papers cut to represent markers of home and to make abstract reference to the many stories, fairy tales, and fables shared between generations. Toni Morrison refers to this as the "spoken library" (O'Reilly, *Toni Morrison and Motherhood*), the realm of children's stories, folk tales, ghost stories, and myths.

Through visual references to both storytelling and craft traditions, I make visible the role of women and girls, mothers and daughters, as bearers of oral and other histories. I lay no individualistic claim to this practice. Rather, I join with other feminist artists who, already in the 1970s but especially in the past decade, have worked to honor the histories and roles of important but unheralded women. While pioneers of the Feminist Art Movement, such as Miriam Schapiro and Judy Chicago, recuperated specific women whose names and works risked being lost to history, such proactive remembering seems less explicit among contemporary artists. Perhaps it is a matter of nuance rather than obvious reference. Carol Armstrong, when comparing two photographers of different generations, establishes a useful framework: "...what I am interested in here are echoes not sources, a haunting not a line of descent, eccentric coincidences not direct influences, a space of dim recollection and regression, not one of canonical progression" (363). In my *Stories* monoprints, I give visual identity to these echoes and hauntings, historical referents and dim recollections passed through my own matrilineage.

Similarly, in painted story quilts American artist Faith Ringgold echoes the tales and traditions of her foremothers. Ringgold's quilts interweave recollected stories with references to inherited craft skills. As such, they function also as an historical nod to the subversive potential of quilts in African-American slave communities, where quilts not only told stories and preserved memories but also participated as "message boards" in the Underground Railroad. By making explicit connections to oral history and knowledge, Ringgold's work might be understood within the concept of the motherline, what some writers theorize as a herstorical alternative to male histories. In her book on the motherline, Naomi Lowinsky discusses the power women can derive by drawing on the experiences of their foremothers, though she specifically foregrounds an essentialist "feminine nature" that is rejected by many women (13). Andrea O'Reilly and others have discussed the importance of the motherline to African-American communities in particular, where women and mothers are the progenitors. "Black mothers pass on the teachings of the motherline to each successive generation through the maternal function of cultural bearing.... In African-American culture, women are the keepers of the tradition: they are the culture bearers who mentor and model the African-American values essential to the empowerment of Black children and culture" (O'Reilly *Rocking the Cradle* 119). Through her artistic references to the complexly layered stories and functions of quilts, Ringgold participates in the maternal bearing of culture from one generation to the next.

In contemporary culture, the role of women as the bearers of familial history has taken new forms. The diary of old becomes the maternal memoir, or "momoir," of the present, an exploding sub-genre in the publishing industry. New mothers and mothers-to-be broadcast their most personal experiences in excruciating, and often hilarious, detail, building communities of mother-readers who seek to share in these bodies of maternal knowledge. The rise of mothers' online journals, or "mommyblogs," mirrors and expands upon this shift in audience. As Andrea Buchanan notes, the phenomenon of mothers blogging represents "a proliferation in shared experience" and "a powerful way to unite women who might not otherwise feel as though they had anything in common." By expanding their communities of women into a global arena, mothers who blog about their lives participate in a virtual expansion of the motherline. Just as these mother-writers seek to enlarge the narratives about mothering, making space for lived experiences that depart from the White, middle-class, self-sacrificial stereotype, so, too, do contemporary artists work to visualize new literacies of mothering.

MEMORY WORK

In *Swirling Stories* (2010), I return to the storytelling pair (see Fig. 2). Surrounded now by a denser layering of patterns and cut paper shapes, including snowflakes and paper dolls, the figures embody the active sharing of knowledge. The narrative and craft referents circulating around them call on the herstorical motherline and acknowledge the gendered nature of knowledge acquisition. Stephan Feuchtwang argues that the transmission of knowledge and memories between generations is "likely to be gendered, a different transmission by men and women, by mothers and fathers, to daughters and to sons. Female transmission is likely to be less accommodated to or acknowledged by public commemoration except in the treasuring of the family and its female progenitor, themselves" (65). Thus, the oral histories and specialized types of knowledge transmitted by mothers tend to differ dramatically

Fig. 2 Rachel Epp Buller, *Swirling Stories*, 2010. Monoprint. Collection of the artist.

from those passed on by fathers.

In developing a visual literacy of mothering through my prints, I aim to draw on a type of cultural, rather than individual, memory. By focusing on shared types of knowledge—in particular, the teaching of craft traditions between mothers and children, even if the specific crafts vary from family to family—I connect with cultural memory, a designation signifying that "memory can be

Fig. 3 Rachel Epp Buller, untitled, 2011. Handmade artist book. Collection of the artist.

understood as a cultural phenomenon as well as an individual or social one" (Bal, Crewe and Spitzer vii). Through this process of visualization, giving visual identity to work that is often devalued, I embrace Annette Kuhn's description of "memory work." Kuhn argues that memory work is an active and inquiring practice of remembering. "Memory work undercuts assumptions about the transparency or the authenticity of what is remembered, treating it not as 'truth' but as evidence of a particular sort: material for interpretation, to be interrogated, mined for its meanings and its possibilities. Memory work is a conscious and powerful staging of memory" (Kuhn 186).

At the end of the series, the *Stories* prints come full circle in tracing and producing maternal literacy. As I cut and tear the prints, folding and binding them into carefully crafted leather covers, I create a set of artist books. These untitled books use no words, only images, yet in my mind, they are made to impart maternal knowledge. Small and portable, the books can be slipped into a pocket or passed easily from hand to hand, mother to mother, parent to child. Going a step further than the monoprints from which they originate, the handmade books explicitly mark traditions of oral storytelling and of folded and cut paper arts as literacies of mothering. As books, the very format honors teaching and learning, from author/artist to reader/viewer as well as between generations. This transmission of oral histories and craft traditions, then, stages the work of maternal memory. The prints and books participate in an "archival impulse," working to ensure that such strands of unwritten knowledge will not be lost. For memory is not just about what is remembered, but also about what is forgotten: memory is a history of both inclusion and exclusion. By reproducing and disseminating markers of mothering and care work that are passed on through generations, the *Stories* act as mnemonic devices (Saltzman 12) of maternity; the books themselves encapsulate maternal literacy.

Peter Burke writes that, "Herodotus thought of historians as the guardians of memory, the memory of glorious deeds. I prefer to see historians as the guardians of awkward facts, the skeletons in the cupboard of the social memory" (110). What role, then, do artists play in the guarding of social memory? And more specifically, how do artists help to guard the memories of the non-glorious deeds and memorialize what might be considered the common, the detritus of daily life? In my own work, and in the work of other contemporary artist-mothers, art becomes a tool for "memory work," an active and inquiring practice of remembering. Whether broadening the visual depictions of maternal experience, speaking to the unseen labors of domesticity, or creating an archive of generational knowledge, contemporary artist-mothers work from the echoes and hauntings of their maternal artist-predecessors to participate in producing new visual literacies of mothering.

WORKS CITED

Armstrong, Carol. "Francesca Woodman: A Ghost in the House of the 'Woman Artist.'" *Women Artists at the Millennium.* Eds. Carol Armstrong and Catherine de Zegher. Cambridge, MA: The MIT Press, 2006. 347-70. Print.

Auther, Elissa. *String, Felt, Thread: The Hierarchy of Art and Craft in American Art.* Minneapolis: University of Minnesota Press, 2009. Print.

Bal, Mieke, Jonathan Crewe, and Leo Spitzer, eds. *Acts of Memory: Cultural Recall in the Present.* Hanover, NH: University Press of New England, 1999. Print.

Buchanan, Andrea. "The Secret Life of Mothers: Maternal narrative, momoirs, and the rise of the blog." Guest blogger on M.J. Rose's *Buzz, Balls, and Hype.* November 21, 2004. Web.

Buller, Rachel Epp, ed. *Reconciling Art and Mothering.* Burlington, VT: Ashgate Publishing, 2012. Print.

Buller, Rachel Epp. "Integrating the Personal and the Professional: Reflections of a Full-Time Academic Mama in the Early Childhood Years." *Academic Motherhood in a Post-Second Wave Context: Challenges, Strategies and Possibilities.* Eds. Andrea O'Reilly and Lynn Hallstein. Bradford, ON: Demeter Press, 2012. 286-97. Print.

Burke, Peter. "History as Social Memory." *Memory: History, Culture, and the Mind.* Ed. T. Butler. Oxford: Basil Blackwell, 1989. Print.

Feuchtwang, Stephan. "Reinscriptions: Commemoration, Restoration and the Interpersonal Transmission of Histories and Memories under Modern States in Asia and Europe." *Memory and Methodology.* Ed. Susannah Radstone. New York: Berg, 2000. Print.

Kuhn, Annette. "A Journey Through Memory." *Memory and Methodology.* Ed. Susannah Radstone. New York: Berg, 2000. Print.

Liss, Andrea. "Maternal Rites: Feminist Strategies." *n.paradoxa* 14 (2004). 24-31. Print.

Lowinsky, Naomi. *The Motherline: Every Woman's Journey to Find her Female Roots.* Los Angeles: Jeremy P. Tarcher, 1992. Print.

O'Reilly, Andrea. *Toni Morrison and Motherhood: A Politics of the Heart.* Albany, NY: SUNY Press, 2004. Print.

O'Reilly, Andrea. *Rocking the Cradle: Thoughts on Motherhood, Feminism and the Possibility of Empowered Mothering.* Toronto: Demeter Press, 2006. Print.

O'Reilly, Andrea and Lynn Hallstein. *Being and Thinking as An Academic Mother: Theory and Narrative.* Toronto: Demeter Press, 2012. Print.

Papazian, Gretchen. "Picturing Mom: Mythic and Real Mothers in Children's Picture Books." *Mothers Who Deliver: Feminist Interventions in Public and Interpersonal Discourse.* Eds. Jocelyn Fenton Stitt and Pegeen Reichert Powell. Albany, NY: SUNY Press, 2010. 119-42. Print.

Parker, Roszika. *Subversive Stitch: Embroidery and the Making of the Feminine.* London: Women's Press, 1984. Print.

Saltzman, Lisa. *Making Memory Matter: Strategies of Remembrance in Contemporary Art.* Chicago: University of Chicago Press, 2006. Print.

IV.
Mothering and Literacies in Cross-Cultural Contexts

9.
"My Girls Are Going to Make It in the Future"

Intertwined Discourses of Mothering, Literacy and Desire

BLAIRE WILLSON TOSO

THIS CHAPTER is based on the analysis of life history interviews with Olivia, a Mexican immigrant mother. Her interviews are part of a larger qualitative study that used a narrative approach to explore Latina immigrant women's use of hegemonic mothering and literacy discourses encountered in a family literacy program. Drawing on her narrative and using a feminist poststructural lens, I look closely at how mothering is tied to literacy—academic and moral—and to the self. Her literacy path, composed from five life history interviews, reveals the influence of prevalent discourses on the labor of childrearing and the achievement of one's desires. Olivia's story evidences how she agentively drew on normative discourses to voice her desires, to claim literate (Bartlett) and good mother (Griffith and Smith) identities—and to enlarge and justify the expansion of her Mexican mothering discourse. However, these moves drew criticism from her ethnic community and caused conflicting behaviors and feelings. Furthermore, participation in the family literacy classes highlighted the mother as a child's primary teacher (National Center for Family Literacy), leading Olivia to postpone her goals to focus her labor on her daughters' schooling.

Olivia's interviews demonstrate how she was simultaneously constrained by *and* appropriated prevalent literacy and mothering discourses to achieve goals or advance ideas that challenged normative views of women. This chapter highlights how ideas of literacy and mothering intertwine in society to shape mothers' roles and the attainment of their desires.

BACKGROUND

The federal family literacy program known as Even Start funded by the *Workforce Investment Act* (WIA), primarily targets poor and immigrant parents (Wasik and Herrman). The introduction to the Even Start Guidance states: "Even Start is an education program for the Nation's low-income families that is designed to improve the academic achievement of parents and their young children, especially in the area of reading" (U.S. Department of Education 1). Even Start was a comprehensive family literacy program that combined adult education, early childhood education, parent education, and parent and child interactive literacy instruction; this combination links parenting skills, literacy, and a child's success.

There is great variety in family literacy programs and they can reflect different ideologies, such as multiple literacies, social change, and intervention prevention (Auerbach). However, many programs reflect, intentionally or unintentionally (see Nakagawa, McKinnon, and Hackett), the prevalent discourse in welfare legislation and family literacy programs—the U.S. Good Mother discourse (Griffith and Smith).

Adult education policy and programming—under which family literacy falls—and the underlying discourses are instrumental in constructing learners' identities, encouraging or limiting their agency, creating active or passive learners, placing and reassigning blame for lack of achievement, and influencing the ways that learners seek to be successful and/or change the structure of society (Walshaw). Discourse links power, knowledge, and language to hegemonic ideologies (Foucault). Here, ideology refers to particular beliefs or ideas held by a group of people, often those in power. One of the mandates in the *Workforce Investment Act* exemplifies how an education program might shape learner identities; it states that programs need to assist "parents in obtaining the educational skills necessary to become full partners in the educational development of their children" (Amstutz and Sheared 155). While fathers are encouraged to attend family literacy programs, participants are primarily women. These programs, thus, reinforce gendered notions of women's roles as mothers and educators (Smythe and Isserlis).

PREVALENT DISCOURSES

The U.S. Good Mother discourse promotes the ideal mother as one who selflessly gives her time and attention solely to her child, negating her own identity, needs, and desires if necessary (Hays). Furthermore, the mother is considered the primary educator of her child. This assumes that a mother must engage in the unpaid labor of educating her child and supporting the schools by volunteering and making up for what schools are unable to do due to lack of resources or unwillingness (Griffith and Smith). The U.S. Good Mother discourse is offered as the answer to educational and economic success for both mother and child; in doing so, it normalizes and regulates particular behaviors. Juxtaposed against this is the Welfare Mother discourse that creates an image of a single woman who is too lazy to work and has babies to get a larger subsidy from the government (Hays). These discourses are used to garner support for program funding and to inform participants about who they are or should be.

A third mothering discourse comes in to play in this work, the Latina Mother discourse. The Latina mother is linked to immigration discourses; Mexican women, central to this discourse, are portrayed as coming to the United States to take advantage of the system by raising their children on welfare (Chavez). Furthermore, Latino children's lack of school success in the United States is attributed, by default, to the mothers. In this way, Latina women are frequently assigned characteristics of the immigrant mother, promoting the idea of illegal, under-educated, deficient mothers that burden U.S. society (Suárez-Orozco, Gaytán, and Kim; Valencia and Black), and are in need of assistance (Valencia and Black; Villenas). Yet, Latino ideas regarding education amplify the academic or literacy-based idea of educational success and include the moral and social upbringing of a child, or *educación* (Reese et al.; Villenas); a mother is to raise a good citizen with strong family values. Reese and colleagues maintain that these values are often interpreted by others as adhering to a "traditional" ideology; educators may then blame this traditional ideology for putting Latino children at a disadvantage compared to their mainstream classmates (Reese et al.). These discourses denote how mothers are generally judged by society based on their child's behaviors and successes (Hays; Segura).

The Autonomous Literacy discourse focuses on the purported skill outcomes of literacy (Street). In this discourse literacy skills are considered as free of context therefore, literacy acquisition is considered a cognitive function achieved through practice and motivation unaffected by social or structural differences. Furthermore, these neutral skills help create a more socially and economically productive citizen (Cook-Gumperz); to be successful one simply needs to work hard. Literacy is seen as the cure for a host of ills: failing children, unskilled workers, poverty, crime (Collins and Blot). Due to the favoring of skill-based literacy, people who have a different form of literacy are often labeled "deficient" (Auerbach). Privileging schooled literacy can, ultimately, determine who is deemed successful in the public's eye (Cook-Gumperz). The literacy and mothering discourses become intertwined, naturalizing mainstream mothering strategies *and* the educational support mothers are to provide. These taken-for-granted ideas shape the ways in which Latina mothers are engaged and perceived in schools and society and in local communities.

THEORETICAL FRAMEWORK

This study drew on a Foucauldian understanding of discourse and power and a feminist, poststructural idea of subjectivity and agency. Power does not originate from a particular location; rather, it circulates through discourses, institutions, and networks and is produced within these fields of relations (Foucault). These arenas of relations define who we are and how we relate to others. Agency denotes the ways in which one acts to achieve desired goals and subjectivities. It is "the socially mediated capacity to act" (Ahearn, "Language and Agency," 112); these acts are interwoven with power, discourses, and social positioning and are historically, geographically, politically, and culturally situated (Ahearn, *Invitations*; Butler, *Undoing Gender*). Many family literacy participants are immigrants or live outside the margins of mainstream, middle-class, White society. What is seen as compliance could, in fact, be a form of resistance or complicity in the name of surviving, or negotiating a social system for one's own good (Mahmood). A complexity of motivations frame decisions and actions, indicating that they need to be understood as more than good, bad, resistant, or compliant (Lewis).

A feminist poststructural framework emphasizes how a social system is structured by patriarchy, classism, racism, and other ideas that define a person. A poststructural reading of agency can help identify the tensions that exist for women in family literacy (e.g., race, poverty, language differences) and how these influence their actions, without erasing either their roles or agency. By highlighting family literacy participants' narratives, we can uncover how they perceive that social structures constrain or enable the way they act, the choices they make, and the state of their well-being.

THE STUDY

This chapter is based on a larger qualitative study that examined five Mexican mothers' use of and adherence to hegemonic discourses prevalent in family literacy (FL) ideology. For this chapter, I highlight Olivia, a 39-year-old mother raising two teenaged girls. I used a narrative inquiry approach in order to gather Olivia's stories and put emphasis on her beliefs, self-renditions and perspectives on life events. My research questions were: How do Latina women in FL programs enact agency within the program and their daily lives? How does participation in FL assist women in enacting agency, if at all? How do Latina women use, negotiate, or disrupt mothering and literacy discourses to mitigate differences or enhance similarities between themselves and the ideals promoted in FL and their communities? I conducted five semi-structured dialogic life history interviews over five months. Olivia chose to be interviewed in English. Each interview lasted between 50 to 75 minutes in length. They were taped and transcribed verbatim. I used thematic analysis along with some aspects of Catherine Riessman's dialogic narrative analysis technique to include amplifying aspects, such as, narrator influences and social context. The mechanics of analysis involved reading and re-reading interview transcripts, identifying narratives—sections of text in which a story could be identified—and reoccurring themes. Identifying narratives included looking to see how the story unfolded and what it accomplished. My research questions, along with some of Riessman's suggested questions, guided the analysis.

OLIVIA

Olivia grew up on a small ranch in northern Mexico. Upon the death of her father, she moved in with her grandmother in Mexico City; her mother went to the United States for work. At 16, an unwilling Olivia moved to the U.S. She and her sister were required to find full-time work to support her brothers. She worked in a hotel and eventually enrolled in English as a second language classes, where she met her husband. She married him when she became pregnant with her first daughter, Teresa—15 at the time of the interviews. Her second daughter, Marissa, was 14 during this study. Olivia was still married despite rocky relations with her husband. She was working part-time as a library assistant and a house cleaner. Olivia expressed a great deal of regret that she had never been allowed to finish school and was working to complete the last two of the General Educational Development (GED®) Tests when I met her. She had already completed a professional masseuse's certificate, demonstrating her ability to acquire complex literacy material. She was dedicated to her daughters and made decisions about her life around her mothering duties.

FINDINGS

Benefits of Adopting Mainstream Discourses

Throughout the interviews, Olivia evidenced her adoption of the Autonomous Literacy discourse and the desire to be seen as a literate subject (Bartlett). She mentioned other benefits literacy and education would bring, such as, "better pay and insurance." She stated, literacy could help her to be "independent, to count" and to "find treasure, you know, go to museums." When we met at the library, she told me, "I rent [check-out] 25 [books] from Crystal City, and another 30 from Rancho Vieja, and another 20 from Verde Springs" and listed off the titles she had selected; these books were markers of her literacy ability and of her desire to be recognized as literate (Bartlett; Holland, Skinner, and Cain). In this way she identified the value she placed on literacy and educational endeavors.

Adhering to the Autonomous Literacy discourse brought Olivia admiration from teachers, other students, friends, and family. The Even Start staff related her daughters' academic successes linking their literacy accomplishments to Olivia's mothering skills. Other women sought her parenting advice and she encouraged other women to continue their education. Her friends would tell her, "Olivia, you are the most smart woman that I ever knew. ... You knew every book that I ever mentioned." Because of her literate identity, she was seen as a knowledge broker for her community. Olivia was proud of her literate status. Being literate and raising high-achieving daughters brought recognition from mainstream society (i.e., teachers, library patrons), thereby contradicting the deficit discourse of uninvolved uneducated immigrant mothers. Embodying the Autonomous Literacy discourse is one way of becoming acceptable in the public's eye. However, the recognition she received also served to inculcate the mothering labor embedded in the Good Mother and Autonomous Literacy discourses as valid entry points into American society and appropriate model behavior.

Constraints of Adhering to Mainstream Discourses

The good mother discourses, while providing access to mainstream society, simultaneously constrained her desires and activities (Piller and Pavlenko). Family literacy classes explicitly tied the mother as the child's "best teacher" and other mainstream ideas of parenting to Olivia's mothering role. She told me about the Even Start program; "Oh, I like that they taught me how to take care of my daughters.... Not to yell at them." She continued, "[They taught me] how to teach them [daughters] literacy.... Miss Carol explain how to read to them.... I did most of what mothers are supposed to do." Her language demonstrates how these literacy activities were naturalized as something that "mothers are supposed to do." Mother as educator was further reinforced by her ethnic community's discourse. Olivia explained her understanding of the Mexican Good Mother:

> *In my culture, the man, he bring the money to the house. So the woman supposed to clean the house. Maintain the house nice and sharpened [clean and organized], cooking. I take the girls to school, I take them to buy books, I take them to the library. I mean, I'm the one responsible for all these things. That's my job.... He [husband] think it's my responsibility to teach my daughters.*

Her use of "responsibility" and "job" indicate the labor embedded in being a woman, cleaning, organizing and educating. Because the woman does not "bring the money to the house," Olivia's wages from working at the library and cleaning homes were not considered earned income.

While this gave her autonomy over how to spend her money, she invested in her children. She said, "I don't spend it [her wages] all in the food, I spend in the clothes. I'm buying things, whatever they [children] need." She used her earnings to be a good mother by providing "whatever they need"; her work was for the children.

Adhering to the good mother discourses also meant that Olivia's educational goals (e.g., go on to college) were often subjugated to the needs of her daughters. For example, Olivia was taking a math class to prepare for the GED® Test. She explained:

> *I'm supposed to go three days, I go only two. But with this situation of my daughters I have to go to meetings about [the band trip to] Africa and all those things. So, I come probably once a week. That's not enough, you know. Because one thing that I know one week, the other week I forget about it.*

Olivia indicated that she would do the utmost to support Teresa and Marissa in having a better and easier life, to be successful, safe, and finish their schooling; education was key to their future. The above illustrates how complying with the requirements of a discourse can meet dictated desires and recognition; however, other personal goals and subjectivities remain unfulfilled or become seen as less important.

Utilizing Mainstream Discourses to Achieve Desires

While we may interpret the above as subjugation and regulation by mainstream discourses, delving further into Olivia's interviews also provides insight into how she appropriated and drew on literacy and mothering discourses to engage more power in the home and build a world for her daughters that negated the constraints she had encountered in her life. The following section provides insight into ways in which women can agentively employ new discourses to achieve desires or open up space for new identities.

Achieving Independence. For Olivia, educating her daughters was bound up in remorse over her interrupted education. She stated that education was also a means to independence and not being subject to a man's rule. She attributed learning how to raise independent children to the U.S. model of childrearing transmitted in family literacy programs. "And they [family literacy staff] help me a lot. Probably that which help me to differentiate my daughters and so I can help them. So they can be independents by themselves." She often drew on ideals from the U.S. Good Mother discourse to contrast herself to her sisters-in-laws and other women in her community. For example, Olivia commented:

> Most of my friends they do things for their sons and for their daughters. Like my cousin, she used to wash my niece clothes when she was 19 years old. Can you believe it? Nineteen? I say, "My goodness." She don't even went to college or do anything. Not me.

In this excerpt, Olivia links independence, schooling and productivity—"She don't even went to college or do anything"—and thus, justifies her mothering practices. Furthermore, she differentiates between a mother's housework labor and educational childrearing labor.

We might read Olivia's labor of creating independent literate children as subjecting herself to a dominant discourse, yet her interviews demonstrate that raising self-sufficient girls is a way to provide Marissa and Teresa with a life that she did not have—a college education, not being subject to a man, choices in the future. Furthermore, insisting on raising independent girls may eventually complete her mothering duties, leaving her free to "work in a community place," "go to college," "climb trees on the weekends"; that is, "do all of those things that fulfill myself." Adhering to the U.S. Good Mother discourse and the embedded literacy discourse is an act of agency that centers her desire to live under a less patriarchal structure.

Expanding Power in the Home. Olivia actively used the U.S. discourses to expand on the woman's role available in her Mexican Good Mother discourse. In her interviews, she remarked on changes she had undergone, in part due to the levying of the U.S. Good Mother discourse. She described some of the differences between discourses:

> *I mean, is like when the man say, "I'm in charge," he's in charge. Even though he's not there [at home]. His presence is not there they should [not] be scared. Most of the women are scared of their husbands. And, especially in my culture. I used to be one of them [scared women], but not any more.*

She recognizes the patriarchal structure of her culture and clearly stated that she "used to be one of them, but not any more." Her change is in part due to taking on new discourses and recognizing the work she does as a mother. She explained,

> *He's [husband] never home, okay? So it's like I'm raising my kids by myself, you know.... I'm the one who gets to makes the main decisions.... Probably that's what I like about that [his absence].*

Being able to criticize her husband's lack of participation gave her the power to control decision making in the home and gain the respect of her daughters. She leverages her active mothering role as a way to claim power in the home.

Melding Discourses. Olivia, however, was careful not to fully reject the Mexican Good Mother discourse. The following section of talk delineates how she melded the two mothering discourses, thereby setting acceptable boundaries for herself and the communities in which she lived. When asked to describe the typical American mother, Olivia responded:

> *A typical American mother, I think they are fifty-fifty. But in my situation, I'm not fifty-fifty because I'm not American. If you're American, I'm supposed to pay half of everything in my house, and I'm not willing to do it.... I do my own things. I'm not like that Mexican mother. I'm not submissive. I not waiting 'til he [husband] come home to eat. I'm not cooking anymore.... I'm more into take my daughters to school and all those things. That's my main priorities, my kids.*

In this excerpt, she maintained the centrality of her mothering role—"my main priorities, my kids"—but refused to identify herself fully within either the U.S. or the Mexican Good Mother discourse; she is "not American" and "not like that Mexican mother." Her refusal of the U.S. Good Mother discourse can be explained in several linked ways: Her refusal 1) offered a rationale (i.e., American mothers provide fifty percent of the household income) for adhering, in part, to the Mexican Good Mother discourse; 2) allowed her to claim her Mexican community; and 3) was her way of making the inescapability of choices bearable.

Olivia actively drew on both discourses to reject particular duties such as cooking for her husband and working full-time and to highlight her daughters' school activities. Ultimately, Olivia continued to abide by the role of Mexican Good Mother (and wife). However, she utilized a view of enforced equity—American women must provide half of the family income—as a way of life that she *elects* not to live. This excerpt is agentic as she chooses aspects of hegemonic discourses to make her life livable, despite ultimately constraining herself to a role she hopes to escape in the future.

Community Approbation

Immigrant women are often subject to a double bind as they navigate the host community and their ethnic community; values can clash and women risk being perceived as bad mothers by one community or the other (Piller and Pavlenko). Community censure can occur when women want to expand beyond the naturalized role of a woman in her ethnic community.

Olivia's narratives show how actions can push, but not exceed, the boundaries of one's circumstances. She said about her daughters, "I think they should grow up to be independent.... So they can feel secure by themselves." In seeking to make them more independent, she was labeled a bad mother by her female relatives: "Oh, you are bad mother Olivia." Olivia counters this by responding, "For me a good quality as a mother. I think I take good care of my children, but I don't follow them around. You know, doing everything for them. I teach them how to be independent." She determined that this aided their success in school, opening educational options beyond the local community college.

Nevertheless, Olivia's stories bore witness to the difficulty and pain of being held on the outside margins of her community because she incorporated new ideas. She made comments such as, "Sometimes it's like I'm embarrassed [of her different opinions]" or "Because probably they think I am a lazy bum." This latter statement was in response to Olivia requiring her girls to learn how to take care of themselves (i.e., becoming independent)—getting up and making their breakfast, doing their laundry.

While Olivia expressed these types of feelings in all of her interviews, she also rejected them and claimed a better standard of mothering due to her independence, pursuit of educational opportunities, and ability to support her children academically:

> *I see the other families.... The father is the one who handle things. Because the woman doesn't work. The woman doesn't speak.... If the girls have a problem at school, okay, they don't do nothing to solve it.... They not can rely in both parents, so they talk to my daughters.... My daughter[s] have the control of their school, of their studies or their knowledge what to do. I just give the resource to do. No, I have taught them [daughters], they have to do homework everyday. I have to read to them.... And, I buy all those things, Legos, a lot of different things for them so they can do [learn].*

In this text, the allure of a dominant discourse, such as the Autonomous Literacy discourse, is evident. Olivia can claim the status of an involved parent and raising academically successful daughters to reject the moments when her community's comments make her feel "bad."

Olivia both pushed and stayed within the boundaries of prevalent mothering discourses. She looks to her daughters to fulfill her desire of becoming independent, academically successful women and within that recognizes her involvement in this process. Through her words, listeners do not always hear regret: "I feel very proud. And, I think they [her daughters] are going to make it in the future.... I have all the honors [laughter]." And, in fact, she says, "I am looking forward to my bright future," a future that rejects the mothering discourses. Olivia maintained, "I have a lot of expectancy of my future instead of be there taking care of grandchildren." Ultimately, she wants what she is trying to give to her daughters: a life that is structured differently (Pavlenko). Her actions are agentic in that, she, perhaps, is creating a greater range of possibility and imagining for her daughters, and eventually herself.

DISCUSSION AND CONCLUSION

This chapter demonstrates how mothering and literacy discourses simultaneously constrained and offered Olivia new opportunities for recognition and identity development. Participation in the family literacy classes highlighted the mother as a child's primary teacher. Mothers were taught to embed literacy activities in routine activities (e.g., bath time), take trips to the library, buy educational games, and create a structure in the home that emphasized skill-based literacy norms. The gendered setting of the classes, and the language of the teachers, naturalized this as mother's work. This role was further supported by the Mexican Good Mother discourse that emphasized mothering labor. Mothering discourses led Olivia to defer her goals to focus on her daughters. Yet the U.S. Good Mother discourse also provided her with opportunities to expand on her ethnic mothering role. Paradoxically, hegemonic discourses regulate subjects into normative behaviors (Foucault) and also offer opportunities to perform new subjectivities (Ahearn, *Invitations*; Butler, *Undoing Gender*; Mahmood).

Ethnic communities provide support, recognition, and belonging; they also structure power relations to which individuals are beholden (Abu-Lughod; Butler, *The Psychic Life*). Olivia's narratives reveal the influence of prevalent ideologies on the labor of childrearing and the achievement of one's desires. She lived in a setting where the Mexican Good Mother discourse was a primary organizing ideology; pursuit of personal desires was restricted by membership in her ethnic community and the emotional and material resources membership conferred (Ahearn, *Invitations*; Malkin). It seems commonsensical that she would not bring her desires to bear too heavily in confronting her home setting and discourses. Furthermore, the ability to achieve one's desires is constrained by associated discourses; for example, husbands were subject to the hegemonic discourse, Male as Provider (Butler, *Undoing Gender*; Segura).

These factors may also explain why she chose to adopt only some aspects of the Autonomous Literacy and the U.S. Good Mother discourses. New discourses took hold where changes could occur. For example, Olivia challenged the Good Wife discourse claiming more independence through the Autonomous Literacy discourse; developing children's academic success was considered an appropriate activity for women. She effected change and expanded her identity, in part, because her home environment permitted it. Family literacy classes highlighted her mothering labor role; however, in doing so her mothering subjectivity was also exposed to more than one possibility (Butler, *Undoing Gender*; Hirsch).

Perceiving agency as contextual and constrained allows Olivia not to simply be labeled as submissive to the discourses, but rather as an agent (Ahearn, *Invitations*), particularly since she posed her decisions as choice even if at times she wished for something else. Her use of, but not insistence on, discourses presents her as having desires while remaining within native discourses. She may over time feel less like a "fool" as her children continue to build success stories in the mainstream that she and others can see as evidence of her ability to mother appropriately. Adhering to or drawing on mainstream hegemonic discourses may be done in order to gain prestige, power or expand the limits of day-to-day lives (Mahmood).

In all of these stories, a tension between desires and hegemonic discourses (native and mainstream) exists (Piller and Pavlenko). Women walking between two cultures feel the tension and the need to conform or take on new roles especially as what is recognized as appropriate mothering practices may be different from their ethnic community's. Women gain recognition for being good mothers via their child's successes. This chapter elucidates how ideas of literacy and mothering intertwine in current U.S. society to shape mothers' roles and the attainment of their desires. The findings also highlight how discourses embedded in educational programs, such as Even Start, support and undermine new identities and old identities, choices and participation in communities. Identifying and making explicit hegemonic ideologies in classrooms can provide learners with tools to understand how taken-for-granted ideologies structure their lives and choices. Furthermore, examining an agent's use of discourses on a continuum of compliance, appropriation (Perry and Purcell-Gates) and resistance allows a more nuanced understanding of how and why women might perform in ways that appear delimiting yet simultaneously expand possibilities for the self. In this way, mothers' childrearing labor and successes in raising a literate child may be recognized as strategic, creating possibility for both Olivia and her daughters "to make it in the future."

WORKS CITED

Abu-Lughod, Lila. *Veiled Sentiments: Honor and Poetry in a Bedouin Society*. Berkley: University of California Press, 1986. Print.

Ahearn, Laura M. *Invitations to Love: Literacy, Love Letters, and Social Change in Nepal*. Ann Arbor: University of Michigan, 2001. Print.

Ahearn, Laura. "Language and Agency." *Annual Review of Anthropology* 30 (2001): 109-37. Print.

Amstutz, Donna and Vanessa Sheared. "The Crisis in Adult Basic Education." *Education and Urban Society*, 32.2 (2000): 155-166. Print.

Anderson, Richard et al. *Becoming a Nation of Readers.* Washington, DC: The National Institute of Education, 1985. Print.

Auerbach, Elsa. "Deconstructing the Discourse of Strengths in Family Literacy." *Journal of Reading Behavior,* 27.4 (1995): 643-661. Print.

Bartlett, Leslie. "To Seem and to Feel: Situated Identities and Literacy Practices." *Teachers College Record,* 109.1 (2007): 51-69. Print.

Butler, Judith. *The Psychic Life of Power: Theories in Subjection.* Stanford, CA: Stanford University Press, 1997. Print.

Butler, Judith. *Undoing Gender.* New York: Routledge, 2004. Print.

Chavez, Leo. "A Glass Half Empty: Latina Reproduction and Public Discourse." *Women and Migration in the U.S.-Mexico Borderlands: A Reader.* Eds. Segura, Denise and Patricia Zavella. Durham, NC: Duke University Press, 2007. 67-91. Print.

Collins, James, and Richard Blot. *Literacy and Literacies: Texts, Power, and Identity.* Cambridge: Cambridge University Press, 2003. Print.

Cook-Gumperz, Jenny. "The Social Construction of Literacy." *The Social Construction of Literacy* (2nd ed.) Ed. Jenny Cook-Gumperz. Cambridge, UK: Cambridge University Press, 2006. 1-18. Print.

Foucault, Michel. *Power/Knowledge: Selected Interviews and Other writings 1972-1977.* New York City: Pantheon Books, 1980. Print.

Griffith, Alison and Dorothy Smith. *Mothering for Schooling.* Mahwah: Routledge Falmer, 2005. Print.

Guendelman, Sylvia, et al. "Orientations to Motherhood and Male Partner Support among Women in Mexico and Mexican-Origin Women in the United States." *Social Science and Medicine* 52 (2001): 1805-13. Print.

Hays, Sharon. *The Cultural Contradictions of Motherhood.* New Haven: Yale University Press, 1996. Print.

Hirsch, Jennifer. "'En El Norte La Mujer Manda': Gender, Generation, and Geography in a Mexican Transnational Community." *Women and Migration in the U.S.-Mexico Borderlands: A Reader.* Eds. Segura, Denise and Patricia Zavella. Durham, NC: Duke University Press, 2007. 438-55. Print.

Holland, Dorothy, Debra Skinner, and Carole Cain. *Identity and*

Agency in Cultural Worlds. Cambridge: Harvard University Press, 2001. Print.

Lewis, Cynthia. *Literacy Practices as Social Acts: Power, Status, and Cultural Norms in the Classroom.* Mahwah: Lawrence Erlbaum, 2001. Print.

Mahmood, Saba. *Politics of Piety: The Islamic Revival and the Feminist Subject.* Princeton, NJ: Princeton University Press, 2005. Print.

Malkin, Victoria. "Reproduction of Gender Relations in the Mexican Migrant Community of New Rochelle, New York." *Women and Migration in the U.S.-Mexico Borderlands: A Reader.* Eds. Segura, Denise and Patricia Zavella. Durham, NC: Duke University Press, 2007. 415-37. Print.

Nakagawa, Kathy, Allison McKinnon, and Mary Ruth Hackett. *Examining the Discourse of Strengths vs. Deficits in a Family Literacy Program.* Paper presented at the AERA, Seattle, WA, 2001. Print.

National Center for Family Literacy. "NCFL & Family Literacy." National Center for Family Literacy. 2011. Web. 13 April 2011.

Pavlenko, Aneta. "'How Am I to Become a Woman in an American Vein?': Transformations of Gener Performance in Second Language Learning." *Multilingualism, Second Language Learning, and Gender.* Eds. Pavlenko, Aneta, et al. New York, NY: Mouton de Gruyter, 2001. Print.

Perry, Kristen, and Victoria Purcell-Gates. "Resistance and Appropriation: Literacy Practices as Agency within Hegemonic Contexts." *Cultural Practices of Literacy Study.* Web. 12 Nov. 2011.

Piller, Ingrid, and Aneta Pavlenko. "Introduction: Multilingualism, Second Language Learning, and Gender." *Multilingualism, Second Language Learning, and Gender.* Eds. Pavlenko, Aneta, et al. New York: Mouton de Gruyter, 2001. 1-13. Print.

Reese, Leslie, et al. "The Concept of Educación: Latino Family Values and American Schooling." *International Journal of Educational Research* 23.1 (1995): 57-81. Print.

Riessman, Catherine. *Narrative Methods for the Human Sciences.* Los Angeles, CA: Sage, 2008. Print.

Segura, Denise. "Working at Motherhood: Chicana and Mexican Immigrant Mothers and Employment." *Women and Migration in the U.S.-Mexico Borderlands: A Reader.* Eds. Segura, Denise and Patricia Zavella. Durham, NC: Duke University Press, 2007. 368-67. Print.

Smythe, Suzanne, and Janet Isserlis. "'The Good Mother': Exploring Mothering Discourses in Family Literacy Texts." *Family Literacy Forum,* 2.2 (2003): 25-33. Print.

Street, Brian. "Introduction." *Literacy and Development: Ethnographic Perspectives.* Ed. Street, Brian. London: Routledge, 1984. 1-19. Print.

Suárez-Orozco, Carola, Francisco Gaytán, and Ha Kim. "Facing the Challenges of Educating Latino Immigrant Origin Students." *National Symposium on Family Isues: Development of Hispanic Children in Immigrant Families: Challenges and Prospects.* Print.

U.S. Department of Education (2003). *Guidance for the William F. Goodling Event Start Family Literacy Programs.* Washington, DC: Department of Education. Web. 12 Nov. 2011.

Valencia, Richard R. and Mary S. Black. "'Mexican Americans Don't Value Education!' On the Basis of the Myth, Mythmaking and Debunking." *Journal of Latinos and Education* 1.2 (2002): 81-103. Print.

Villenas, Sofia. "Latina Mothers and Small-Town Racisms: Creating Narratives of Dignity and Moral Education in North Carolina." *Anthropology & Education Quarterly* 32.1 (2001): 3-28. Print.

Walshaw, Margaret. *Working with Foucault in Education.* Rotterdam, The Netherlands: Sense Publishers, 2007. Print.

Wasik, Barbara Hanna, and Suzannah Herrman. "Family Literacy: History, Concepts, Services." *Handbook of Family Literacy.* Ed. Wasik, Barbara Hanna. Mahwah, NJ: Lawrence Erlbaum, 2004. 3-22. Print.

10.
From Traditional to Transmedia Storytelling

Constructing and Deconstructing Motherhood Across Cultural Contexts

ELIZABETH TREJOS-CASTILLO, PAULINA VÉLEZ, AND
MARTA CECILIA GUTIÉRREZ-RESTREPO

TODAY—more than ever—mass media influence societal norms and expectations, particularly for young girls in the construction of the motherhood discourse (Kinnick 2). Even though each culture has unique ideals about childbirth and childrearing, technological advancements and globalization have opened a door of endless possibilities for sharing meanings regarding motherhood across the world. In the current chapter, we use symbolic interactionism and Uri Bronfenbrenner's *Ecological Model* as a theoretical framework to examine traditional and transmedia storytelling transmission of motherhood discourse across different social and cultural contexts—United States and Latin America—and its impact on young women's understanding of mothering practices.

THEORETICAL UNDERPINNINGS

Michel Foucault defines "discourse" as both signs and practices representing subjects that are constructed differently across different contexts (49). Through exploration, individuals are always constructing and deconstructing discourses that allow them to disclose their ideologies and question societal values and practices. Motherhood discourse, thus, can be described as a social construct formed through everyday interactions embedded in a particular context. Key to understanding the construction of motherhood discourse across cultural contexts is the recognition of the importance of using a theoretical framework, and thus, we will describe the main tenets of symbolic interactionism and Bronfenbrenner's *Ecological Model*.

Symbolic Interactionism

Symbolic interactionism posits that individuals create symbolic worlds in their interactions that, in turn, shape their behaviors. Individuals develop a concept of self and identity through social interactions as well as assign values to those interactions and activities (LaRossa and Reitzes 149). Four major concepts for this theoretical perspective are roles (shared norms applied to the occupants of social positions); identities (self-meanings that are given to a role); interactions among individuals; and contexts—behaviors are shaped by culture and culture is shaped by behaviors (Stokes and Hewitt qtd. in LaRossa and Reitzes 151).

James White and David Klein (69) argue that the social norms or expectations of nurturance and protection define the traditional role of a mother. From a traditional standpoint motherhood is expected to be central to a women's identity, and women who do not become mothers might be perceived not only as rejecting motherhood but also as putting their identity as women at risk (Woollett and Marshall 182). According to Wesley Burr and colleagues (qtd. in White and Klein 70), the greater the perceived role strain resulting from performing a role, the less the ease in making a transition into the role and the greater the ease in making a transition out of the role.

Multiple researchers argue that mass media generally portrays "supermoms who do it all" and many more concur that multiple challenges are faced by women in trying to balance work, family and personal life (Douglas and Michaels 4; Kinnick 6; Tropp 861). It can be argued that if the mass media portray motherhood as conflictive, this might influence the social constructions of motherhood and how young women construct their meanings for this role. Another central concept in symbolic interactionism is the assumption that individuals view their situation and respond based on the meanings they attribute to their situations (LaRossa and Reitzes 143). Thus, when people experience the same events, their reactions can be different because of their individual construction of meanings. This is important to consider when studying how mass media influence the constructions of motherhood as similar situations might be interpreted differently by people and, therefore, motherhood may not be represented as conflicted by every woman.

Bronfenbrenner's Ecological Model

According to Bronfenbrenner (514), the ecological environment is conceived as a nested arrangement of structures. The first level of these structures is the microsystem, which encompasses the relations between the person and the immediate setting containing that person. The second level, the mesosystem, involves the interrelations among major settings containing the person; it can also be conceived as a system of microsystems. The third level, the exosystem, contains other social structures including the immediate settings in which the person is found. The next level, the macrosystem, refers to the patterns of the culture and subculture that define the structures and activities occurring at the other levels (Bronfenbrenner 515). Later developments of the ecological theory included time as part of the conceptual model, described as the chronosystem, which refers to the idea that developmental processes are likely to vary according to specific historical events.

The environment or context involves the four interrelated systems: microsystem, mesosystem, exosystem and macrosystem. It could be said that today's women have expanded their interactions, from physical interactions with peers, family and groups, to virtual interactions that are made possible through the Internet. This impacts the amount of information that young women have access to creating their representation of motherhood, but at the same time, can make it a difficult process considering the wide range of options and images that women and girls find. Traditional and conservative values of motherhood emphasized women's place as "housekeepers," new standards of motherhood place them as mothers that can balance work and family, among other activities. Thus, women have not only expanded the microsystems in which they spend their time but have also expanded the influence of the exosystems.

Regarding macrosystems, the globalized world challenges traditional images and practices of motherhood, though conservative ideas regarding gender roles are pervasive. Young women are influenced by different images of mothers from different cultures, learning about different possibilities and choices that influence how they construct and deconstruct the motherhood discourse. For instance, access to online communities (e.g. blogs) allows women to share ideas and experiences about motherhood with women from different parts of the world. Also, technology and globalization have made possible that adolescents from around the world can access television shows and movies from a variety of cultural contexts. As stated by Marc Bornstein and Jennifer Lansford (261), social and economic development and information confront today's mothers with many similar socialization issues and challenges. This has led to changes in traditional values and belief systems that define what is expected from young women and women in general as mothers. At the chronosystem level, motherhood representations and constructions might vary according to socio-political and historical events. Different women's rights movements have transformed the role of women in society, and consequently their roles as mothers. Rights such as bodily integrity and autonomy, voting (suffrage), holding public office, working, access to fair wages or equal pay, owning property, education, serving in the military, entering into legal contracts, and to having marital, parental and religious rights are broadening the possibilities for women in society, including their decision about whether or not to become a mother and what kind of mother they want to be (Lockwood vii-xvii).

TRADITIONAL AND TRANSMEDIA STORYTELLING AND THE CONSTRUCTION / DECONSTRUCTION OF MOTHERHOOD DISCOURSE

Traditional Storytelling

By definition, "storytelling" can be described as the practice of conveying events in narrated or written words, images, and sounds with the purpose of entertaining, educating, and preserving cultural legacies across generations ("storytelling" def.1 def. 2). Though storytelling traditions vary across cultural contexts, the core themes of the stories transmitted seem to be similar across groups and encompass sharing common wisdom and traditions related to cultural values. That seems to be the case of motherhood narratives, which is a recurrent theme in storytelling. Mothers across cultures seem to be expected to share their birthing and mothering stories as a way to prepare younger women to know what to expect and how to prepare for what's to come (Fox, Heffernan and Nicolson 564; O'Connor and Madge 358). While transmitting their stories, women construct a discourse of motherhood which not only represents the transition into a new life stage, but also a social transition. This social transition brings significant changes related to mothers' new role(s) and statuses as well as personal and social meanings attached to those changes (Breheny and Stephens 113; Nelson 23).

A particularly salient characteristic of the traditional discourse on motherhood is that it generally portrays teen mothers as rebellious young women who reject the ideal of virtuous good mothers and wives. In a study conducted by Maggie Kirkman and colleagues, teen mothers talk about the harsh judgments place on them by society (Kirkman et al. 280). Recurrent themes across their interviews were the condemnation from others because of their age at motherhood, lack of freedom, the idea that their "life was over," hanging out with friends, demands of motherhood, trial and error in feedings, diaper changing, bathing, etc. Interestingly, becoming a mother at 16 to 19 years of age was not perceived by the interviewed mothers as "too young." The teen mothers emphasized their rights to become mothers and their bitterness for having to justify it with or to others. Furthermore, they described how labor (birthing) proved to them their strength as women and described the other, more "adult" mothers as seemingly distressed as opposed to their calm and collected manner.

Sharing birthing and mothering experiences from the traditional storytelling point of view allows women to "link" with others, to proclaim their new social status, and to become initiated into a selective female group. Among some groups of women, stories about birthing and motherhood describing natural birth (rather brutal descriptions in some cases) represent a way to highlight the stronger, more courageous, more womanly stories with themes revolving around issues of pain and "fitness for birthing" (e.g., reasons for an epidural, length of labor). Numerous activities such as prenatal classes and baby showers practiced by today's young women and expecting mothers seem to have originated from cultural traditions supporting a subtle rite of passage into motherhood. Showers, for instance, represent an opportunity for women to share stories, pass down wisdom and advice, and offer gifts (Nelson 19-20).

Transmedia Storytelling

Though transmedia storytelling is not a new phenomenon per se—throughout centuries humans have found multiple ways to transmit their stories such as cave paintings, art work, sculptures, symbols, music, etc.—current technologies and mass media platforms have taken storytelling to the next level. A main difference between traditional and transmedia storytelling is that the audience moves from a passive role (mostly listening without directly participating in the transmission of the story) to a central role by allowing individuals to fully participate by developing and sharing their own stories via multiple forms of media (e.g., websites, email, blogs, etc.).

Among adolescent girls, the use of mass media deserves special attention. Adolescence is a developmental period that is characterized by intense information seeking, especially about adult roles (L'Engle, Brown, and Kenneavy 191). Victoria Rideout and collaborators noted that adolescents (ages eight to eighteen years) spend on average more than 7.5 hours per day with media (Rideout, Foehr, and Roberts 2). Moreover, given the amount of time they spend using more than one medium at a time, today's youth pack a total of 10 hours and 45 minutes worth of media content into those daily 7.5 hours (Rideout, Foehr, and Roberts 2). The average amount of time spent with each medium in a typical day is: 4.3 hours watching television content, 2.3 listening to music/audio, 1.3 using the computer (outside of school work), 1.13 playing videogames, 0.38 using print media, and 0.25 watching movies. Furthermore, today 20 percent of media consumption occurs on mobile devices (e.g. cell phones, iPods or handheld video game players) (Rideout, Foehr, and Roberts 2-3).

Given the lack of information about sexuality readily available to teens, adolescents may turn to the media for information about sexual norms (Brown, Greenberg, and Buerkel-Rothfuss 511-513). Indeed, media such as television, movies, and magazines have been repeatedly cited by teens as major sources for sexual information (L'Engle et al. 191). The Internet, for instance, is one of the most influential means of communication for new generations, as is shown by the heavy use of email and participation in virtual communities and online learning activities.

Some studies have examined the possibilities that the Internet offers young women, mothers, and future mothers, in constructing their motherhood representations and roles (Bailey and Ulman 171-192; Fox, Heffernan and Nicolson 553-568; Hall 179-195; Lopez 729-747; O'Connor and Madge 351-369). Mothers today go online for fast updates, tips and quick advice; they also want to hear from peer moms, and are more likely to call or email for help (Bailey and Ulman qtd. in Hall 185). A Google search of "moms" yields approximately 30 pages of more or less mainline motherhood sites where different categories can be found: Momagenda.com (sells day planners); Amominredhighheels.com (a blog site dedicated to "empower moms through beauty and style"); Mom's Best Friend-mbfagency.com (places nannies and household staff); and Healthymomsfitness.com. Other mom's sites are more values-oriented (e.g., ministry for moms with family values—"Emphasisonmoms.com") whereas other sites are dedicated to single mothers (e.g., Singlemom.com and Singlemom.org) or working moms (e.g., Bizymoms.com, Jobsformoms.com, and Internetbasedmoms.com) (Hall 180).

Motherhood virtual sites also offer young women opportunities to receive information, support, and advice when joining online communities. Other benefits include the "anonymity of the Internet" (O'Connor and Madge 363) as the Internet gives mothers the opportunity to speak without fearing reprisals or embarrassment when seeking help. Thus, the Internet represents an important outlet for young women to "legitimiz[e] their identity as new mothers" (O'Connor and Madge 64). Internet blogging, specifically "mommy blogging" (Lopez 729) is a phenomenon that has also received attention for its contribution to redefining motherhood. Lori Kido Lopez discusses how "mommy bloggers" are creating a different picture of motherhood from what women see in the mainstream media: "The messages we get about motherhood typically either come to us in sanitized or idealized form (television, magazines) or sensationalized (newspapers).... So that's what we're dealing in here. The unexciting, every day, in between stuff" (Lopez 732).

A recent book by Judith Stadtman Tucker (2009) entitled *Mothering and Blogging: The Radical Act of the Mommyblog* provides very interesting insights about mother's blogging and the reason why they do it. Tucker suggests that mothers blog because they want to gain something from it. That something can include "connecting with like-minded mothers in the digital sphere, carving out a virtual room for one's own, or experiencing the liberating sensation of letting it all hang out online" (2). Casual crosstalk between mommybloggers and their core audience creates a sense of community. Readers offer support when mothers blog about difficult transitions or personal crises. Although bloggers and their readers may develop an emotional connection, the relational practices necessary for establishing intimate ties require a degree of mutuality that is inconsistent with the blogging paradigm (Tucker 1-20). Buchanan argues that motherhood blogs are a rich source of affirming, authentic stories and invigorating social interactions (qtd. in Tucker 8).

In summary, technology has become a possibility for young women to expand and enhance the range of communicative activities among them regarding motherhood (Honey 220-239). Interestingly, with all the technological advancements and media incorporation in the transmission of motherhood discourse, the phenomenon of "blogging" and/or blogging community-building resembles the classic oral traditional storytelling—a time when young women, mothers, and mothers-to be shared stories between each other instead of relying on institutions, virtual sites, or experts for advice on childrearing (Lopez 743).

STORYTELLING, MOTHERHOOD LITERACY, AND SOCIAL CONTEXT

According to Bronfenbrenner (qtd in. Tudge et al. 200), human development takes place through processes of reciprocal interactions between the individual and the persons, objects and symbols in its immediate external environment. At the level of interactions, regarding the construction of motherhood, today more often women tend to rely less on their own mothers and more on peers and mass media in search for advice and information (Hall 187). According to Dennis Hall (187), this may be in part because new generations see their moms as old-fashioned or out of touch with current and rapidly changing developments in child rearing practices. On the other hand, the objects in the immediate external environment that help women construct their roles as mothers are television, Internet, movies and magazines. From the symbolic interactionist perspective, contexts in which people are involved provide meanings and expectations associated with a role. This way, expectations for role behavior become normative and commonly understood (LaRossa and Reitzes 147).

Ralph Turner (qtd. in White and Klein 74), argues that the social structure and culture provide a broad, vague, and ambiguous outline for behavior. The individual's role taking is not simply the enacting of a well-defined role but is "making" the role through interaction with others and the context. Based on that perspective, through interactions, individuals construct their own reality and negotiate their roles. Consequently, people can create their roles and change their role behaviors based on interactions with others. According to Rebeca Grynspan et al. (5), young people experience a heterogeneous universe in their objective conditions, but also in their individual interests, cultural referents and identities. However, information and communication technologies emerge as a mutual characteristic of socialization, which is highly valued by young people who perform naturally in this environment.

The discourse of motherhood has changed substantially in the last 50 years. Before, personal history, fundamental life decisions, and life projects of most women were centered on their motherhood experiences. At the same time, motherhood positioned women in a status of adulthood—the most important public recognition for a woman. Today the ranking of those priorities has been altered, generating a new identification axis for young women (Fuller 225-242).

Based on the assumption that the discourse of motherhood has changed, particularly during the last five decades as a result of media influences, it is only natural to wonder if the discourse of motherhood has varied similarly across contexts. Below we examine the construction/deconstruction of motherhood discourse in two contexts: the United States and Latin America.

United States

The typical eight- to eighteen-year-old's home contains an average of 3.8 TVs, 2.8 DVD or VCR players, 1 digital video recorder, 2.2 CD players, 2.5 radios, 2 computers, and 2.3 console video game players. Additionally, 71 percent of all eight- to eighteen-year-olds have their own TV in their room, half have a video game player (50 percent) or cable TV (49 percent), and a third have a computer (36 percent) and Internet access (33 percent) in their room. Furthermore, 29 percent of eight- to eighteen-year-olds own a laptop, 66 percent own a cell phone, and 76 percent have an iPod or other MP3 player (Rideout, Foehr and Roberts 9-10). It is not surprising, then, that media has such a great effect on young women's conceptualizations about motherhood and mothering practices. Some researchers have been concerned with how today's young women are presented with multiple possibilities that transcend traditional gender roles and conceptions about being a mother (Tropp 861-877); others have addressed the associations among television viewing with teenage motherhood (Brown et al., "Sexy Media Matter" 1018-1027; Ex, Janssens and Korzilius 955-968; Larson 97-110; Silbergleid 93-111).

Other studies have concentrated on the influence of television on teenage pregnancy. Jane Brown and colleagues ("Sexy Media Matter" 1018) found that after controlling for other factors, teens at greater risk of early sexual activity and pregnancy were those with the highest consumption of television, movies, music, and magazines. However, other authors have proposed that instead of the total amount of television exposure is the exposure to certain sitcoms and soap operas that appear to be related to girls' and young women's images of motherhood. In a study with Dutch young women, Carine Ex and collaborators found that the consumption of a large number of soap operas and sitcoms that depict more traditional models of motherhood is associated with a more traditional view of motherhood. Moreover, younger participants (ages 15-17) and those with a lower level of education were more traditional with respect to their ideal image of motherhood as compared to other groups. Older participants (ages 20-22) generally expected their ideal image of motherhood to be more self-assertive. According to these authors, television programs may influence young women's perceptions of motherhood because they can create and reinforce certain social values and stereotypes (Ex, Janssens and Korzilius, 955–968). Mary Strom Larson (107) reports that surveyed soap opera teen viewers were more likely to assume that single motherhood has many desirable consequences (e.g., having a healthy baby, their own apartment, a good job, an active social life, and male friends who will help with child care) than non-viewers regarding their perceptions of unmarried motherhood. Similarly, Robin Silbergleid (95, 104) argues that the show *Gilmore Girls* presented teenage pregnancy as a feminist triumph: independent young women, rearing their own children, and overcoming adversity on their own.

According to the author, the show *Gilmore Girls* promotes not only the acceptance but also the desirability of teenage motherhood. For Lorelai (the mother character), the unplanned birth of Rory (the daughter), serves as catalyst for Lorelai's entrance into adulthood and emancipation from her parents. Lorelai serves as an example of the way that is possible to be a "good mother outside the confines of a female homemaker, male breadwinner family" (Silbergleid 99). Even though the show presents a new single mom style, as Silbergleid mentions, it is important to take into account the class and race realities that makes Lorelai's success possible: she comes from a white and wealthy family.

Movies have also influenced young women' ideas of motherhood. Jessica Willis (254) states that the film *Juno* implies that while all women—as a result of their bodies—should expect to become "mothers," there are clear distinctions between who qualifies as a "good" or "bad" mother. The idealization of motherhood in *Juno* is most clearly represented by the character of Vanessa, the prospective adoption mom for Juno's baby. Vanessa is positioned as a stable, white, upper-middle class wife in a happy marriage. The advertisement from which Juno finds the future adoption family portrays clearly the image of "good motherhood": "Educated successful couple wishes to adopt a child. We live in a suburban area near good schools and playgrounds. The child will be raised in a loving atmosphere full of laughter, learning and teddy bears." On the contrary, Juno is portrayed as young, unmarried, working-class girl with minimal material or educational prospects. According to Willis (254) this contrast is significant because it speaks about social and cultural ideas regarding who is best suited to raise a child in the American society.

Latin America

In regards to Latin America, Norma Fuller (225-242) discusses that some studies conducted in rural Latin American populations in the past decade still show a close association between sexuality and reproduction. Before the sexual revolution of the 1960s, reproduction and motherhood were conceptualized together in such a way that virginity was an important marker in the status of women (Benitez Mereles qtd. in Fuller 232). Fuller (225-242) further argues that changes in the concepts of motherhood and sexuality in the recent decades have been influenced by means of communication which emphasize greater democratization of relationships, freedom and self-assertion, greater autonomy of young women, and less parental control, placing young women at a greater risk for unwanted pregnancies or experiencing motherhood in a precarious way. Those changes seem to challenge the traditional view on feminine identity in regards to conservative social roles such as pregnancy and motherhood.

In a recent study about Latin American soap operas and gender roles, Rocío Quispe-Agnoli points out that the soap opera has served as a main mechanism to keep up cultural stereotypes of feminine identity. Chauvinism, oppression, virginity, submission and negation to eroticism have been the symbols that radio and TV soap operas have widely popularized in their dramatic broadcastings. In this context, motherhood is described as an ideal when it occurs within the context of heterosexual marriage, but brings suffering and misfortune when it happens outside of it. Thus, motherhood is also presented as an opportunity to secure a man and a husband. Ana Cervantes (280-295) argues that soap operas portray the traditional representation of femininity such as expressiveness, ideal motherhood, and submission to a man/hero/warrior.

Some examples of Colombian soap operas broadcasted by the end of the 1980s and the early '90s showed characters that did not fit into traditional feminine stereotypes; on the contrary, those characters focused on realities closer to real young women and women supporting the construction of new female identities (e.g., "*Yo soy Betty la fea*"; "*Gallito Ramirez*"; "*Señora Isabel*"). Similarly, the so-called narco-culture phenomenon deviates from the traditional feminine model—obedient, self-sacrificing and submissive mother and wife—to introduce a woman who gives up her freedom and identity to achieve luxury, beauty (plastic surgery), and wealth (Cervantes 280-295). In contrast, Mexican soap operas focusing on younger populations became very popular in the 80s and have been successfully adopted throughout Latin American countries. According to Tania Meza (83-94), this genre presents stereotypes focused on physical perfection and beauty, where the perfect woman is the one preferred by men: blond, slim, and submissive. Female characters define themselves as successful professionals, mothers, and wives thanks to youthfulness and beauty.

A different scenario is offered to middle- and upper-class adolescents whose access to the global world has moved their femininity ideals away from the traditional views presented in popular soap operas. Professional careers, work life, and good economic positions are ideals that place them at the same level of European and North America girls. For those young women, access to the Internet and other media has influenced the construction of their identities and motherhood discourses (Turkle 23-61). These issues are recognized by Latin American scholars, but much of their scholarship has focused on economic and social factors rather than the realities of teenage motherhood, with only few studies addressing the effects of media and globalization on the construction of identity, sexuality, and motherhood discourses of young women.

CONCLUSIONS

From the analysis conducted in the current chapter it is evident that in the United States as well as in Latin American countries, technology and the media have influenced the social and subjective constructions of motherhood discourse among young women. Nowadays, motherhood discourse is no longer tied to the generational transmission of traditional narratives and cultural values. Rather, it seems to be more influenced by transmedia and cyberspaces that provide youth with more flexible "virtual realities" to further explore, construct and deconstruct the motherhood discourse and mothering practices (Erazo and Muñoz 723-754)—this is a phenomenon that has mushroomed faster than scholarship on this area and, thus, warrants further exploration.

With the broadening of physical and virtual spaces across the globe, the role of mass media has become especially important in constructing societal norms and expectations for women across their different life stages (Kinnick 2). As suggested by Silbergleid (105), today's young women are "bombarded" with media images about motherhood and mothering advice wherever they turn. Youth, in general, seem to be involved in an unstoppable interchange of meanings, individual and collective subjective interpretations while trying to express, strengthen, legitimize, empower and re-build their discourses and own cultures (Muñoz 17-21). How Internet has replaced face-to-face interactions regarding the transmission of motherhood practices is still a controversial point. According to German Muñoz (17-21), this is not an arbitrary movement; it is an ongoing movement that warrants further exploration.

Some authors argue that as a consequence of heavy use of the Internet, young women are tending to rely less on their mothers and more on peers and mass media in search for advice. This change may be in part because new generations see their moms as old-fashioned or out of touch with current and rapidly changing developments in childcare and childrearing. "Millennial Moms," thus, "represent both the promise posed by a future dominated by technology and the anxiety posed by the need to keep pace with technology" (Hall 193).

Media narratives have also been found to characterize motherhood in moral terms, juxtaposing the "good mother" (who makes her family the highest priority and conforms to expected roles of femininity) with the "bad mother" (who is depicted as self-centered, neglectful, preoccupied with career, or lacking in traditional femininity; Kinnick 9). As contexts provide different opportunities and constraints for different people, however, many of those motherhood ideals can become difficult to reach for some women (Tudge et al. 201). Furthermore, some studies have argued that media also presents racial and class biases in the social construction of motherhood (Willis 253).

Other scholars, however, claim that while young women take seriously the advice coming from magazines and websites, they also pay attention to the examples set by their own mothers and grandmothers (Fox, Heffernan and Nicolson 564; O'Connor and Madge 358). Indeed, others have argued that the phenomenon of cyberspace communities has become a "new social space" that helps youth build self-confidence, learn how to reach others and communicate better with them, and therefore, prepares them for later face-to-face interactions and shapes their social roles (Fernback 51).

While it is true that the motherhood discourse has evolved considerably during the last century, it still embodies virtues reflecting prominent and dominant ideals regarding childbirth and childrearing practices. Particularly, researchers in this area should consider that today's young women have easy access to multiple meanings and societal norms defining motherhood. Echoing White and Klein (83), the ongoing construction or reconstruction of meaning may be most important in times of rapid social change. In this sense, it is surprising that in spite of the evident influence of media and communication technologies on the construction of motherhood and youth subjectivity, the literature on this area continues to be limited and scattered (Grynspan et al. 5, 6; Muñoz 17-21).

WORKS CITED

Bailey, Maria T., and Bonnie W. Ulman. *Trillion-dollar Moms: Marketing to a New Generation of Mothers*. Chicago, IL: Dearborn Trade Publishing, 2005. Print.

Bornstein, Marc H. and Jennifer E. Lansford. "Parenting." *Handbook of Cultural Developmental Science*. 259-277. New York: Psychology Press, 2010. PsycINFO. Web. 22 May 2012.

Breheny, Mary, and Christine Stephens. "Individual Responsibility and Social Constraint: The Construction of Adolescent Motherhood in Social Scientific Research." *Culture, Health & Sexuality* 9.4 (2007): 333-346. Print.

Bronfenbrenner, Urie. "Toward an Experimental Ecology of Human Development." *American Psychologist* 32.7 (1977): 513-531. Print.

Brown, Jane D., Bradley S. Greenberg, and Nancy L. Buerkel-Rothfuss. "Mass Media, Sex and Sexuality." *Adolescent Medicine* 4.3 (1993): 511–525. Print.

Brown, Jane D. et al. "Sexy Media Matter: Exposure to Sexual Content in Music, Movies, Television, and Magazines Predicts Black and White Adolescents' Sexual Behavior." *Pediatrics* 117.4 (2006): 1018-1027. Print.

Cervantes, Ana C. "La telenovela colombiana, un relato que reivindicó las identidades marginadas." *Investigación y Desarrollo* 13.2 (2005): 280-295. Print.

Coll, Ana. "Embarazo en la adolescencia: cuál es el problema?". *Adolescencia y juventud en América Latina*. 427-448 Cartago, Colombia: Libro Universitario Regional, 2001. Print.

Douglas, Susan J. and Meredith W. Michaels. *The Mommy Myth: The Idealization of Motherhood and How It Has Undermined All Women*. New York: Free Press, 2004. Print.

Erazo, Edgar D. and Germán Muñoz. "Las mediaciones tecnológicas en los procesos de subjetivación juvenil: Interacciones en Pereira y Dosquebradas, Colombia." *Revista Latinoamericana de Ciencias Sociales, Niñez y Juventud* 5.2 (2007): 723-754.

Ex, Carine T. G. M., Jan M. A. M. Janssens and Hubert P. L. M. Korzilius. "Young Females' Images of Motherhood in Relation to Television Viewing." *Journal of Communication* 52.4 (2002): 955-971. Print.

Fernback, Jan. "Beyond the Diluted Community Concept: A Symbolic Interactionist Perspective on Online Social Relations." *New Media & Society* 9.1 (2007): 49-69. Print.

Foucault, Michel. *The Archaeology of Knowledge*. London: Routledge, 1972. Print.

Fox, Rebekah, Kristin Heffernan, and Paula Nicolson. "'I Don't Think It Was Such an Issue Back Then': Changing Experiences of Pregnancy Across Two Generations of Women in South-East England." *Gender, Place & Culture: A Journal of Feminist Geography* 16.5 (2009): 553-568. Print.

Friedman, May and Shana L. Calixte. "Introduction." *Mothering and Blogging: The Radical Act of the Mommyblog.* Eds. May Friedman and Shana L. Calixte. Toronto: Demeter Press, 2009. 21-36. Print.

Fuller, Norma. "Maternidad e identidad femenina: relato de sus desencuentros." *Adolescencia y juventud en América Latina.* 225-242. Cartago, Colombia: Libro Universitario Regional, 2001. Print.

Grynspan, Rebeca et al. *Innovar para incluir: Jóvenes y desarrollo humano. Informe sobre desarrollo humano para Mercosur 2009-2010.* Buenos Aires: Libros del Zorzal, 2009. Print.

Hall, Dennis. "Moms.Com." *Mommy Angst: Motherhood in American Popular Culture.* Eds. Ann C. Hall and Mardia J. Bishop. Santa Barbara, CA: Praeger/ABC-CLIO, 2009. 179-195. Print.

Honey, Margaret. "The Maternal Voice in the Technological Universe." *Representations of Motherhood.* Eds. Donna Bassin, Margaret Honey, and Meryle Mahrer Kaplan. New Haven, CT: Yale University Press, 1994. 220-239. Print.

Kinnick, Katherine N. "Media Morality Tales and the Politics Of Motherhood." *Mommy Angst: Motherhood in American Popular Culture.* Eds. Ann C. Hall and Mardia J. Bishop. Santa Barbara, CA: Praeger/ABC-CLIO, 2009. 1-28. Print.

Kirkman, Maggie et al. "'I Know I'm Doing a Good Job': Canonical and Autobiographical Narratives of Teenage Mothers." *Culture, Health & Sexuality* 3.3 (2001): 279-294. Print.

LaRossa, Ralph and Donald C. Reitzes. "Symbolic Interactionism and Family Studies." *Sourcebook of Family Theories and Methods: A Contextual Approach.* Eds. Pauline G. Boss, William J. Doherty, Ralph LaRossa, Walter R. Schumm, Suzanne K. Steinmetz. New York: Plenum, 1993. 135-163. Print.

Larson, Mary Strom. "Sex roles and Soap Operas: What Adolescents Learn About Single Motherhood." *Sex Roles* 35.1/2 (1996): 97-110. Print.

L'Engle, Kelly L., Jane D. Brown, and Kristin Kenneavy. "The Mass Media Are an Important Context for Adolescents' Sexual Behavior." *The Journal of Adolescent Health: Official Publication of the Society for Adolescent Medicine* 38.3 (2006): 186-192. Print.

Lockwood, Bert B. *Women's Rights: A "Human Rights Quarterly"*

Reader. Baltimore, MD: Johns Hopkins University Press, 2006. Print.

Lopez, Lori Kido. "The Radical Act of 'Mommy Blogging': Redefining Motherhood Through The Blogosphere." *New Media & Society* 11.5 (2009): 729-747. Print.

Meza, Tania. "Las telenovelas juveniles mexicanas y las adolescentes obesas." *Revista Mexicana de Ciencias políticas y sociales* 48.197 (2007): 83-94. Print.

Muñoz, German. "La comunicación en los mundos de vida juveniles: Hacia una ciudadanía comunicativa." Diss. Centro de Estudios Avanzados en Niñez y Juventud – Universidad de Manizales, 2006. Print.

Nelson, Fiona. "Stories, Legends and Ordeals: The Discursive Journey into the Culture of Motherhood." *Organization Development Journal* 21.4 (2003): 15-32. Print.

O'Connor, Henrietta, and Clare Madge. "'My Mum's Thirty Years Out of Date': The Role of the Internet in the Transition to Motherhood." *Community, Work & Family* 7.3 (2004): 351-369. Print.

Quispe-Agnoli, Rocío. "La telenovela latinoamericana frente a la globalización: Roles genéricos, estereotipos y mercado." *La Mirada de Telemo: Revista Académica sobre Televisión Peruana y Mundial* 2 (2009): n. pag. Web. 20 September 2011.

Rideout, Victoria J., Ulla G. Foehr, and Donald F. Roberts. *Generation M^2: Media in the lives of 8 to 18 year olds.* Menlo Park, CA: Kaiser Family Foundation, 2010. Print.

Silbergleid, Robin. "Hip Mamas: Gilmore Girls and Ariel Gore." *Mommy Angst: Motherhood in American Popular Culture.* Eds. Ann C. Hall and Mardia J. Bishop. Santa Barbara, CA: Praeger/ABC-CLIO, 2009. 93-111. Print.

"Storytelling." Def. 1. *Oxford English Dictionary (OED).* Oxford University Press. 17 October 2011. Web. September 2011.

"Storytelling." Def. 2. *Wikipedia, The Free Encyclopedia.* Wikimedia Foundation, Inc. 17 October 2011. Web. 14 October 2011.

Tropp, Laura. "'Faking a Sonogram': Representations of Motherhood on *Sex and the City.*" *Journal of Popular Culture* 39.5 (2006): 861-877. Print.

Tucker, Judith Stadtman. "Foreword." *Mothering and Blogging:*

The Radical Act of the Mommyblog. Eds. May Friedman and Shana L. Calixte. 2009. Toronto: Demeter Press. 1-20. Print.

Tudge, Jonathan R. H., Irina Mokrova, Bridget E. Hatfield, and Rachana B. Karnik. "Uses and Misuses of Bronfenbrenner's Ecological Theory." *Journal of Family Theory and Review* 1 (2009): 198-210. Print.

Turkle, Sherry. *La vida en la pantalla: La construcción de la identidad en la era de internet*. Trans. Laura Trafí. Barcelona: Paidós, 1997. Print.

White, James M., and David M. Klein. *Family Theories: Understanding Families*. Thousand Oaks, CA: Sage Publications, 2002. Print.

Willis, Jessica. "Sexual Subjectivity: A Semiotic Analysis of Girlhood, Sex, and Sexuality in the Film Juno." *Sexuality & Culture* 12.4 (2008): 240-256. Print.

Woollett, Anne, and Harriette Marshall. "Motherhood and Mothering." *Handbook of the Psychology of Women and Gender*. Ed. Rhoda K. Unger. Hoboken, NJ: John Wiley & Sons Inc, 2001. 170-182. Print.

11.
Rethinking Literacy Research/Training with Marginalized *Mujeres*

CINTHYA M. SAAVEDRA AND CARA L. PREUSS

IN THIS CHAPTER, we explore the interlinking literacy discourses that shaped two different studies across time and space with Mexican *mujeres*. We reexamine the "blank spots" (Anzaldúa xxiii) often ignored in our own research contributing to the erasure of brown bodies. Bringing our two studies together has helped us to step back and refocus on the ways that *mujeres* are disciplined, domesticated as well as erased through dominant ideas of literacy development and literacy research. We also illuminate the ways the data gathered—if reinterpreted with *mujerista* eyes, heart and intuition—could provide glimpses of the resistance and multidimensional struggles of the participants. We use multiple feminisms (Chicana, critical, and poststructural) as a looking prism opening up a more critical (re)reading of each of our studies. We searched in the ruins of our research and data so as to not allow our past epistemic positions in our studies to go unscathed. Critical reflexivity (Pillow) even in our past studies is crucial and important.

As we reworked the "ruins" of past research studies (Lather) with immigrant women, similarities in discourses across time and space were found: a) (dis)empowerment through limited definitions/understandings of literacy, b) (re)inscriptions of the good mother through literacy goals, and finally c) resistance through our re-imagining of data. This resistance came to life through the use of Chicana and poststructural feminist lenses that allowed us to de/re/construct in situated and contextualized ways, avoiding grand narratives of resistance/oppression. Reworking the ruins of our literacy research and training provided new insights and questions that disrupted definitions of literacy, in hope of decolonizing it and moving beyond the confines of Enlightenment/Modern projects of social justice.

We begin by exposing our theoretical framework/looking prism followed by our methodology and brief descriptions of our individual studies. Then we proceed with the merging and reimagining of our studies. Finally we conclude with interruptions that ask of us to (un)learn and de/colonize literacy research as tied to larger socio-political contexts.

THE LOOKING PRISM: MULTIPLE FEMINISMS

In our project, it was necessary and important to seek scholarship from the margins that not only questions but also offers *nuevas posibilidades* for research. Chicana feminism was used as a reminder that knowledge can also be produced from the everyday pedagogies and lived experiences of women (Trinidad Galvan). In many ways, this type of *mujerista* scholarship refuses to *read* the "Other" in dominant ways. That is, a reading that always showcases lacking knowledge, skills and needing intervention—a colonialist technique (Smith). We also infused Chicana feminism as a decolonial possibility that stems from the experiences, conditions and uncertainties/ambiguities that many Third World peoples in the United States have learned to navigate because of their subordinate positions (Anzaldúa).

Poststructural feminist perspectives also provided important disruptions in methodology and knowledge. Poststructural analysis allowed us to seek resistance and inscriptions on the bodies of the *mujeres* in our projects. We find useful in poststructuralism Michel Foucault's concept of discourse. An examination of the discourses surrounding literacy can be helpful in examining power through dominant prescriptions of its narrow definition as well as resistance exhibited by the multiple and myriad ways the *mujeres* in our study (re)defined literacies.

Finally, we draw from critical childhood and educational studies (Burman; Cannella; Cannella and Viruru; Grumet) that have critiqued education and in particular the constructions of children, women and teachers by revealing the reinscriptions of patriarchal and capitalistic relations (Saavedra). This scholarship illuminates the socio-historical and political contexts of mothers and teachers through the myths of science, psychology and education. Together, Chicana feminism and postructuralist perspectives afforded us with the temporary realism to (re)examine our separate and distinct studies and merge data/stories/ perspectives across time and space.

METHODOLOGY:
PLÁTICAS, CRITICAL REFLECTIONS AND (RE)WRITING

We know each other from a previous study where we attempted to reexamine Cara's dissertation study through critical feminist perspectives. It was during our *pláticas* (conversations) that we began to make connections to larger issues of power in our society that are symptomatic in literacy research and training. In fact, it was during our encounters that we also began to critically reflect on our involvement in our projects. I (Cinthya) began to tell Cara about my own study in North Carolina and how I saw many entanglements to/with her study in Washington. What resulted through our *pláticas* and critical reflections was a process of "rewriting" the *mujeres* and us in the previous project. For this project, we continue with a similar process but this time we merged our separate studies through time and space.

We use the term *pláticas* as a research methodology that has been documented in Francisca Gonzalez's work with *Mexicana* families (647-648). Her use of *pláticas* and *encuentros* was a way to respect the knowledge that comes from the spontaneous meaning making that occurred when she encountered and engaged in conversations with her participants. Furthermore, Wanda Pillow's powerful discussion on critical reflexivity was also important in our study. We use critical reflexivity as an "...ongoing critique of all of our research attempts... in a way that would continue to challenge the representations we come to while at the same time acknowledging the political need to represent and find meaning" (192). With these two methodologies in mind we offer a rethinking not only of our studies but also of the field of literacy research/ training with marginal *mujeres*.

Our Previous Studies

Cinthya's project was set in North Carolina where she was part of a team of researchers investigating the perspectives of immigrant families with regards to high quality childcare. This project was funded by a local agency interested in a perceived dearth of immigrant children in childcare facilities—especially as there was an influx of new immigrants to the area. The goal was to make sure that newcomers' children had access to English literacy as a path to "success in the U.S." Even though there were immigrants from different originating countries involved in the study, Cinthya mostly worked with the Mexican/Latina mothers conducting focus groups.

Cara's project was set in the state of Washington where she contributed research support to a literacy initiative already underway. The goal of the original project was to improve the literacy and in turn, the quality of care provided by the Spanish-speaking childcare providers, most of who were Mexican immigrant women. For her contribution, Cara investigated the literacies of the childcare providers in order to assess how the curricula in use were a good match. She used observation, interviews, and archival data to explore the research questions from multiple perspectives of the women and those who worked with them. A private organization provided the majority of the funding for the project.

(DIS)EMPOWERMENT THROUGH LIMITED DEFINITIONS/UNDERSTANDINGS OF LITERACY

Though much research in literacy is about the empowerment (in terms of assimilation) of individuals through teaching literacy—a cultural capital skill deemed necessary in our society—we contend that much of this research actually further disempowers individuals (Delpit). Literacy in the Global North/West is limited and only encompasses very individualistic, linear and entrepreneurial notions of what it means to have literacy as well as how it should be incorporated/delivered by individuals (Peña). Few areas—such as multiliteracies and New Literacy Studies—are beginning to expand the definitions of literacies (McCarty). But perhaps we should question the very epistemological and ontological underpinnings of literacy knowledge as a western construct that disciplines more often than liberates marginalized groups. Gaile Sloan Cannella and Radhika Viruru contend that literacy is/was instrumental during colonialism in creating hierarchies between "literate and non-literate." Literacy was seen as a marker of "advancement" and civilization.

Through our *conversaciones, pláticas* and revisiting of our projects, this became evident. For one study, we noticed that literacy meant reading, writing and passing tests as well as equating literacy as English. Critically reflecting, Cara observed how in the program's goal the word "educated" was undefined and unquestioned. There was a hidden assumption as to what it meant and that it meant the same to all. Thus, it was the dominant interpretation of educated, which meant someone who reads and writes and uses these skills to "advance" in U.S. society (Preuss). This was not that different for the goals of the research project in Cinthya's study. The fact that the funding agency was worried about immigrant children accessing English literacy superseded perhaps other more urgent needs of immigrants (Saavedra). The need to have early English literacy skills is so that new immigrants will "advance" in society.

However, for both us it is apparent that literacy is an inherent cultural value in a capitalistic nation. Cara saw this for the underlying goals of the program she was investigating. It was believed that a literate childcare provider is not only a "better" one but also one who can grow her business and the quality of care she can deliver. Similarly, Cinthya observed how the granting agency in her study made an issue of the early literacy for immigrant children as young children are seen as future resources—almost like an annuity account. Deposit now for later withdrawal, which we claim is not only a narrow way to view literacy but also to relate to younger human beings.

Ultimately, the only way to show this accumulation of knowledge—known as literacy—is through creating standardized tests and making learning into rote memorization. Otherwise how else would one show their literateness? Cara explained how one participant struggled,

> Week after week she did not work out of the MEVyT curric-

ulum, but instead practiced solving equation after equation in a spiral notebook. One night I went into the testing room that has four computers providers use for taking the computer-based exams. This provider was there taking her math exam with the help of the instructor. When she finished she had a five out of ten; six is passing. It was her third time failing the same exam. (Preuss 97)

This need to "teach" and accumulate literacy knowledge starts very young. As Cinthya observed in her own notes about the funding agency and its purpose, "The X funded the project with the intention to address the national awareness that immigrant children do not receive high quality care or literacy education" (field notes). Whether it is formal schooling or home "education," immigrant *mujeres* are positioned as not knowing how to raise/educate young children. As mentioned above, the childcare providers need literacy training to grow their business and become better teachers to compensate for the immigrant children not knowing English and not having a "good foundation" at home. It was during these connections that we felt our studies spoke to each other, were related perhaps even demonstrating strong entanglements/linkages through time and space. One such linkage we further describe below is the notion of the good mother through literacy.

(RE)INSCRIPTIONS OF THE GOOD MOTHER THROUGH INSTITUTIONALIZED LITERACY GOALS

Because we noticed how literacy education discursively positions the *mujeres*, whether childcare providers directly or the immigrant mothers, through early literacy propaganda, we contend that in many ways, these discourses are also about the constructions of the global West/North good mother. The notion that women needed to focus on generations of children for the progression of the superior man was crystallized after Ellen Key's publication of *The Century of the Child*. Here, molding children constructed women as those responsible for shaping progress and delivering children to the nation state (Grumet). This meant that women were/are put under the medical, psychological and educational gaze. These were subtle subtexts that we read as we discussed our studies in our conversations. In many ways, these subtexts existed through discourses of what is good for children in their early experiences. Historically, women have been inextricably tied to children and are often measured by children's visible behaviors as well as their measured intellectual capacity (Burman; Cannella).

The monitoring of children's behavior under the providers' care by the instructors in Cara's research happened quite often and can be interpreted as the belief in literacy as order and cleanliness and ultimately good mothering. For example, Cara noted many comments like the following, "At breakfast time the children lined up to wash their hands, and then lined up again to wait for Bravo to take them outside ... learning and play materials were well organized" (Preuss 83). This comment seems harmless, but we cannot divorce this comment from the discourses that have been used to judge women, especially poor and women of color. Cara also noted other comments that inevitably point to the construction of good mothers via manners or *modales,*

> [A provider] expressed an opinion that those who lacked a formal education also lacked "refinement," a word she used repeatedly, and therefore were harsher than others in the ways that they communicated. That same provider expressed her opinion that "modalities" (manners) should be included in every training, "at least one sentence," she said, to help providers focus on improving in this area. (Preuss 215-216)

For Cinthya, these discourses were similar for her participants in different ways. The strong emphasis on early education for second language learners ultimately led her to start questioning how this discourse constructs immigrant/Latina mothers in her project. For example, to provide rationale for examining high quality care the principal investigators (including Cinthya) drew upon the current research (Garcia and Gonzalez) that promotes high quality care in preschools. Though at first glance this seems "reasonable," the research creates an image that immigrant/Latino/a homes are not equipped to get their children "ready to learn." Ultimately blame goes to the mothers. What one sees in this research are the salvation promises of high quality early care. For example, this research is replete with phrases like "solving the achievement gap," "promoting vocabulary development," and "fostering cognitive development." These are, after all, what good mothers "should" do in their home with young children (Peña). During the time that Cinthya was conducting her research, Univision (a major Spanish language television network) was running a literacy/education ad that showed the Latina mother (of course) grocery shopping with her child in the cart while at the same time teaching the child vocabulary words in decontextualized ways. Both research and popular discourses have the *lupa* (magnifying lens) on the homes and inevitably on the *madres* of immigrant/Latino/a children.

Though we do not deny the importance of having access to the culture of power (Delpit), we would hope that literacy and those who are its experts begin to see that literacy encompasses so much more (McCarty). A growing body of scholarship is taking into account the ways that individuals incorporate multiple literacies that are important and acquired through cultural ways to respond to the world around them (Street). We are reminded of Paolo Freire's definition of literacy as "reading the word and the world." However, we would also want to push beyond the ideas of empowerment through literacy and consider other ways to exist in the world that do not necessitate Western constructions of particular skills (Cannella and Viruru)—a decolonial hope.

REFUSING TO BE READ:
RESISTANCE THROUGH OUR RE-IMAGINING OF DATA

Though we were discouraged by such assaults on the *mujeres*, we also have to re-read the *mujeres* as having agency and resisting/ negotiating in their own ways many oppressive discourses. Our previous discussion has centered on the discourses that narrow definitions of literacy and ultimately construct the image of the deficient immigrant/Latina (m)Other. There were spaces and moments where we both acknowledged the limits of oppressive discourses. Our participants engaged in the way they wanted to participate in the training and research. Through our *pláticas* about our research we began to reimagine how to see the *mujeres* in a different way thereby refusing to read them as complete victims.

Though there were many dominant ideas present in Cara's research, the spiritual code in her analysis opened up a different way for us to revisit her study. For many participants, the initial goal was to advance through their interrupted schooling began previously in Mexico. However, the training program was co-opted by the *mujeres* in ways perhaps not intended by the Caminos Program. Cara notes the spirituality that occurred between the *mujeres*:

> One time a provider got visibly upset during class about a personal problem and wiped tears from her eyes. Providers listened, talked, and began to encourage her. The advice that the women were giving her was that forgiveness is to help the person feel better ... that forgiveness is not really for sake of the other person that hurt you, it is to help yourself and how you can feel better and be healthy. Another woman provided support by explaining how the blood of Christ will take everything, wash it, and make it clean. (Preuss 139)

In a similar way, Cinthya observed how her participants, though engaging with the research questions, would deviate and talk about their husbands and children to get advice from the other women present in the focus groups. It was apparent that the women—though happy to participate in this research—were making the time/space their own. When asked about services that would be helpful in their communities, one participant asked back "for us or the children?" This shows that they wanted to think about themselves and not necessarily just their children. One *mujer* commented:

> *that is the problem, sometimes we forgot about ourselves. So then the head of the family hmm is something else. My daughter is a new experience for me. Now that I have her, not that I'm bad, it's a great job. But I have forgotten about me when it comes to me as a woman. For example, I have my aspirations, goals and I keep thinking to myself this will pass, this will pass. She is now one-year old and maybe*

for next year but hmm if your husband, for example, tells you to stay home and you accept that role and sometimes we give in. Many times there is help, day cares or look for someone to take care of them. But we may not have a car. Then what do I do?

Because participants asserted their needs as women the research itself became decentered. After all, the project was to ascertain their perspectives about high quality early care *for* their children. A further discussion ensued that focused more on their needs even though the facilitator tried to revert the question back to making sure that the women addressed services that would be helpful for children:

Moderator: So a service that provides transportation, care for children where you can learn something.
P2: For example, if you say "I'm going to spend one year of my life taking care of my baby." So if there were a place where I could get together like here with friends, "hey let's get together Saturday" and we are going to talk about what ever or do what ever. Or we are going to have a make over. So then you feel like "yes, I'm going to get ready, look good" you understand. Or maybe watch a movie or talk about so many thing[s].
Moderator: Like a support group?
P2: Yes. We are all in the same situation and the children are young and you say "well if I have to take care of her fine, my husband supports us, great because I don't have to work." But like what happened here has helped me because I thought I was alone that I was the only one and everyone else works and I was the only one who stays home taking care of a baby. This is great and I feel great. Like her [referring to an earlier comment by another participant] I get depressed and cry because I'm not used to it. I see my daughter and of course I love her but there is this little part of me that is sort of forgotten and dim.
P5: Yes, and that is what happens, you dedicate yourself to your children, husband...

P7: The home...
P5: And we are the end of the list and sometimes no one takes into account what we do and you get frustrated. You get depressed.
P2: And even if you tell him [husband] "look I feel like this" and he says "but be patient you are fine you are here at home."
P5: But we depend on them. You go to the store and see something and you like it. And then he says "ay I have to pay this, rent, phone, gas" so you say "well I can't get it now." You let it go. And then you stay there. One has to depend on them [to] take you places, give you money.

For the purpose of the North Carolina study, the researchers were sensitive to this need that surfaced among other groups as well. As a result, Cinthya's team wrote a follow-up grant for parental involvement that would focus on learning from the participants as well as creating a space of solidarity and community for the new immigrants. Unfortunately, this did not fit the funding agency's agenda and idea of parental involvement, as the proposed grant did not use an established, tried and true curriculum for parents.

When reexamining our studies through our *pláticas* it was evident to us that there were many moments that the *mujeres* inserted their needs or their own way to participate. Though at first it is/was tempting to see them as victims of domination, we took an interesting pause to contemplate a different reading—refusing to read them in only one particular way. We were left constructing and deconstructing our assumptions. Are they victims? Yes and no. Are they liberated? Yes and no. Both. So where do we go from here? What are the lessons to be learned as researchers interested in critical ways to engage with marginalized populations?

CONCLUSION/BEGINNINGS: (UN)LEARNING AND DE/COLONIZING LITERACIES

The lessons we have learned have been powerful. Discourses intersect in complex ways in our lives and bodies (Foucault) and similar for the *mujeres* in our studies. Important for us is being reflexive

(Pillow) about our research and about the discourses that operate in them. Even our own social justice work cannot go unscathed by scrutiny. We contend that even empowerment ideas can limit as well as construct participants as deficient (m)Others. Further, research that espouses empowerment is about intervention, control and change of the Other.

For example, much research espouses critical literacy as the savior to issues and conditions that are beyond its scope. Militarism, neoliberalism, nationalism, to name a few, are not violent discourses that come from the lack of literacy (defined broadly) in the lives of people. In many ways, what we are saying with our critical literacy approach is that if people only read the world critically it will solve our larger industrial complex problems. It seems a great deal like the discourses found in education for social change (though we think this is important). We would hope that we also begin to think beyond the confines of Enlightenment epistemology. Literacy was, after all, a technique of colonization. As Cannella and Viruru poignantly highlight, "Language and literacy have certainly been used to contribute to the larger project of colonizing minds, intellects, and emotions, creating desires to think like and be like the Empire" (41).

Even if literacies are intended to liberate people, it's always with an inherent notion that experts know how and with which tools. We are reminded of Audre Lorde's assertion that we cannot dismantle the master's house with the master's tools. Though social justice work is important and needed, the question remains: how can we think about it in different ways, unthought of possibilities (Cannella and Viruru) that can revolutionize without imposing a vision, that can transform without being prescriptive, that can create *nuevas posibilidades* without using the same colonist logic? We believe that is our task.

WORKS CITED

Anzaldúa, Gloria. *Making Face, Making Soul, Haciendo Caras: Creative and Critical Perspectives by Feminists of Color*. San Francisco: Aunt Lute Foundation Books, 1990. Print.

Burman, Erica. *Deconstructing Developmental Psychology*. 2nd ed. London: Routledge, 2008. Print.

Cannella, Gaile Sloan. *Deconstructing Early Childhood Education: Social Justice and Revolution*. New York: Peter Lang, 1997. Print.

Cannella, Gaile Sloan and Radhika Viruru. *Childhood and Postcolonization: Power, Education, and Contemporary Practice*. New York: Routledge Falmer, 2004. Print.

Delpit, Lisa D. *Other People's Children: Cultural Conflict in the Classroom*. New York: New Press, 1995. Print.

Foucault, Michel. *Discipline and Punish: The Birth of the Prison*. New York: Pantheon Books, 1977. Print.

Foucault, Michel. *The History of Sexuality*. New York: Pantheon Books, 1978. Print.

Gonzalez, Francisca E. "Haciendo que Hacer-Cultivating Worldview and Academic Achievement: Braiding Cultural Knowledge into Educational Research, Policy, Practice." *Journal of International Qualitative Studies in Education* 14.4 (2001): 641-656. Print.

Grumet, Madeleine R. *Bitter Milk: Women and Teaching*. Amherst: University of Massachusetts Press, 1988. Print.

Key, Ellen. *The Century of the Child*. New York: G. P. Putman, 1909. Print.

Lather, Patti. "Drawing the Line at Angels: Working the Ruins of Feminist Ethnography." *Working the Ruins: Feminist Poststructural Theory and Method in Education*. New York: Routledge, 2000. 284-312. Print.

Lorde, Audre. *Sister Outsider: Essays and Speeches*. Trumansburg, NY: Crossing Press, 1984. Print.

McCarty, Teresa. L. *Language, Literacy, and Power in Schooling*. Mahwah, NJ: L. Erlbaum Associates, 2005. Print.

Peña, Katherine S. "No Child Left Behind? The Specter of Almsgiving and Atonement: A Short Genealogy of the Saving Grace of U.S. Education." *The Child in the World/the World in the Child: Education and the Configuration of a Universal, Modern, and Globalized Childhood*. Ed. Marianne N. Bloch, Devorah Kennedy, Theadora Lightfoot, Dar Weyenberg. New York: Palgrave, 2006. 177-194. Print.

Pérez, Emma. *The Decolonial Imaginary Writing Chicanas into*

History. Bloomington: Indiana University Press, 1999. Print.

Pillow, Wanda. "Confession, Catharsis, or Cure? Rethinking the Uses of Reflexivity as Methodological Power in Qualitative Research." *Journal of International Qualitative Studies in Education* 16.2 (2003): 75-96. Print.

Preuss, Cara L. *License and Learning: Latina Family-Based Childcare Providers' Literacy Learning Goals and Opportunities within the Caminos Program*. Washington State University: Unpublished Dissertation, 2010. Print.

Purcell-Gates, Victoria. *Cultural Practices of Literacy: Case Studies of Language, Literacy, Social Practice, and Power*. Mahwah, NJ: Lawrence Erlbaum Associates, 2007. Print.

Saavedra, Cinthya M. "De-Academizing Early Childhood Research: Wanderings from a Chicana Feminist Researcher." *Journal of Latinos and Education* 10.4 (2011): 286-298. Print.

Smith, Linda Tuhiwai. *Decolonizing Methodologies: Research and Indigenous Peoples*. London: Zed Book, 1999. Print.

St. Pierre, Elizabeth A. and Wanda S. Pillow. *Working the Ruins: Feminist Poststructural Theory and Method in Education*. New York: Routledge, 2000. Print.

Street, Brian V. *Literacy and Development: Ethnographic Perspectives*. London: Routledge, 2001. Print.

Trinidad Galvan, Ruth. "Portraits of *mujeres desjuiciadas:* Womanist Pedagogies of the Everyday, the Mundane and the Ordinary." *Journal of International Qualitative Studies in Education* 14.5 (2001): 603-621. Print.

12.
Literacy and Motherhood Abroad

The Case of Japanese Overseas Mothers

MASAKO KATO

LITERACY IS SUBJECT to the social practices varying across time and space and even within cultures (Bartlett 69; Street 77), so it is of importance to examine how minority groups negotiate the literacy of a dominant community. For a mother who strives to transmit her mother tongue to her child in a foreign context, literacy takes on a different meaning and greatly affects the way in which she makes sense of her motherhood in the new context in which she raises her child, using both her mother tongue and the community language.

This study concerns what mother tongue literacy comes to mean to "overseas" mothers and how it has an impact on their new lives or on the (re)construction of their motherhood. It asks how a woman literate in her native language comes to understand her literacy skill and her literacy transmission when she lives in a foreign country where her native language is marginal and her literacy skill in her native language is rarely appreciated. In this case, being literate does not necessarily give her security and confidence.

In this chapter I present interview data from Japanese overseas mothers who communicate their attitudes toward their mother tongue transmission practices and concomitant awareness of their new roles and skills. The data demonstrate that literacy transmission plays a crucial role in an altered view of motherhood, but that it does so in a sociocultural context. That is, during the transmission of literacy, it becomes clear that mothers also face the challenge of cultural norms and expectations from both their home and host countries, which leads them to find creative ways to tackle such challenges and construct an empowering motherhood for themselves. In the end, I argue that literacy gives women opportunities and agency to challenge the dominant ideology of literacy and motherhood as well as to embrace motherhood by asserting agency and vitality in a host country.

LITERACY TRANSMISSION AND MOTHERS

There has been a growing interest in research on literacy and women, but mothers have rarely been the focus in such research (Hutchison). According to Kirsten Hutchison, the term "family literacy" was first used by Denny Taylor to mean "the rich and diverse uses of literacy within homes and communities." A family literacy program, when it is roughly defined, offers literacy education to families, including parents and children, while it can be different in terms of emphasis and goals. Sondra Cuban and Elisabeth Hayes argue that family literacy programs tend to ignore the central role of mothers by considering them merely aides to support their children's literacy and paying little attention to the mothers' autonomy (7-8). In a similar vein, Hutchison criticizes the invisibility and deficiency of mothers positioned as secondary in family literacy by claiming, "family literacy programs, when primarily designed to train parents as teacher aides and support and enhance child literacy only, without regard for broader dimensions of adult learning, can be viewed as programs of domestication, in their confinement of participants to a sphere where labor is voluntary, autonomy is minimal and rewards are, for the most part, located in the altruistic domain of good mothering" (n.pg.). Instead, she suggests acknowledging their multiple subjectivities, which include being researchers, learners, and teachers of their children. In addition, these studies point out that family literacy programs possibly promote gender division of literacy work in a family, rather than literacy for empowering women to "analyze, understand, and transform their world" as Lalita Ramdas argues (qtd. in Hutchison).

Home literacy practices represent diverse practices, such as reading, writing, singing, narrating, and storytelling, through parent-child interactions and parents' literacy practices within the home. Home literacy practices play an important role in promoting children's literacy development (Bus, van Ijzendoorn, and Pellegrini 14-18; Neuman 509-511; Sénéchal 2) although they are situated and varied in contexts (Hammer, Miccio, and Wagstaff 27; Langer 7; Heath 348; Rodriguez-Valls 127-128; Zentella 28). However, mothers are not the central concern in home literacy studies, either. Where they include the perspectives of mothers, home literacy studies have mostly revolved around parental, especially maternal, beliefs about literacy and their literacy-related activities in order to better understand how mothers help their children learn literacy at home. For example, Daniel Weigel, Sally Martin, and Kymberley Bennett explored the effect of mothers' beliefs about literacy on their children's literacy development. Identifying two different beliefs, that of conventional mothers and facilitative mothers, they found that conventional mothers tend to expect schools, rather than parents, to be responsible for teaching literacy to their children whereas facilitative mothers tend to take an active role in teaching and reading to their preschool children and reading with them, which creates a different home literacy environment (205-208).

Studying Taiwanese mothers, Chien-Huei Wu identifies two kinds of maternal beliefs about reading: teaching strategy and positive emotional affect. She argues that positive emotional affect, rather than teaching strategies, works better to facilitate children's reading. Young-Suk Kim studies the impact of home literacy practices of Korean families on the development of the children's emergent literacy. She identifies two dimensions of home literacy practices, home reading and parent teaching, and reveals that the parents manage the two tactics depending on children's progress or struggles in literacy acquisition (26).

To explain what beliefs and strategies work to promote children's language learning, these studies adopt quantitative methods and carry out surveys and questionnaires. Therefore, they have not revealed *how* and *why* the literacy practices work, effectively masking mothers' viewpoints about their literacy experiences. Recently, qualitative methods have been employed to highlight the detailed, *subjective* literacy experiences of mothers. Pei-Shan Chiang examined literacy teaching practices of Australian Taiwanese families and demonstrated that the parents maintain traditional ways of literacy teaching as well as creating new ways to accommodate the external social forces. Interviewing the mothers of the families, she showed that their parental beliefs about literacy change over time (271). Likewise, focusing on Vietnamese mothers in Taiwan, Ching-Ting Hsin examined their beliefs, values, and expectations about literacy learning to understand how they interpret literacy in a foreign context. She found that Vietnamese mothers in Taiwan, although they are considered as culturally "deficient" and incapable of teaching children literacy, have high expectations for children's literacy development and actively try out new strategies that they believe help promote this (30-31). Although Chiang and Hsin uncovered the mothers' perspectives about literacy teaching, they nevertheless did not go further to study the impact of the interpretation of their literacy experiences on the construction of motherhood.

Thus, previous research of family literacy and home literacy is mainly concerned with the children's language learning, as they examine mothers' literacy practices to ultimately explore the linguistic and cognitive outcomes of the children. Scarce are studies that examine the literacy experiences expressed from the viewpoints of mothers, exposing the reconstruction of their motherhood.

I define literacy experiences as "what one does with literacy," following the idea that literacy is a social practice (Bartlett 69; Barton 100-101; Barton and Hamilton 3; Jones Diaz 32-34). I consider that through literacy experiences mothers can express their own voices. Such literacy experiences of mothers who engage in transmitting literacy to their children in overseas motherhood have been overlooked. This study fills the gap by looking at two aspects of overseas mothers' literacy experiences: literacy transmission and literacy skills.

RESEARCH CONTEXT

The data stem from my dissertation research on Japanese overseas mothers' bilingual language experiences in New York. Data sources include participant-observation, field notes, recorded conversations between mothers and their children, and interviews with 22 mothers. The interviews were conducted in Japanese in different locales, including play dates, music classes, my home, and their homes, and originally revolved around questions about mothers' language and its effect on socialization practices.

For this chapter, the focus is on four mothers of school-aged children who described their literacy experiences: Jun, Shihomi, Nao, and Mamiko (all names are pseudonyms). There are two reasons I have paid close attention to these four women. First, they were in the middle of adamantly pursuing children's literacy in the home language while the children were expected to learn reading and writing in both English and Japanese at school. Second, the women could no longer fully control their language transmission but rather needed to be flexible with the children's linguistic and cultural development in both languages. Their children faced tremendous linguistic and cultural pressures from mainstream society as they had started using English with their peers and teachers in the local American schools. At the same time, they faced the need to learn the Japanese writing systems at an age of about five years old. At this time, the women formalized their roles as language transmitters because of this strict effort to teach reading and writing in Japanese. Indeed, interviews with these mothers show that literacy plays a significant role in their lives, unlike in Japan, where, according to them, literacy is something taken for granted: children learn Japanese reading and writing at school with little concern from their mothers. Literacy comes to acquire quite different meanings, however, once it leaves the Japanese context. The women articulated their mother tongue literacy experiences in everyday contexts while doing their best to pass the Japanese language on to their school-aged children. Further, they highlighted their efforts in literacy transmission at the center of their bilingual motherhood and discovered the significance of their literacy skills as a consequence of their transmission practices. The profiles of the fours mothers are shown in Table 1.

To understand these mothers' literacy experiences, I looked for and analyzed parts of their literacy experiences in the interview data by employing the notion of "literacy narratives." Literacy narratives are often used as pedagogy in classroom settings by

Table 1
Japanese Mothers, Children and Family Information

Mothers Names Ages (Years)	Focal Child (Gender) Age (Year: Month)	Length Mother's Stay in U.S.–Years	Family Types
Jun (42)	Asako (F) (4:3)	14	Eijuu
Shihomi (36)	Ai (F) (6:9)	4	Tyuuzai
Nao (37)	Tomo (M) (8:4)	4	Tyuuzai
Mamiko (40)	Leina (F) (8:5)	14	Kokusaikekkon

writing or composition teachers who attempt to strengthen their students' awareness of their reading and writing experiences (Carpenter and Falbo 100; Clark and Medina 64; Fleischer 69; Williams 343). Literacy narratives allow one to "be self-reflective and critical of their roles and responsibilities as writers, their writing strategies, and their interactions with generic forms, as they (re)position themselves in the discourses of different genres" (DeRosa 3). Researchers of literacy narratives share a point of view that literacy narratives give people an opportunity to reflect on their everyday literacy practices as well as reflect on their lives surrounded by personal literacy experiences. Although this kind of literacy narrative is in the form of writing, the perspective that emphasizes agency through writers' literacy practices is quite useful for my study because it helps to understand mothers' literacy practices as a phenomenon where they not only undergo their literacy events but also make sense of themselves through literacy events in an everyday context. Following that approach, this study analyzed the literacy narratives by focusing on the ways in which mothers interpret and understand their experiences of literacy and motherhood. The analysis reveals that literacy experiences of Japanese mothers are expressed mainly through two themes: the transmission of Japanese literacy and their own literacy skills. Unsurprisingly, mother tongue literacy transmission to their children is the most important topic among these women, and the theme of their own literacy skills emerges as they narrate their literacy transmission experiences, which often touch upon the negotiation of their motherhood. These women account for their literacy practices in connection with fathers, children, and school and, indeed, the interaction with these three parties in both contexts lets them recognize and reflect on the diverse (gender and language ideological) issues in relation to mother tongue literacy and helps them confront the different cultural norms of literacy and motherhood.

JAPANESE, LITERACY AND MOTHERHOOD

When does literacy emerge as a more complex problem for Japanese overseas mothers? All four Japanese mothers hoped to raise their children bilingually in the U.S. Their hopes gradually started fading, however, when they joined English-speaking institutional settings and saw how their children learned English. Interviews revealed that while the mothers were happy to see their children acquiring English, they increasingly became anxious about how to develop and maintain their children's mother tongue, Japanese. Shihomi looked back at the time when she had no clue about the fact that her daughter was learning English but losing Japanese, as follows:

> *I did not have a concern when Ai [her daughter] started her English-speaking preschool [at age three]. She did not complain or show a problem adjusting to the new [English-speaking] environment ... so I didn't even imagine she was having trouble with her Japanese because she kept using it with me.... I did not know how Japanese children in Japan at her age spoke Japanese, because there were no such children around us....*

Concerns regarding children's Japanese development emerged, and literacy transmission turned into a visible issue and conscious work for Japanese families as children started learning Japanese reading and writing in addition to English. Accordingly, Japanese literacy shifted from a personal issue to a social one in motherhood among the mothers—the Japanese mothers decisively identified themselves as "very serious and strict Japanese tutors" for their children (Kato 115).

INTERSECTIONS BETWEEN SCHOOL, LITERACY AND MOTHERHOOD

School played the most important role in raising awareness about the mother tongue among Japanese mothers. Because schools, including ideologies in schools and school-related contexts, positioned Japanese and English unequally, the process of language and literacy teaching and learning in both languages generated strain between teachers, children, and mothers. The interviews with the four women made it evident that they were subject to the force of English monolingualism from school at different levels; they reported that there was great pressure from the American schools that their children attended to prioritize their children's English development. For instance, Nao was told by her son's teacher that she should use English with him at home in order to enhance his vocabulary and writing skills to succeed academically. Local American school teachers kept telling the mothers that they should, first and foremost, help their children improve their English, instead of helping them learn Japanese. They suggested, "If you want your child to make it in the U.S., you should speak English rather than your home language" which is a message from school equally recognized by Shihomi and Nao. They recommended to the mothers that the children should speak English at home and have playdates with their English-speaking friends.

For mothers who assumed the strategy "English at school and Japanese at home," using English at home was incompatible with society's expectation; they believed that home should be protected as a venue for children to be exposed to Japanese. Mothers interpreted the teachers' advice to prioritize English in this way: "Japanese is out of the question for them (teachers). They don't even care about it (the Japanese language). They think of it as secondary or even less," as Nao expressed. This kind of pressure from school to prioritize English is observed in other U.S. bilingual communities (Bayley and Schecter 38; Kohli 178-179; Reyhner 22; Shin 69; Wong Fillmore, "Loss of Family Languages" 207).

Also, being English learners (ELs) and mothers of ELs positioned these women against the status quo and reinforced their marginal status and minority language in school, affecting their relationship with mainstream mothers. Shihomi explained:

> They [the mainstream mothers] appear to ignore me because they think their children are different from ESL students. And they think that their interests do not match ours.
>
> One mainstream mother implied that the budget for ESL courses was a waste and should be allocated to mainstream classes.

A lack of respect for minority mothers and minority languages was subtly conveyed by English-speaking mothers. Japanese mothers understood these incidents to mean that those mothers were telling them that both they and their children were uninvited guests, and even nuisances at school. Similarly, Japanese mothers believed that their lack of English proficiency could restrict them from full participation in a school community. One woman, Shihomi, made fun of her English, and felt isolated because of her low proficiency whenever she mingled with English-speaking mothers in her daughter's school:

> Some non-Japanese mothers completely ignore me. They behave as if I were invisible in the schoolyard [when I wait to pick up my daughter].

When Shihomi had to socialize, she said that she kept silent and just listened. Most of the time, she managed to avoid such occasions by minimizing her involvement in the school. Even other Japanese mothers, whose English was relatively good, believed their limited English to be a source of mockery among English-speaking mothers because they agreed, "the limited vocabulary must sound the same as the level of elementary school students." As a result, these mothers intentionally stayed away from English-speaking mothers and kept their distance from local American schools. Instead, they gathered with Japanese mothers, which inevitably helped to keep the mainstream mothers away from them. This estrangement was recognized not only by Japanese mothers, but also by non-Japanese mothers. Nao was asked by a non-Japanese mother with acrimony, "Why do Japanese exclusively hang out with Japanese?" without realizing that it was a reaction to the exclusion from their English-language networks.

Thus, the school ideology, which strongly emphasized English language development even to the exclusion of Japanese language development, created a challenge to the Japanese mothers' desires to transmit her native tongue to her child. The Japanese language was obviously positioned at a lower status level and the Japanese mothers' efforts at transmitting it was barely recognized, which led to the trivialization of their motherhood in the US. In this way, mothers were compelled to encounter the local dominant force in society while standing for their mother tongue maintenance and taking on its literacy transmission.

INTERACTING WITH CHILDREN: EMOTIONAL BOND AND CULTURAL/FAMILIAL BELONGING

There is little wonder, then, that the powerful force of English that children learned quickly at a local American school made Japanese bilingual children easily lose the incentive to learn the Japanese language, despite their mothers' devoted efforts to transmit their own language. While children started formal schooling in a local school, mothers also sent their children to Japanese Saturday schools. At Japanese Saturday school, children were expected to learn all subjects taught in Japan—including reading and writing. At home, mothers helped their children with their Saturday school homework, particularly the study of Japanese characters. Although they learned it with ease in the beginning, many children gradually felt overwhelmed by Japanese literacy, especially when they started learning *kanji*.

At that point, helping with children's Japanese homework created a strain between mother and child. Children began to respond in various verbal and non-verbal ways to go against their mothers' encouragement to learn Japanese; they showed unwillingness, reservation, and sometimes defiance. Common phrases to mothers included, "Japanese is too difficult. I live as an American, so I don't need to learn Japanese" and "I will be

American and speak only English." In contrast, mothers' sense of responsibility toward Japanese language/literacy transmission developed in a profound way and occupied a large part of their motherhood, but they were unable to organize language transmission practices at their own discretion because of the children's rejection and the strong pressure from the schools to use English. Shihomi looked back:

> ...*I sometimes feel stupid about what I am doing for my daughter [as her Japanese literacy tutor], because I need to beg her, "Could you please please use Japanese for me?" It's ridiculous, isn't it? We don't know who is superior to whom. But I have to do it to make her use Japanese!*
>
> *...[Discouraged by her attitude] I feel like abandoning [the role]. Because it [Japanese literacy tutoring] is a source of strain and resistance [between us]. I used to cry with her when we studied it together, because she resisted learning and I got mad about it.*

These accounts reveal that Shihomi was forced to adjust her position as a Japanese literacy tutor, always depending on her daughter Ai's reactions, drifting between being compassionate and strict. It was when Ai was reluctant to learn Japanese that Shihomi felt silly, because she had to put herself below her daughter by begging her to learn it. This makes it clear that literacy tutoring often involves emotional conflicts and disputes between mother and children. Transmitting a home language thus complicates the parent-child relationship; it may overhaul the relationship of power between mother and child (Relaño Pastor 156; Shin 3; Wong-Fillmore, "When Learning a Second Language" 343). The hardship of transmitting Japanese and negotiating parental power is highlighted when English is clearly involved, as below.

Nao told a story in which she felt like an "idiot" herself in interacting with her son, Tomo. This happened when she seriously took on teaching him Japanese writing, but he was not interested in learning it, and further looked down on her for her "miserable English," in the mother's words. When their differences in English proficiency separated them, their positions were totally reversed;

Nao felt that she lost parental authority over her son. When Nao asked her son about an English word that he used and that was unfamiliar to her, she recounted:

I asked him, "What's that word mean in Japanese?" And he derisively replied, "Don't you even know such an easy word?" Probably, he was joking, but still it was terrible, wasn't it?

Nao also said that it was her English pronunciation that became the focus of his ridicule. However, she admitted that when her son refused to do homework with her, she was not able to force him to do it. She was afraid that he would dislike Japanese if she pushed him excessively. Nonetheless, Nao was not dissuaded from transmitting Japanese to Tomo. Indeed, she found her transmitter role was vital not only for him to develop and maintain Japanese, but also for herself because, in addition to the significance of transmission, the Japanese language revitalized her own being.

Thus, literacy tutoring emerged as a huge effort for them and had a great impact on motherhood in the US as women became conscious of their role as a language transmitter, taking on the role of a literacy tutor. At the same time, they found that they came to lose control over their children and that their parental authority was put into question. Negotiation with children over literacy transmission was certainly a pressing issue that challenged their role as a literacy tutor and a mother living overseas.

IDEOLOGY OF GENDER

Although mother tongue transmission is the core concern of an overseas family, fathers were rarely involved in this project, as the interviews demonstrate. Mothers reported that fathers agreed with the idea of transmitting Japanese to their children, believing it crucial for them to speak it, but that they did not physically help. Mothers attributed such lack of help to the fact that fathers tended to believe that rearing and teaching children, including language and literacy transmission, was the wives' "job" and that husbands were not to take the role of caregiver. It is also the case that, in Japan, fathers identify themselves and are identified as economic providers who barely contribute to childrearing in a practical manner; some studies have even explored "fatherless" children whose fathers are largely absent in childrearing in Japan (Doi 152-153; Ishii-Kuntz 105; Nishioka Rice 92; Seto and Woodford 168).

This sort of division of labor seems strengthened by another gender norm: the ideal "mother." That is, mothers are considered to be the best caregivers and educators of their children (Fujita 75-76). Shihomi related that her husband told her that Ai's acquisition of the Japanese language was her mission during their stay in the US. If she could not achieve it, he said, she and Ai should go back to Japan. Although Shihomi was upset about his attitude and was full of complaints, telling me "he is tough, isn't he?" she did not show it to him. She understood that her husband was too busy with his work to have time to help their daughter with her Japanese. Similarly, Jun appeared to convince herself that her husband was so overworked that he had little time to help with Japanese tutoring.

Mamiko was in a different situation from Shihomi and Nao since her husband was an American. He showed understanding and cooperation toward their daughter Leina's Japanese development. Having learned the language himself, he understood how difficult it was to learn it and how advantageous it would be for Leina to be Japanese-English bilingual. Mamiko and her husband put Leina in a Japanese after-school program once a week. He even tried to use Japanese with them at home as much as possible when advised to do so by the children's Japanese teacher. Mamiko was happy that her husband was understanding about this matter, but at the same time, she recognized his support as unreliable because he predominantly spoke English with Leina and his understanding did not guarantee her future Japanese development. Therefore, Mamiko believed that transmitting Japanese was her own project since there was no one but her, as a native-Japanese, to make sure that Leina developed Japanese and to give her incentive to learn it.

Consequently, both the fathers and mothers together formed a tacit agreement that the mothers would be devoted to childcare and reinforced the idea of mothers as sole caregivers and as exclusive language and literacy tutors in the foreign context. Operating within the ideology of "mother" which indicates the Japanese-specific expectation of motherhood, both mothers and fathers emphasized that no one but mothers could raise/teach children properly, or teach Japanese language/literacy.

LANGUAGE AND IDENTITY

Lastly, the ideological link between the Japanese language and Japanese identity cannot be ignored; mastering Japanese is considered a way to be Japanese in Japan. This idea is a norm in Japanese communities beyond the context of Japan as a country. Commonly accepted, *Nihonjinron*, or "theories about Japanese," underscores Japan's homogeneity, uniqueness, and superiority. It substantially claims that the Japanese language makes up the distinctive Japanese identity, creating Japaneseness, suggesting it as the main basis of its uniqueness (Goodman 60; Liddicoat 20.6; Miller 10-11). Therefore, it is a normative expectation that children are skilled at Japanese, even when they live outside of Japan. Under these circumstances, women are compelled to be successful mother tongue transmitters. Shihomi laments:

> It [her daughter learning Japanese] is natural, and no one compliments me when my daughter develops Japanese. If she did not, they would blame me, though.

Shihomi also remembers the dismay she felt when her daughter was writing a letter to her grandmother in Japan:

> Her Japanese is terrible. [Her choice of] particles [that she chooses to write] is just a mess. It's just terrible. It is fine when she speaks, but it isn't when she writes. I say [to her], "Write as you talk!" But she just cannot. I am desperate.

The former account reveals a belief in Japan that language and identity are intertwined and develop together, and that the development of both is imposed upon Shihomi. The latter explains that Shihomi follows such a belief by identifying Ai's lack of literacy development as her responsibility. These vignettes indicate that mothers both consider themselves and are considered by others to be responsible for being the primary language/literacy transmitters for their children. While mothers complained about the lack of support from their husbands, they believed that they should play a primary role in their children's Japanese language and literacy maintenance and development, which was apparently related to culturally gendered patterns of childrearing responsibilities (Okita 97). Being assigned and assuming the sole responsibility, mothers often spoke about the difficulties associated with their tutor roles and sometimes deliberately avoided talking about them, claiming that it did not solve problems.

LITERACY AS SELF-CONSTRUCTION

Literacy transmission also offers women space to redefine their motherhood. They cherish the tutoring role by understanding it as something that brings them a sense of accomplishment, an emotional bond, and a sense of their own existence:

> *To teach Japanese is worth doing although it is a lengthy and exhausting task. You can see the progress of your child as you put in your time and energy. It is rewarding.*

Looking back on her long struggle to study Japanese reading and writing with her daughter, Shihomi expressed that as she and her daughter, Ai, worked hard together, they were able to see affirmative results, which made both of them feel happy and share the happiness. She said that tutoring strengthened her emotional bond with her daughter, because Shihomi considered the task of studying Japanese not solely her daughter's obligation, but a collaboration between the two of them. Sitting together for a certain time every single day to reach the shared goal allowed them to enhance their mother-child relationship with no interruption by others.

Further, as this was a prevalent thought among the women, they were convinced that the success of a child's Japanese development outside of Japan was up to them. Shihomi expressed:

> *Because we [my child and I] came to New York, we got to seriously take on this task [Japanese literacy studying]. I would have been spoiled doing nothing with her school matters if I had stayed in Japan. It's rewarding.*

She saw the contrast between her "mother" role outside Japan and the role in Japan. She constructed her role as a Japanese tutor as more valuable by deemphasizing the role she would have had in Japan. Shihomi considered Japanese literacy a significant composite of her new motherhood; the task of Japanese tutoring established her role as a Japanese mother and as the primary language/literacy transmitter in the U.S. This experience reverberated with Jun and Mamiko whose stays would be permanent. Despite the pressure they might have felt to know they were the primary resource for their children to learn and develop Japanese, they seemed to happily take on the transmitter role. Jun was determined, saying:

> *Because they [her children] are Japanese, it would be sad if they cannot use Japanese. They have all their family members in Japan, they should learn and use it. I think it [transmitting Japanese to them] is my mission assigned to me while living here [the U.S.].*

Likewise, Mamiko said of the role, "It's difficult, but there is a good thing about it, too."

In addition, women became empowered when they connected the tutor role to part of their identity. Nao found her tutor role vital not only for her son, Tomo, to learn Japanese, but also for herself because Japanese gave her strength and her life meaning, apart from the significance of transmission. Through tutoring literacy, she found a confidence in using Japanese and being Japanese that shifted her view of her role as a mother in New York City:

> *That [when I feel ashamed of my English] pushes me to realize my Japanese language ability. I must not shame myself ... myself as a mother [due to her poor English, often made fun of by her son]. Because I speak and write Japanese and it is my language.*

It is clear that Nao perceived herself as a significant and responsible Japanese mother in the U.S. Tutoring her son and using Japanese allowed Nao to buttress her role and to value it in the U.S. where her minority status and her mother tongue are regarded as marginal. Indeed, this marginality led Nao to feel a new strength about the Japanese language and helped to foster a new awareness of her Japaneseness while contributing to a harsh critique of this marginality. The Japanese language is a significant part of sustaining her Japaneseness in her role as a mother. Thus, Japanese literacy represented no longer just something passed onto their children but a practice in which women positively identified themselves in relation to others and form a bridging of the two countries to make their motherhood viable and powerful.

CONCLUSION

This study explored how literacy was enacted in the lives of Japanese mothers, demonstrating the strong link between literacy and self-construction; literacy can provide powerful new identities and facilitate self-construction. For Japanese mothers, literacy signifies two aspects: the transmission of literacy to their children and a recognition of their own literacy skills.

First, mothers are responsible for transmitting the Japanese language to their children, which is often interrupted by American schools and mainstream groups of people. Accordingly, they make use of their literacy transmission practices to justify their motherhood in the U.S. Secondly, their own literacy ability communicates their legitimacy and authority as mothers in a foreign context where their English ability and even their existence are constantly marginalized and their motherhood is often put into question.

The literacy narratives reveal that mothers manage these two entangled issues on an everyday basis and, at the same time, adopt both literacy practices to contest both the dominant ideology of language and gender and the traditional ideal of Japanese mother as gentle and obedient. Also, they create an alternative view of motherhood, expressed as liberated and autonomous, by asserting validity and vitality in the bilingual situation.

As Hutchison argues, the mothers of this study certainly adopt multiple roles as teachers, learners, and researchers. They are teachers of their children as mother tongue transmitters, learners in the ways in which they search out different cultural expectations of mothering, and then researchers when they explore and create their own motherhood. Indeed, they are at the center of literacy transmission. I argue that mothers take advantage of the literacy transmission experiences as a venue where they negotiate gender ideology and create a new type of motherhood, allowing them to maintain their autonomy and legitimacy. It is thus apparent that literacy does not confine mothers at the margins of the domestic sphere but allows them an active sense of their mothering.

WORKS CITED

Bartlett, Lesley. "Social Studies of Literacy and Comparative Education: Intersections." *Current Issues in Comparative Education* 5.2 (2003): 67-76. Print.

Barton, David. "Directions for Literacy Research: Analyzing Language and Social Practices in a Textually Mediated World." *Language and Education* 15.2,3 (2001): 92-104. Print.

Barton, David, and Mary Hamilton. *Local Literacies: Reading and Writing in One Community*. London: Routledge, 1998. Print.

Bayley, Robert, and Sandra R. Schecter. "Family Decisions about Schooling and Spanish Maintenance: *Mexicanos* in California and Texas." *Building on Strengths: Language and Literacy in Latino Families and Communities*. Ed. Ana Celia Zentella. New York: Teachers College Press, 2005. 31-45. Print.

Bus, Adriana G., Marinus H. van Ijzendoorn, and Anthony D. Pellegrini. "Joint Book Reading Makes for Success in Learning to Read: A Meta-analysis on Intergenerational Transmission of Literacy." *Review of Educational Research* 65.1 (1995): 1-21. Print.

Carpenter, William and Bianca Falbo. "Literacy, Identity and the 'Successful' Student Writer." *Identity Papers: Literacy and Power in Higher Education*. Ed. Bronwyn T. Williams. Logan, UT: Utah State University Press, 2006. 92-108. Print.

Chiang, Pei-Shan. *Home Literacy Education of Taiwanese Australian Families: A Sociological Analysis.* Diss. Queensland University of Technology. 2010. Web. 13 March 2012.

Clark, Caroline, and Carmen Medina. "How Reading and Writing Literacy Narratives Affect Pre-service Teachers' Beliefs about Literacy, Pedagogy and Multiculturalism." *Journal of Teacher Education* 51.1 (2000): 63-76. Print.

Cuban, Sondra and Elisabeth Hayes. "Women in Family Literacy Programs: A Gendered Perspective." *New Directions for Adult and Continuing Education* 70. (1996): 5-12. Print.

DeRosa, Susan. "Literacy Narratives as Genres of Possibility: Students' Voices, Reflective Writing, and Rhetorical Awareness." *Ethos.* Web. 15 March 2012.

Doi, Takeo. *The Anatomy of Dependence.* Trans. John Bestor. Tokyo: Kodansha International, 1973. Print.

Fleischer, Cathy. "Literacy Narratives." *A Middle Mosaic: A Celebration of Reading, Writing, and Reflective Practice at the Middle Level.* Eds. Elizabeth Close, and Katherine D. Ramsey. Urbana, IL: National Council of Teachers of English, 2000. 67–72. Print.

Fujita, Mariko. "'It's all mother's fault': Childcare and the Socialization of Working Mothers in Japan." *Journal of Japanese Studies* 15 (1989): 67-91. Print.

Goodman, Roger. "Making Majority Culture." *A Companion to the Anthropology of Japan.* Ed. Jennifer Robertson. Malden: Blackwell Publishing, 2005. 59-72. Print.

Hammer, Carol Scheffner, Adele W. Miccio, and David A. Wagstaff. "Home Literacy Experiences and their Relationship to Bilingual Preschoolers' Developing English Literacy Abilities: An Initial Investigation." *Language, Speech, and Hearing Services in Schools* 34.1 (2003): 20-30. Web. 13 March 2012.

Heath, Shirley Brice. *Ways with Words.* Cambridge: Cambridge University Press. 1996. Print.

Hsin, Ching-Ting. "Active Agents: The New-Immigrant Mothers' Figured Worlds of Home Literacy Practices for Young Children in Taiwan." *The Asia-Pacific Education Researcher* 20.1 (2011): 17-34. Web. 10 March 2012.

Hutchison, Kirsten. *Reframing Mothers in Family Literacy.* Paper presented at the annual conference of Australian Association for

Research in Education, Sydney, Australia. (2000): n. pag. Web. March 12, 2012.

Ishii-Kuntz, Masako. "Are Japanese Families 'Fatherless?'" *Sociology and Social Research* 76 (1992):105-10. Print.

Jones Diaz, Criss. "Literacy as Social Practice." *Literacies in Childhood: Changing Views, Challenging Practice*. Eds. Laurie Makin, Criss Jones Diaz, and Clare McLachlan. Sydney: MacLennan and Petty, 2007. 31-42. Print.

Kato, Masako. *Bilingual Motherhood: Language and Identity among Japanese Mothers in New York City*. Diss. The Graduate Center, City University of New York, 2009. Print.

Kim, Young-Suk. "The Relationship between Family Literacy Practices and Developmental Trajectories of Emergent Literacy and Conventional Literacy Skills for Korean Children." *Florida State University & Florida Center for Reading Research* Web. 16 March 2012.

Kohli, Rita. "Breaking the Cycle of Racism in the Classroom: Critical Race Reflections from Future Teachers of Color." *Teacher Education Quarterly* 35.4 (2008): 177-88. Print.

Langer, Judith. A. "A Sociocognitive Perspective on Literacy." *Language, Literacy and Culture: Issues of Society and Schooling*. Ed. Judith A. Langer. Norwood, NJ: Ablex Publishing, 1987. 1-20. Print.

Liddicoat, Anthony J. "The Ideology of Interculturality in Japanese Language-in-Education Policy." *Australian Review of Applied Linguistics* 30.2 (2007): 20.1-20.16. Web. 13 March 13 2012.

Miller, Roy Andrew. *Japan's Modern Myth: the Language and Beyond*. New York and Tokyo: Weatherhill, 1982. Print.

Nishioka Rice, Yoshie. "The Maternal Role in Japan: Cultural Values and Socioeconomic Conditions." *Japanese Frames of Mind: Cultural Perspectives on Human Development*. Eds. Hidetada Shimizu, and Robert Alan Levine. Cambridge: Cambridge University Press, 2001. 85-110. Print.

Neuman, Susan B. "Children Engaged in Storybook Reading: The influence of Access to Print Resources, Opportunity, and Parental Interaction." *Early Childhood Research Quarterly* 11 (1996): 495-513. Print.

Okita, Toshie. *Invisible Work: Bilingualism, Language Choice and Childrearing in the Intermarried Families*. Amsterdam: John Benjamins, 2002. Print.

Ramdas, Lalita. "Women in Literacy: A Quest for Justice." *Convergence* 23 (1990): 27-43.

Relaño Pastor, Ana Maria. "The Language Socialization Experiences of Latina Mothers in Southern California." *Building on Strength: Language and Literacy in Latino Families and Communities*. Ed. Ana Celia Zentella. New York: Teachers College Press, 2005. 148-61. Print.

Reyhner, Jon. "Cultural Survival vs. Forced Assimilation: The Renewed War on Diversity." *Cultural Survival Quarterly* 25.2 (2001): 22-5. Web. March 13 2012.

Rodriguez-Valls, Fernando. "Cooperative Bi-literacy: Parents, Students, and Teachers Read to Transform." *English Teaching: Practice and Critique* 8 (2009): 114-36. Print.

Sénéchal, Monique. "The Effect of Family Literacy Interventions on Children's Acquisition of Reading: from Kindergarten to Grade 3." *Encyclopedia of Language and Literacy Development*, London, ON: Canadian Language and Literacy Research Network. (2008): 1-7. Web. March 14 2012.

Seto, Atsuko and Mark S. Woodford. "Helping a Japanese Immigrant Family Cope with Acculturation Issues: A Case Study." *Family Journal* 15.2 (2007): 167-73. Print.

Shin, Sarah J. *Developing in Two Languages: Korean Children in America*. Clevedon, UK: Multilingual Matters. 2005. Print.

Street, Brian. "What's 'New' in New Literacy Studies? Critical Approaches to Literacy in Theory and Practice." *Current Issues in Comparative Education* 5.2 (2003): 77-91. Web. 13 March 2012.

Taylor, Denny. *Family Literacy: Young Children Learning to Read and Write*. London: Heinemann, 1983. Print.

Weigel, Daniel J., Sally S. Martin, and Kymberley K. Bennett. "Mothers' Literacy Beliefs: Connections with the Home Literacy Environments and Pre-school Children's Literacy Development." *Journal of Early Childhood Literacy* 6.2 (2006): 191-211. Print.

Williams, Bronwyn T. "Heroes, Rebels, and Victims: Student Identities in Literacy Narratives." *Journal of Adolescent & Adult Literacy* 47.4 (2003): 342-45. Print.

Wong Fillmore, Lily. "Loss of Family Languages: Should Educators

be Concerned?" *Theory into Practice* 39.4 (2000): 203-10. Print.
Wong Fillmore, Lily. "When Learning a Second Language Means Losing the First." *Early Childhood Research Quarterly* 6.3 (1991): 323-46. Print.
Wu, Chien-Huei. "Attitude and Behavior toward Bilingualism for Chinese Parents and Children." *Proceedings of the 4th International Symposium on Bilingualism*. Eds. James Cohen, Kara T. McAlister, Kellie Rolstad, and Jeff MacSwan. Somerville, MA: Cascadilla Press, (2005): 2385-94. Web. 14 March 2012.
Zentella, Ana Celia. "Introduction: Perspectives on Language and Literacy in Latino Families and Communities." *Building on Strength: Language and Literacy in Latino Families and Communities*. Ed. Ana Celia Zentella. New York: Teachers College Press, 2005. 1-12. Print.

V.
Public Discourses and Literacies of Motherhood

13.
Mothers-For-Natural-Hair

The Afro-Cyberella's Social Media Guide to Afrocentric Hair

LAUREN CROSS

> We have a generation that does not know and has never seen [its] own hair in its natural state—think about it. I am not trying to lay a guilt trip on any mom, and I know that you did not know better, but now that you know, pass the word to other moms and do better. Moms must take the time to teach our little girls about their hair type—how to care for it, how beautiful it is, and how important it is to make others respect their hair. We never know how it will affect them later.
> —Lisa Akbari, *The Black Woman's Guide to Beautiful Hair*

SOME PEOPLE might agree that Afrocentric[1] hair care is a lost art, in need of desperate revival. In the epigraph above, Lisa Akbari confirms this, suggesting that a generation of African American women has never known nor seen its hair in "its natural state." Unsurprisingly, Akbari places the responsibility of "hair mothering" on the mothers of African American children. Motherhood, assumed to be the inherent institution for women, similarly casts African American women mothers as the inherited cultural distributors of hair care knowledge. Akbari is not alone in her assumption that mothers are the expected caregivers for African American children's hair. Several authors of self-hair care guides—printed self-help-oriented hair care guides, which are usually full of photographs and written "how-to" tutorials—suggest, as Akbari did, that mothers of African American children "must take the time to teach [their daughters] about their hair type." Additionally, Akbari warns that when young African American women do not learn to care and respect for their hair, their social and cultural lives may be affected. In this context, some scholars would argue that when criticizing the disproportion of natural hair care knowledge across generations, Akbari assigns "mother blame" to the mothers of African American children (Caplan 276; Phillips 3, 30).

On the one hand, it is important to recognize the "important work" that all mothers contribute to hair mothering practice, even when straightening hair (Caplan 276); on the other hand, we must call into question a system which encourages the denial of Afrocentric hair care knowledge passed down to younger generations of African American women. In this way, mothers of African American children are left with a tremendous dilemma, especially when Afrocentric hair care knowledge is inaccessible due to the fact that traditional cultural discourse communities, such as beauty salons, magazines, and print media, neither affirm nor educate people on Afrocentric hair care or styling practices. Nevertheless, I suggest that African American women, whom I am calling Afro-cyberellas,[2] fill this gap in Afrocentric hair care knowledge, creating new cultural discourses through social media platforms whilst serving as "cyber-other-mothers" to African American children.

To be sure, while it might be tempting to critique or "blame" mothers who choose to advocate the straightening of their daughters' hair, I argue that such a critique does not acknowledge the ways in which hair straightening has been a place of empowerment for mothers, as well as a rite of passage for some African American women. My goal is not to condemn mothers who straighten their daughters' hair, nor am I claiming that mothering through Afrocentric hairstyles is the only way to practice hair mothering. To the contrary, my project is to make clear the specific agency practiced by mothers of African American children, particularly when educating themselves and their daughters on how to style their hair in its natural state. Through hair mothering, I suggest new platforms for literacy that are available through social media, allowing mothers of African American children to access Afrocentric hair care knowledge through the cyber-other-mother network of Afro-cyberellas: African American women who share Afrocentric hair care knowledge through platforms such as YouTube, Facebook,[3] and blogging.

HAIR MOTHERING EXAMINED: MOTHERING "NATURALLY" AND A POSITIVE GLOBAL SELF-ESTEEM FOR AFRICAN AMERICAN GIRLS

> For women raising children, mothering is simultaneously practice, image, and ideology. It may be privately undertaken, often within the realm of the home, but it is publicly scrutinized. A child's cleanliness, manners, maturity, dress, playthings, temperament, and behavior, among many other things, are constantly judged by outsiders, and if found lacking, blame is often laid at the feet of the mother.
> —Laurie Wilkie, *The Archeology of Mothering: An African American Midwife's Tale*

Through culture and community judgment, mothers learn that their children's hair has meaning. In the African American community, mothers are judged, as Wilkie stated above, by the appearance of their children, whether the mother is African American, white, biological, or non-biological. Hair is often an indicator of whether people are "wearing their race wrong" (Rooks), which in effect means that African American women and girls are policed by Eurocentric hair aesthetics. Perhaps the rhetorical racist and stereotypical imagery of the early 1900s, which illustrated African American children with so-called wild hair, has been inscribed in the minds of many African Americans. To put it more bluntly, dominant culture has used hair as an excuse for racist ideologies about "difference;" as a result, we find that these images have been internalized and directed at each other as a reminder of racial injustice. Thus, mothers of African American children carry what some would call an "unfair burden of responsibility" (Phillips 31) to ensure their children are representing "the race" in positive ways, especially when so-called ethnic hairstyles are deemed unacceptable inside and outside of the African American community (Rooks).

So, without question, hair choices for young children and young adults rest at the hands of the mother. In the African American community, mothers have been the caretakers of hair mothering, and have controlled the hairstyling choices of their daughters. Mothers of African American children, particularly girls, are often left with the economic responsibility for their children's hair, which explains why many mothers adopt hairstyling techniques in their mothering practice (Banks 84, 101). Then, at certain ages, mothers are challenged by societal pressures and even by their daughters to perm or press hair into straighter styles (Sullivan 122-123). Such pressures call for action, which in many cases requires hair mothering to adopt a form of "nurturance" that is "defined and experienced as resistance" (O'Reilly, "'Home Is Where The Revolution Is'" 117). Some mothers intentionally mother their children's hair by resisting social and cultural norms. This form of hair mothering values Afrocentric hair care traditions that, as a result, require mothers to "mentor and model the African American values essential to the empowerment of Black children and culture" (O'Reilly, "'Home Is Where The Revolution Is'" 119).

Mothers-for-natural-hair are concerned with the well-being of their daughters, and take on "the task of providing an environment in which their daughters can become emotionally and spiritually sound, happy, healthy, and productive African American women" (Turnage 264) to protect them. The pressures increase when so-called bad mothering assumes that mothers are not actively protecting children from psychological, cultural, and social harm; such pressures may cause mothers "to avoid mother blame," which creates "mothering self-recrimination, anxiety, and guilt" (O'Reilly, *Rocking the Cradle* 13). To put it another way, the fear of damaging a daughter's self-esteem puts a lot of pressure on mothers. Adding to this pressure, as Barbara Turnage argues, there is "no room for many African American mothers to forget what it means to confront racial and sexist barriers . . . 'to provide an interpretation of the society to the child'" (264). Accordingly, they may try to "secure [a] consistent environment to form the foundation for a positive global self-esteem" (263).

The support and love of hair mothering can be a form of maternal activism, helping mothers to encourage a positive self-image for their children, and to reject negative assumptions about "African-oriented features" (Turnage 264). According to Turnage, African American mothers can help to solidify new values that are based on "African American beauty standards" (265-266, 270).[4] Yet, in order to encourage these new values, African American girls need an overall positive "ethnic identity, appearance evaluation, and trust of mother" (264, 270). Turnage sees mothering as being a most significant task. Mothers can provide a social context for the things happening around their daughters that might be socially and emotionally painful (Turnage 264). Additionally, "[a]n African American mother must not only verbally encourage her daughter, she must model the image of womanhood she wishes her daughter to obtain" (Turnage 266).

In other words, Turnage charges mothers again with the responsibility to model the confidence they want to instill in their daughters. In the case of natural hair, a mother's ability to affirm her own beauty and the beauty of her daughter can determine whether her daughter "chooses conformity" or chooses to pursue "her African American pride through her hairstyles" (Turnage 265). So that young African American girls are not "left unprotected," mothers, in the words of Turnage, "encourage their daughters to develop an African American ethnic identity, providing their daughters (emphasis mine) with an appearance evaluation that is reflective of her daughter's ethnic heritage; the enhancement of a trusting mother-daughter relationship; and teaching her daughter effective coping strategies" (267). Through applying these strategies towards hair mothering, mothers can help to cultivate a positive global self-esteem amongst African American girls.

EMPOWERING MOTHERS, EMPOWERING DAUGHTERS: AFRO-CYBERELLAS AS CYBER-OTHER-MOTHERS IN ACTION

To Naptural85: "your hair is beautiful ... and so are you ... I love listening to you give instruction ... you have become my daughter's inspiration ... she is 11 and has decided that she wants to be natural ... As I explained the pros and cons and how she might get a "lot" of negative comments. She said that she didn't care ... that she loves your tiny coils and springy curls, and thus has begun the

journey... [punctuation and capitalization as original]"—
0kitten00's comment on Naptural85's post "Simple 'Natural Hair' Style for Humid Weather"

Just as mothers have the ability to foster a positive global self-esteem in young African American girls, I see Afro-cyberellas as cyber-other-mothers, contributive agents of social change. Thus, mothers can use the self-representations of Afro-cyberellas to encourage their daughters with their natural hair journey. When mothers like 0kitten00 show their daughters the work of Afro-cyberellas or vloggers, like Naptural85, such powerful images have the power to change negative perceptions of natural hair. Currently, there are hundreds of Afro-cyberellas on YouTube advocating natural hair, and many others posting on blogs; as online activists, one could say, they perhaps dominate black beauty paradigms on the web. As a result, mothers can use the work of Afro-cyberellas to empower their daughters to be more accepting of their natural beauty, and to see the value in fighting through social and cultural challenges that might discourage their decision.

EMPOWERING BLACK WOMEN, EDUCATING MOTHERS

Though there are surges of salons specializing in natural hair care in some major metropolitan cities, they are in the minority of salons overall. As a result, this lack of salons specializing in natural hair care and the lack of media representation have often made Afrocentric hair mothering very difficult (White 302). The notion that you have to be "brave" to wear your hair naturally (White 302) is something that Afro-cyberellas contest greatly. What this means for mothers and young girls is even more challenging, because the stakes of social acceptance are extremely high for mothers and young girls. The lack of available options to learn about natural hair (White 303) has required mothers of African American children to rely on "othermothering" and "community mothering" networks to support the development of Afrocentric hair knowledge production (Collins 178; Rogers 234-235).[5] This allows "hair mothering" to be "collective rather than [an] individual enterprise" (Hill 114-115).

YouTube has begun to fill this void. In the *New York Times* article, "'Going Natural' Requires Lots of Help," Jamila Bey writes, "tired of expensive, time-consuming salon visits, many would-be 'naturals' are searching YouTube for inspiration, instruction and other people who have made peace with their kinks and curls" (E3). Afro-cyberellas are thus there to provide information that will be helpful and useful to other women. For example, Maeling Tapp, a Ph.D. candidate in materials engineering at Georgia Tech and creator of the blog and YouTube channel NaturalChica, says "'I wanted to contribute to the wealth of information that's out there'" (E3). While there is a wealth of information already available, multiple platforms continue to pop up every day, including new media publications, which provide a platform for women of color to share their knowledge. Laquita Thomas-Banks writes, in the new cutting-edge online publication *Clutch*, that with "a simple online search you will come across the natural hair community sites, forums, personal blogs and natural hair albums within Kotki and Flickr" as well as Twitter and Facebook ("Natural Hair Online Support Groups"). Specifically Thomas-Banks lists an exhaustive list of Afro-cyberellas contributing natural hair care knowledge on the Internet.

In the case of natural hair, we can understand Afro-cyberellas to be providing knowledge that not only mothers can use, but the entire community. According to Patricia Hill Collins, women who mother non-biological children in their local communities participate in "community othermothering" (189). While Patricia Hill Collins focuses on the kinds of work that women do in local communities (i.e., babysitting, child care, and civic teaching), I believe that community othermothering not only exists in face-to-face communities, but in online communities. Afro-cyberellas are thus community othermothers, who exist, educate, and localize through cyberspace. This is important, as "[t]he practice of other-mothering remains central to the African American tradition of motherhood and is regarded as essential for the survival of black people" (O'Reilly, "'Home Is Where The Revolution Is'" 111), while responding to the needs of mothers. While community mothers are often thought to be beyond childbearing years (O'Reilly, "A Politics of The Heart" 172), ironically, Afro-cyberellas are often younger generations of African American women who are either currently single or young mothers themselves. Afro-cyberellas are cyber-other-mothers because they may never meet the mothers, fathers, or the children they help to mother; however, through the localization of online communities or "meet-ups" (Postill; Sessions), Afro-cyberellas have the potential to influence families through face-to-face relationships. Thus, as community cyber-other-mothers, Afro-cyberellas share knowledge that allows them to express the accountability they feel to give back to the community, to distribute knowledge that was available to them (Collins 189-190, 193), and to produce community work that addresses community needs (O'Reilly, "'Home Is Where the Revolution Is'" 110).

While Afro-cyberellas and families can meet through face-to-face meet-ups, their relationships remain cyber; yet, they have been localized into everyday communities. Face-to-face meet-ups allow "the empowerment of minority children through resistance and knowledge to occur both at home and in the larger cultural space through communal mothering and social activism" (O'Reilly, "'Home Is Where the Revolution Is'" 118). Similarly, when mothers engage with the work of Afro-cyberellas they are practicing a form of maternal activism that allows mothers to connect with "community action" (Nathanson 245), where the boundaries of self, family, and community are blurred to help children to fight oppression. Mothers and other African American women encounter these "fights" when they respond to challenging hair care topics on blog forums. For example, the DIY Hair Care Blog's June 18, 2011 post "Natural Hair Discussion: Dreads on Children, Yay or Nay?" addresses the contentious issue of whether mothers should allow their children to wear dreadlocks. Afro-cyberella Jarmelia asks readers what they think about dreads (a.k.a. dreadlocks) or locks on small children; in the comments readers are able to join in the discussion giving their unabashed opinions on the subject. The result—mothers can consider the ins and outs on what might be considered one of the most controversial Afrocentric hairstyles.[6]

Thus, social media sites become platforms where both Afro-cyberellas and mothers can engage in online activism and cultural discourse. According to Guobin Yang, online activism can be defined as "cultural, social, political, and nationalistic" where cultural activism "expresses concern over values, morality, lifestyles and identities" (33). National protests in cyberspace often involve large-scale online mobilizations, in which online communities become "important new form[s] of civic association, where [the] action is" (Yang 34). Yang asserts, "online activism ... is directly linked to changes in citizen's attitudes and behavior towards power" (36). In other words, what happens online through various platforms has a direct impact on the lives of viewers. The same can be said of the online "mobilizations" of Afro-cyberellas; the knowledge that is being created and distributed through social media channels is changing lives—quite literally. Afro-cyberella Maeling Tapp used online groups and forums during her own journey, which prompted her to contribute her own knowledge to the natural hair community: "After that (seeing women sharing knowledge about natural hair online) I felt really empowered, like, I can really do this, all these people are doing this as well, so I feel like I can do it too" ("African American Women 'Go Natural' Online"). Thus, in true reciprocity, Tapp's do-it-yourself model of online activism has been beneficial to other African American women, to mothers of African American children, and to the empowerment of their daughters.[7]

Now that African American girls can access and use the Internet in empowering ways, not only can mothers benefit from the knowledge of Afro-cyberellas, but also young African American girls are able to connect directly to the cyber-other-mother network of Afro-cyberellas available online. Blogging mediums particularly are major platforms in which young girls engage in political activity on the Internet (Harris); therefore, Afro-cyberella bloggers and vloggers have the potential to provide important tools for self-concepts.

Not only can Afro-cyberellas project positive representations of African American women, which are typically absent in traditional media, but African American girls and their mothers can also connect with these women online through posting comments. Afro-cyberella and blogger Maeling Tapp's feature in both *The New York Times* and NPR's *Here & Now,* are examples of this phenomenon: a major feature which garnered much attention to the online natural hair community. After seeing Tapp's interview posted on

Here & Now's online archive of the interview, a user praised Tapp, saying, "Maeling, you and your natural hair are beautiful. Thank you for being a role model for young girls...Bravo to you, and to Robin for featuring this topic (FWIW, I'm a white girl who grew up hating her naturally curly hair)" ("African-American Women 'Go Natural' Online"). In a similar way, WestIndianChula posted on Afro-cyberella, vlogger Hairsity's post "Black hair care for kids (children)...Natural Thick hair," "keep it up. I see many black girls with natural hair that gets long but when not manageable for the parent they perm it. Leave it natural forever." Such posts show how important the work of Afro-cyberellas can be in affirming the hair mothering of mothers and affirming Afrocentric-feminist aesthetics towards Afrocentric hair.

More and more Afro-cyberellas are producing Afrocentric hair care knowledge specifically for mothers of African American children, as well as forums to discuss specific issues or challenges that arise when attempting to awaken African American children to Afrocentric hair aesthetics. CurlyNikki.com's "Curly Parents" forum allows mothers of African American children to discuss "hair raising" issues such as dealing with relatives, maintaining healthy natural hair for one's child, mirroring natural hair for children, and styling tutorials.

Other blogs help to suggest ways in which mothers can learn how to style hair when there is limited time available. The blog, "Happy Girl Hair: Natural Hair Care for Kids," is a "semi-retired blog" produced by an Afro-cyberella who is also a mother. She suggests the blog entry "Progressive Styling" as a solution for mothers lacking time and patience; a progressive style she states is done in stages over time. She confesses that she is "not a hair care professional, I'm a mom who has learned to take a gentle approach to caring for natural hair."

Lastly, some Afro-cyberellas are mothers themselves, such as the mother represented on YouTube channel, Familygoingnatural, who shows YouTube users the power of mirroring Afrocentric hairstyling not just on herself, but also in the confidence she builds in her children. In a series of vlog posts called "Natural Hair: Back to School after the Big Chop" (PT1 and Update) her young daughter tells her experience of going back to school after her "big chop." Thus rightly so, when the young girl displays confidence to fight the criticism of her peers, YouTube users credit *her mom* for building such confidence in her daughter. Sample comments include the following:

> moniquerogers— "wow this little girl knows who she is… im almost 30 an jus now getting it!!! Your mom is doing a great job with you all!!!"
> iamsillywarm— "So nice to see a young black girl excited about her natural hair. Good job mom!"

On a different YouTube channel, kemosabbie comments on Afro-cyberella and YouTube vlogger, AfricanExport's post "Natural Hair: Children Who Are Natural" when African Export demonstrates natural hair care on her daughter's hair, "Your daughter is so cute. Her hair looks very healthy. She is lucky to have a mother that takes good care of her hair."

CONCLUSION

In conclusion, Afro-cyberellas have significant hair care knowledge to offer mothers of African American children. While self-hair-care guides exist in print, the printed word has tremendous limitations (Smith 29, 35-37; hooks 108-111), which makes hair care books relatively inaccessible to many people. While economically marginalized users may have limited access to the Internet and may not know how to access the information that Afro-cyberellas provide, scholars suggest that the so-called digital divide is closing in many ways, particularly in the United States, and addressing the specific ways in which marginalized users use the Internet (Mehra). Such claims suggest that there is great potential when using social media sites for social and maternal activism.

I acknowledge that future research on this topic is needed to explore the specific ways in which African American women and girls are affected by the cyber-other-mother network of Afro-cyberellas. It would be unreasonable to suggest that Afro-cyberellas eliminate all negative perceptions of Afrocentric hair, nor do I claim that such knowledge eliminates the desire of some African

American mothers and adolescents to straighten their hair. The practice of hair straightening too must be understood as both a political and a social strategy used by mothers and adolescents to survive in a world that privileges straight hair (Yoo and Johnson 354-355, 360, 377; Banks 102, 120). What I hope to suggest in this essay is that hair mothering offers the possibility "to guide ... children to make the right decisions," and sometimes it takes great patience, especially when young adolescent girls want to wear their hair like most other people (Williams 94). Nevertheless, I think that the work and practice of cyber-community-mothering by Afro-cyberellas has important implications for developing new forms of literacy, which can enhance cultural discourses within mothering, and affirm the resistance of social and cultural norms.

[1] I use the term Afrocentric hair to describe what might be called "natural hair" or hair that has not been altered permanently through chemical or heat manipulation. I use the term Afrocentric to suggest the African-inspired practice of wearing one's hair naturally or tightly coiled, and appreciating one's hair in its natural state. I suggest that Afrocentric hair care is a lost art, because the practice of styling hair naturally has repeatedly been hidden knowledge until times of Afrocentric or black consciousness, such as the '60s, '70s, and '90s. Currently, I would say the consciousness that exists today is less of an Afrocentric or black consciousness in terms of identity than an appreciation for epistemological knowledge about natural hair care and health.
[2] This term was derived from Hafkin and Huyer's theory of the "cyberella": a woman who contributes to information knowledge societies through the Internet, with the hopes of helping other women. I use the term "Afro-cyberellas" to describe African American women or women of the African diaspora who contribute knowledge to other African American women through the Internet.
[3] I will not be talking about any Facebook groups specifically in this paper; however, while there are several natural hair Facebook groups, there are relatively few groups dedicated to hair mothering.
[4] Although Turnage asserts that African American mothers help to create positive self-esteem for young black daughters, biracial moth-

ering by white women and even black fathers has been successful in encouraging positive self-esteem, either by affirming Afrocentric beauty standards or through situating daughters around good role models or positive images of black women.

[5] I am intentionally applying other-mothering to hair mothering, even while other-mothering and community mothering are typically referenced in regards to childcare.

[6] There are often strong views about locks, as they are now termed (to take away the negative implications within "dreadlocks"), because they have often been rejected extensively by the dominant culture, particularly corporate America, as being "unprofessional" or "inappropriate". Much of the negativity towards locks stems from an association with locks in Rastafarian culture, and representations of people of African descent with locks in detrimental ways. Also, locks are often viewed as being a "permanent" hairstyle because most people think you have to cut them off when you don't want the style any more. In reality, it is possible to take locks out; it just takes time to grow the hair out and comb out the locks.

[7] Examples include Ashababe56's comments on YouTuber GirlsLoveYourCurl's YouTube video "Love2 Love Washing Children's Natural Hair and Exfoliating the Scalp," and comments on the *Ask Anu* video "Grooming Your Child's Natural Hair."

WORKS CITED

"African-American Women 'Go Natural' Online." *Here & Now*. NPR, 29 July 2011. Web. 19 August 2011.

Akbari, Lisa. *The Black Woman's Guide to Beautiful Hair: A Positive Approach to Managing any Hair and Style*. Naperville, IL: Sourcebooks, 2002. Print.

Banks, Ingrid. *Hair Matters: Beauty, Power, and Black Women's Consciousness*. New York: New York University Press, 2000. Print.

Bey, Jamila. "'Going Natural' Requires Lots of Help." *The New York Times*, Style Desk; SKIN DEEP, E3. June 9 2011. Web. 11 August 2011.

"Black Hair Care for Kids (Children) ...Natural Thick Hair." Hairsity. *YouTube*. 2008. Web. 11 October 2011.

Caplan, Paula. "Don't Blame Mother: Then and Now." *Mother Outlaws: Theories and Practices of Empowered Mothering*. Ed. Andrea O'Reilly. Toronto: Women's Press, 2004. 275-283. Print.

Collins, Patricia Hill. "Black Women and Motherhood." *Black Feminist Thought: Knowledge, Consciousness, and the Politics of Empowerment*. 2nd ed. New York: Routledge, 2000. 173-199. Print.

"Curly Parents." Forums. *CurlyNikki.com*. Web. 11 October 2011.

"Grooming Your Child's Natural Hair." *Ask Anu*. 8 April 2010. Web. 11 October 2011.

Hafkin, Nancy J. and Sophia Huyer. *Cinderella or Cyberella? Empowering Women in the Knowledge Society*. Bloomfield, CT: Kumarian Press, 2006. Print.

Harris, Anita. "Young Women, Late Modern Politics, and the Participatory Possibilities of Online Cultures." *Journal of Youth Studies* 11.5 (2008): 481-495. Web. 11 Nov. 2010.

Hill, Shirley. "African American Mothers: Victimized, Vilified, and Valorized." *Feminist Mothering*. Ed. Andrea O'Reilly. Albany, N: SUNY Press, 2008. 243-256. Print.

hooks, bell. "Educating Women: A Feminist Agenda." *Feminist Theory: From Margin to Center*. Boston, MA: South End Press, 1984. 107-115. Print.

"Love2Love Washing Children's Natural Hair and Exfoliating the Scalp." GirlsLoveYourCurl's. *YouTube*. 2010. Web. 11 October 2011.

Mehra, Bharat. "The Internet for Empowerment of Minority and Marginalized Users." *New Media & Society* 6.6 (2004): 781-802. Web. 11 Nov. 2010.

Nathanson, Janice. "Maternal Activism: How Feminist is it?" *Feminist Mothering*. Ed. Andrea O'Reilly. Albany, NY:SUNY Press, 2008. 243-256. Print.

"Natural Hair: Back to School after the Big Chop PT1." Familygoingnatural. *YouTube*. 2009. Web. 11 October 2011.

"Natural Hair: Back to School after the Big Chop Update." Familygoingnatural. *YouTube*. 2009. Web. 11 October 2011.

"Natural Hair: Children Who Are Natural." AfricanExport. *YouTube*. 2010. Web. 11 October 2011.

"Natural Hair Discussion: Dreads on Children, Yay or Nay?"

DIYHair Care Blog. 18 June 2011. Web. 11 October 2011.

O'Reilly, Andrea. "A Politics of the Heart: African American Womanist Thought on Mothering." *Mother Outlaws: Theories and Practices of Empowered Mothering.* Ed. Andrea O'Reilly. Toronto: Women's Press, 2004. 171-191. Print.

O'Reilly, Andrea. "'Home is Where the Revolution Is': Womanist Thought on African-American Mothering." *Rocking the Cradle: Thoughts on Feminism, Motherhood, and the Possibility of Empowered Mothering.* Toronto: Demeter Press, 2006a. 109-127. Print.

O'Reilly, Andrea. *Rocking the Cradle: Thoughts on Feminism, Motherhood, and the Possibility of Empowered Mothering.* Toronto: Demeter Press, 2006b. Print.

Phillips, Shelley. *Beyond the Myths: Mother-Daughter Relationships in Psychology, History, Literature and Everyday Life.* New York: Penguin Books, 1991. Print.

Postill, John. "Localizing the Internet beyond Communities and Networks." *New Media & Society* 10.3 (2008): 413-431. Web. 24 November 2010.

"Progressive Styling." Happy Girl Hair: Natural Haircare for Kids. 11 August 2011. Web. 11 October 2011.

Rogers, Mary. "Othermothering." *Mothers & Children: Feminist Analyses and Personal Narratives.* Ed. Susan E. Chase and Mary F. Rogers. New Brunswick, NJ: Rutgers University Press, 2001. 234-248. Print.

Rooks, Noliwe. "Wearing Your Hair Wrong: Hair, Drama, and a Politics of Representation for African American Women at Play on a Battlefield." *Recovering the Black Female Body: Self Representations by African American Women.* Ed. M. Bennet and V. D. Dickerson. New Brunswick, NJ: Rutgers University Press, 2001. Print.

Sessions, Lauren F. "How Offline Gatherings Affect Online Communities." Information, Communication & Society 13.3 (2010): 375-95. Web. 1 August 2011.

"Simple 'Natural Hair' Style for Humid Weather." Naptural85. *YouTube.* 2011. Web. 3 November 2011.

Smith, Linda Tuhiwai. "Imperialism, History, Writing and Theory." *Decolonizing Methodologies: Research and Indigenous Peoples.*

New York: Zed Books, 1999. 19-41. Print.

Sullivan, Laura. "A Rio Crime." *Tenderheaded: A Comb-Bending Collection of Hair Stories*. Ed. Juliette Harris and Pamela Johnson. New York: Pocket Books, 2001. 116-125. Print.

Thomas-Banks, Laquita. "Natural Hair Online Support Groups." *Clutch Magazine Online* 13 (April 2009). Web. 21 July 2011.

Turnage, Barbara. "The Global Self-Esteem of an African American Adolescent Female and Her Relationship with Her Mother." *Mother Outlaws: Theories and Practices of Empowered Mothering*. Ed. Andrea O'Reilly. Toronto: Women's Press, 2004. 263-274. Print.

White, Shawntae Brown. "Releasing the Pursuit of Bouncin' and Behavin' Hair: Natural Hair as an Afrocentric Feminist Aesthetic for Beauty." *International Journal of Media and Cultural Politics* 1.3 (2005): 295-308. Web. 11 Nov. 2010.

Wilkie, Laurie. The Archaeology of Mothering: An African American Midwife's Tale. New York: Routledge, 2003. Print.

Williams, Jena. *Kinki Kreations: A Parent's Guide to Natural Black Hair Care for Kids*. New York: Harlem Moon, 2004. Print.

Yang, Guobin. "China Since Tiananmen: Online Activism." *Journal of Democracy* 20.3 (2009): 33-36. Web. 11 Nov. 2010.

Yoo, Jeong-Ju, and Kim K. P. Johnson. "Effects of Appearance-Related Testing on Ethnically Diverse Adolescent Girls." *Adolescence* (2007) 42.166: 353-380. Web. 11 October 2011.

14.
Hidebound Prohibitions and Electronic Literacies

Separate Spheres Ideology and the Surveillance of Mommyblogs

ELIZABETH HOWELLS

During the fall of 2010, the Franzen frenzy, better known as #Franzenfreude on Twitter, erupted and spoke to the legitimacy of narratives of domesticity in mainstream discourses. While Jonathan Franzen confirmed his status as a high art icon and literary darling with the debut of his domesticity-themed novel *Freedom*, other women writers (such as Jennifer Weiner and Jodi Piccoult) pointed out that the domestic is not always so highly valued, particularly when literature about women and families is often deemed "chick lit." Meghan O'Rourke and Ruth Franklin are among those writers who have participated in the heated debate, and their discussions attributed the discrepancy to the privileging of narratives written by male writers. Franzen himself weighed in on the flap in an interview with National Public Radio (NPR): "It's about the quality of attention that writing by women gets compared to the quality of attention by male writers. I actually have a lot of those feelings myself and have over the years" (Franzen).

Ultimately, these suspicions about quality were supported by statistics about quantity, and the numbers did seem to add up. For two years (2008-2010), the *New York Times* reviewed 545 works of fiction, and 62 percent were by men. Of the 101 books that got a review in both the *Times* and *Sunday Book Review*, 72 of them were men (DoubleX Staff). The debate continues over whether the gender of the author or the content of the work is the issue. The Franzen example, however, highlights the absence of domestic narratives in the "canon." Where can we find narratives of domesticity? How do literacies of parenthood, specifically motherhood, get disseminated?

In his 2006 article in *The New York Times Review of Books,* O. Scott lists the best of American fiction in the past twenty-five years as identified by a few hundred "prominent writers, critics, editors and other literary sages" (Scott). Ultimately, the narratives decidedly lack a focus on domesticity, mothering and motherhood: works from Cormac McCarthy, Don Delillo, John Updike, and Philip Roth dominate the list. While two women writers do make the cut, one of those writers, Marilynne Robinson, focuses on the lack of a mother in *Housekeeping*, and the top novel (Toni Morrison's *Beloved)* addresses the modern Solomon dilemma of the sacrificial mother. The narrative that is valued the most of any other is one that tells the story of the mother who must sacrifice, who must split herself. The double consciousness of the mother is revered and any other domestic narrative remains nonexistent.

If narratives of domesticity are not found or prized in mainstream literature, this manuscript examines the more likely frontier: the blogosphere, specifically what has come to be known as the virtual space of motherhood, "mommyblogs." These blogs by mothers describe the joys and travails of planning for, conceiving, delivering, raising, and celebrating children. Thus, if we concede the ways in which language constitutes reality, it is in this space in which discourses on motherhood regulate what is and what is not appropriate mothering. In these spaces, women negotiate legitimate motherhood and the discursive parameters therein, and transgressions are ultimately punished. The ether of the internet that at one time offered a kind of freedom as a virtual frontier for rewriting and redefining motherhood is no longer so wide open. Instead, this new space has now reinscribed the conventional codes of surveillance. The assumptions which undergird definitions of motherhood are reinstated, and the binaries that articulate, police, and maintain the split subjectivity of the mother are reinstituted.

With the number of "mommyblogs" increasing daily, and with some popular sites attracting more than 100,000 hits a day and hundreds, sometimes thousands, of comments per post, these blogs began as a space where the myths of a naturalized idealized version of mommy could be challenged: myths about conception, infertility, birth, boredom, satisfaction could be rejected and rewritten (Lopez 734). These blogs, from *Girls Gone Child* to *Finslippy*, from *Barefoot Foodie* to the *Bloggess*, from *Motherhood Uncensored* to *Dooce*, all demonstrate the gaps and sutures in the accepted narratives of motherhood in raw, ripe, graphic, compelling language, often anchored by irreverent humor and scandalous in shocking revelations.

Certainly, this virtual space has allowed for this kind of freedom. Rules did not govern what can be said about the body, about others, and about one's children on this web frontier and in this journal-like forum. Like the novel in the nineteenth century, the birth of this new genre has allowed for a fresh start without established territories, without conventional codes of propriety, and with a distinctly unconventional set of pioneers and a desperately hungry and enthusiastic audience. The private could be comfortably made public through the anonymity afforded by the web. Where extended families once provided communal support and unorthodox advice to the new mother, discussion boards, comment streams, and inter-blog references now allow institutional recommendations, accepted wisdom, common sense, and experiential knowledge to find voice, coexist, and flourish: "[t]here's a playground where everyone pretends everything's fine, and a computer screen behind which women can say, under cover of mommyblogs, 'How come this is so hard for me?'" (qtd. in Quindlen). *Mommy Needs Coffee* blogger Jenny Lauck wrote of the heyday of mommyblogs, back in 2005: "We were first and foremost writers. Good writers. We just happened to write about our family lives and our children." Ultimately, bloggers found an outlet for their voices and an antidote to the isolation of new motherhood in modernity. It was for this reason that at the inaugural BlogHer Conference in 2005 *Finslippy* blogger Alice Bradley declared blogging a "radical act." The medium and message were radical: Mommyblogs offered something revolutionary in the opportunity to re-narrativize motherhood. However, what might have been more radical and potentially transgressive was the opportunity to redefine a mother working in the home and the nature of the separate spheres.

Dooce (http://www.dooce.com) blogger Heather Armstrong represents one of those mothers and certainly serves as the pioneer of the new genre and profession. Armstrong began blogging as a single, former Mormon, Los Angeles-based web designer (once a Brigham Young University English Major) and become famous for getting fired for her blog in 2001. Her reincarnated blog (minus references that infringed upon her coworkers or family's privacy) received new life the following year in chronicling her move to Salt Lake City, new marriage, new baby, and subsequent post-partum depression (Waters). In 2008, Armstrong described the community the web allowed her: "Immediately I realized that writing things down and sharing it with people was getting me through the day" (Shellenbarger 1). The warm response from "this community of mothers ... lifted me up and gave me courage" (Shellenbarger 1). In the past few years, Technorati named Armstrong, now age 37, one of their top 100 bloggers, and *Forbes* named her number 26 in a list of the most influential women in media, sharing the spotlight with the likes of Oprah, Ellen, Tina Brown, and Barbara Walters (Blakeley). In 2005, Armstrong and her husband quit their jobs to work on *Dooce* full time which, while not disclosed by the Armstrongs, has been estimated to earn well over a million a year. Described as "The Power Mom" and "The Prom Queen of Mommybloggers," Heather "Dooce" Armstrong receives 6 million page views a month—or 100,000 visitors a day—according to Federated Media, has almost 1.6 million followers on Twitter, has made the careers of those individual artisans on Etsy whose craftwork she recommends, has multiple books, traveled to the White House as part of a dialogue about women in the workplace, and hosts spin off content on design on HGTV (Fulton).

Armstrong has been regularly celebrated as the model of mommyblogging for her honesty and wit. While chronicling its beauty in artful crafted photographs, her writing speaks of the agony and glory of childbirth and childrearing as well as offering design tips, discussion of health issues, and images of her dogs Chuck and Coco. Armstrong has also received shockingly virulent hate mail calling her children ugly, insulting her husband's "manhood," calling her a sell-out, and criticizing her separation from her husband Jon in early 2012. She has received aggressive, colorful, and highly personal attacks for everything from taking antidepressants to traveling for work to how she decorated her bathroom.

While the criticism can be attributed to everything from a dislike of the genre to a case of *schadenfreude*, the radical nature of this working mother and the persistence of the ideology of separate spheres is also at stake. Perhaps rewriting this narrative, exposing this myth, and tipping the delicate balance of the working mother binary is considered a transgression to be punished. The accepted narrative of motherhood allows for an inner division, a split subjectivity, and even a reflection on the impossibility of any elegant reconciliation. The mother is self-divided, as it were, privileging the needs of other above and in lieu of her own. Narratives of sacrifice and division abound. This cyborg notion, in fact, has been naturalized, no longer recognizable as myth, but constituted as an icon, a shiva as in the summer 2009 *Ms. Magazine* cover story (Jesella). Time and again, we recognize and reference the sitcom mother who wears high heels and the baby bjorn, the chick lit heroine in *I Don't Know How She Does It*, and the mommy martyr who juggles it all. The modern world has dismantled the myth of the nineteenth century's angel of the house or the 1950s June Cleaver to allow for the image of the working woman who rises to the top, and not just the working girl who must fall. But is that the limit of our literacy of motherhood?

The threat is when the split is not maintained and not depicted as cyborg. What if the mother is not juggling, that break is not maintained, that chink not articulated, and that fault line not respected? The "split subjectivity" identified by critics Sandra Gilbert and Susan Gubar as well as Nancy Chodorow, and countless women writers from Anne Bradstreet to Mary Shelley, from Charlotte Perkins Gilman to Jane Campion, and male writers from Sophocles to Shakespeare, from Faulkner to Hitchcock, have created a literary archetype or a paradigm of the mother as split subject, attempting to reconcile her roles but forever failing, noble in her self-sacrifice.

Armstrong is attempting to write the world of herself as a working/writing mother, a woman whose mothering is work, whose work is mothering. She is reconciling that split subjectivity, those separate spheres. Like many bloggers, she was offered and successfully courted advertising and enjoys ad revenue for her writing about the domestic sphere. Debra Aho Williamson, senior analyst at *eMarketer,* describes moms as "the ultimate internet networkers." (qtd. in Thompson). In her *Denver Post* article, journalist Christine Tatum observes: "Advertisers, news organizations and politicians have heard the mommies' roar, and they're trying to tap into their vast and incredibly-fast networks." BlogHer, an aggregator of mommyblogs, creates conferences and opportunities—advertisers, PR experts, and corporations identify the blog world as "ripe to be targeted" and have witnessed the rise of "momtrepreneurs" (Kirby). Conventionally, the means of making money as a mommyblogger or blogger in general is through sponsored posts, brand ambassadorships, display ads, conferences and event planning. On a yearly basis, Mom 2.0 Summit is held and celebrated as a chance for mom bloggers to talk shop with social media influencers, industry leaders and leading brands as they share best practices, discuss ways to create smarter web-based marketing, and discover social media tools that engage audiences and build relationships. When ads started appearing on Armstrong's blog alongside her reveries on mothering, her hate mail increased with comments like the one the *Wall Street Journal* described in 2008 as a "scathing parody" of one of Armstrong's monthly letters to her daughter: "Since your father and I started exploiting you for cash, neither one of us had to work a real job for a few months now. Score!" (Shellenbarger 1).

The "Maytag incident" of August 2009 sent ripples through the mommyblogging world when Armstrong used the power of her social network to call out Maytag for not returning her requests for maintenance or attending to her broken washing machine. With an eight-week-old newborn and a new long-desired high-end washer, Dooce tweeted (to her 1.6 million followers) to demand a Maytag boycott. Bosch, Home Depot, and ultimately Maytag were quick to respond, each with new washers and/or repairs, but so were some of Dooce's biggest detractors, calling her a "bully," a narcissist, and a sell-out for making public these domestic woes. Clearly, Dooce betrayed the legitimate narrative of motherhood by not only "exploiting" her children, but also in bringing the sphere of commerce into the idyll of the domestic. Others in the blogging community were quick to police this boundary between spheres, to punish this transgression, and to identify the threat of making motherhood work, of making her not natural but commercial.

Around that same time a few years ago, at BlogHer 2009, there was MommyGate. Unlike the 2005 BlogHer celebration of the radical potential of mommyblogs, the great outcry arose against the label, the very nature, and the recent commercialization of mommyblogging. Anecdotes of mothers threatening corporations with negative posts in order to get a pair of Croc shoes abound (Smith). As a result, many mothers vowed to reject the label of "mommyblogger" and its crass commercialism, its exploitation. In posts after the events of that summer's BlogHer conference, *Mom101* blogger Liz Gumbinner describes 2009 as "the year that shame died." *Motherhood Uncensored* blogger Kristen Chase wrote: "In fact, after this BlogHer, I really don't want to be called a mommyblogger ever again." *The Mom Slant*'s Julie Marsh contributes to this thread: "Many women in this new wave of mommybloggers just want to make money, or at the very least, gather up as many goodies from the swag piñata as they possibly can." And another blogger writes: "Mommybloggers make me hate capitalism, and people, I normally love capitalism" (Damen). Entering the public sphere in this way threatens the entrenched narrative of capitalism as well as the narrative of motherhood. The term *mommyblogger*, thus, became synonymous with this threatening conflation of spheres. The literacy of motherhood was, thus, being regulated, parameters were being established, and transgressors were being punished. As the ethics were being explored and articulated, demands to reinstitute separate spheres precipitated this call for "blogging with integrity." Ultimately, the mommyblogger revolution certainly precipitated efforts by the Federal Trade Commission to crack down on bloggers who do not disclose themselves as paid endorsers.

Domestic-themed blogs, whether they are design blogs or cooking blogs, seem not to suffer this same policing from sub-culture insiders or blog followers. In worshipping the shrine of the domestic in celebrating the hearth and the angel as one who creates amenities conducive to beauty and comfort, the illusion of separate spheres can be maintained. Cooking or design blogs are safe because they rarely bring "mommying" into it. Women as consumers are ok, mommies as consumers even better, but mompreneurs, maybe not.

Writers who articulate the maternal in the public sphere are often viewed with disdain.

Initially, Armstrong responded to the accusations about her exploitation with a blog she entitled "Monetizing the Hate." In a public space linked directly to *Dooce*, she published her hate mail, exposing the vitriol and rants in their own space, rife with ads thereby capitalizing on the hatred of her commercialization and the hatred of that commodification. The more "hits" she got from viewers reading her hate mail, the more money she received from sponsors. Here is how she described it in her September 16, 2009 post entitled "Your Momma Said You Ugly:" "Here I will be posting all the hate mail I get in my inbox and all the hateful anonymous and not-so-anonymous comments left on this website. And let me tell you, it is a hoot! And the money? OH THE MONEY! I am going to roll around naked in all that money!" The money, she announced, was going to charity. After a matter of weeks, ultimately, what replaced that spinoff website was the creation of community, a space for people to share their thinking, a location of affinity, as Donna Haraway might describe it (156). What diffuses the threat is the story of community here, which doesn't threaten the narrative of motherhood but is part of its "nature" as a legitimate form of this literacy.

Ultimately then, if mommyblogging is a radical act, that radicalism has its limits. Armstrong is not the only mommyblogger (or working mother) that suffers this kind of surveillance. On March 12, 2010, on the front page of the Style section of the Sunday *New York Times*, Jennifer Mendelsohn's article "Honey, Don't Bother Mommy. I'm Too Busy Building My Brand" set off a maelstrom in the "mommyblogging" world. The article itself positioned as it was in the Style section and written by a fellow mommyblogger was soundly criticized across the internet by many bloggers including Kelby Carr in her post entitled "Newspaper Bias Against Mom Bloggers" and Liz Gumbinner in her post entitled "Honey, Don't Bother Mommy. I'm Writing a Mildly Annoyed Letter to *The New York Times*." The title itself illustrates the necessary division, and the accompanying graphic reinforces the accepted narrative of the harried mother ignoring her distressed child. Rather than focus on the *kairos* of the mommyblog at this moment in our culture from the standpoint of this new breed of media mogul or the reality of economic exigency, the tone of the article suggests as Liz Gumbinner, *Mom101* blogger, puts it in a March 14th post: "And we're supposed to be home with our younguns suckling at our teats while we try in earnest to get our whites whiter, our pancakes fluffier, and our menfolk happier." Mendelsohn expressed surprise at attending a conference for mommybloggers that focused on "search-engine optimization, building a 'comment tribe' and how to create an effective media kit." With descriptions of "the minivan crowd," the "girly bonding," the "sass" and "summer-camp director" style of the keynote, and their laptops as "splayed," the tone is decidedly derogatory if not downright disdainful. Bloggers like Kelby Carr and Liz Gumbinner were quick to point out this fact.

The narrative construction of this marketing event by Mendelsohn in the *Times* overlooks the possibility of mommybloggers as articulating the business of mommying. Heidi Hartmann offers us a means to understand the critiques of this article and its strategic rhetoric as a call to reassess the woman question not as "the neurotic lament of the maladjusted, but a response to a social structure in which women are systematically dominated, exploited, and oppressed" (174). In other words, this new narrative of the mommyblogger poses a threat to the fundamental narratives of patriarchy and capitalism. The very nature of and extraordinary success of the mommyblog can be perceived as undermining the basic tenet of "job segregation by sex" which "by ensuring that women have the lower paid jobs, both assures women's economic dependence on men and reinforces notions of appropriate spheres for women and men" (181). While the reality of mommyblogging is big business, its power must be checked, undermined, and put into its place for its potential to challenge conventional family structures and fundamental economic structures.

Narratives like this express the anxiety linguistically and the repeated counter-narratives about the "Rise of the 'Daddy Blogger,'" such as the article of the same title from *The Week* issue published June 17, 2009, describes the "sphere" as "dominated by moms" which articulates the threat overtly. Notice the rhetorical implications of the following paragraph: "'Daddy-bloggers are great at giving stay-at-home dads advice and support,' said Steven

Hodson in *The Inquistir*, but they're no match for the raw, market-moving power of the mommybloggers, whose 'ire' has burned more than one company. And that's alright. Mommyblogs gave voice to a group of 'under appreciated or just ignored' women, while many daddy-bloggers see their blogs as a 'temporary way station' to being breadwinners again." The threat of the "power" of the mommy-bloggers as "raw, market-moving" and capable of tremendous "ire" is articulated here and simultaneously dismissed in the connotations of this profession as okay for invisible women but temporary for down-on-their-luck dads. The final line of the article cautions against the very nature of the work "making time to be a mommy or daddy blogger takes you away from 'the thing that qualifies you to be one, parenting.'" Ultimately, it doesn't matter if daddy bloggers are on the rise then because maybe no one should be a domestic blogger, or work and parent simultaneously for that matter. In articulating an understanding of this emerging profession as a reality, writers cannot help but construct narratives that perceive of such a profession as a threat.

Perhaps real economic factors will dismantle the potential threat. While in the past few years the internet presence of the business side of mommyblogging has increased exponentially, as with many financial opportunities at this moment, we are seeing the promise of this new business venture wane, with articles like "Possible Signs of the Mommyblogging Bubble Bursting" by Anna Viehle from the blog ABDPBT. Of late, Heather Armstrong's *Dooce* has reinvented itself as a blog less about narrativizing motherhood and family (particularly with the Armstrongs' separation) and more focused on design, music, fashion, and photography. When she did return to foray back into her old stomping grounds through the guise of a charitable organization called "Every Mother Counts" in 2011 in an effort to encourage awareness and charity through a recent trip to Bangladesh, her detractors in the blogosphere and now mainstream media critiqued her poverty tourism, her inefficacy, her loss of focus, and her fame. Her "trolls," as they are known in the internet world, got restless. When challenging conventional codes of the working/mother narrative, those conventional prohibitions arose, and when subscribing to conventional notions of how women can enter the public sphere legitimated by her motherhood,

Armstrong was in turn critiqued for such an outdated, imperialist version of public motherhood.

In many ways, then, the promise of this virtual space as a new location for authority, as potential for new visions and new voices merely opened a new venue for not only the same visions but also for the same voices. Many mommybloggers came to blogging as mothers of middle class means who were once women who worked outside of the home—they were mothers in the private sector who were reentering the public sector in an alternative way. The mommyblog phenomenon is notorious because of its absence of diverse representations of motherhood and its distinct class bias. Veronica Arreola's 2008 *Bitch* magazine summary bears consideration even a few years later: "the image of the mommyblogger is about as progressive as June Cleaver—it overlooks the legions of mom bloggers who aren't white, heterosexual, married women" (48). Clearly, the "digital divide" can be attributed to race, sexuality, and nationality as well as class, according to Arreola's synthesis. In her article "The Radical Act of 'Mommyblogging': Redefining Motherhood through the Blogosphere," Lori Kido Lopez summarizes the Pew Internet and American Life Project study of the demographics of the blogging community citing "60 percent of bloggers identifying as white, 11 percent African American, 19 percent Hispanic and 10 percent of other ethnicity" (734). All of the promise of progress in this new frontier for literacies of motherhood, then, may merely be a mirage.

The space of mommyblogging in its short history has presented in many ways as more regressive than progressive. For all of its challenging of convention in terms of notions of privacy and the nature of work, it also provides a locus for advocating highly conventional family structures. The narrative of *MckMama* offers one example of a fundamentalist Christian photographer writer espousing the importance of submitting to her husband and God's will while at times single-handedly supporting her husband and five children. Counterblogs like *MckMama without Pity* has been, as its name suggests, relentless in pointing out the hypocrisy of her subject position. But the fact of the blog itself and its strong following points to the presence of and desire for such mommyblogs that espouse conventional "family values" and structures.

For many of the massively popular blogs, whether *MckMama*, *Dooce*, or *Pioneer Woman*, an equally fervent backlash arises.

The nature of the backlash, ultimately, also suggests a kind of crisis of literacy wherein the narrative in flux is currently being established. Michel Foucault examines in his study of the discourse of sexuality the "veritable discursive explosion" of the nineteenth century in which

> a whole rhetoric of allusion and metaphor was codified. Without question, new rules of propriety screened out some words: there was a policing of statements. A control over enunciations as well: where and when it was not possible to talk about such things became much more strictly defined; in which circumstance, among which speakers, and within which social relationships. Areas were thus established, if not of utter silence, at least of tact and discretion.... (301)

This moment, thus, could be considered as a kind "discursive explosion" in which, among the proliferation of voices, the new literacy of motherhood bears an uncanny similarity to the pre-technology literacies in subjectivity, style, and substance. When Susan Faludi was diagnosing the backlash against feminism of the end of the twentieth century, she described the phenomenon in terms of "these codes and cajoling, these whispers and threats and myths, [that] move overwhelmingly in one direction: they try to push women back into their 'acceptable' roles" (xxii). It seems we have arrived at a similar moment in the history of literacies of motherhood.

Ultimately, a space that once offered new opportunities for articulating and envisioning the narrative of motherhood theoretically has served to reinscribe conventional avenues and occasions for public voice for women and mothers. Armstrong's efforts to raise awareness for "Every Mother Counts" are not unlike nineteenth-century writers like Elizabeth Gaskell turning to the Condition of England novels to find female public voice in the appropriate guise of eliciting sympathy, motherhood writ large. As one blog analyst, Kristen Howerton, writes in her summer article at the Shepost blog, "[a]dvocacy ... *does* seem to be an emerging part of [Armstrong's] brand, and many in the blogging community are inspired and proud that Armstrong is using her significant influence to bring attention to important global concerns." For Armstrong, this narrative rings as safer and more familiar than her previous subject matter and a portion of her audience is drawn to this familiar mythology of this "once upon a time..." narrative.

Blogger Anna Viehle of *ABDPBT* pointed out the condescension of Armstrong "exposing [her] own privilege" in this way as well as the "Commodification of Victimhood in the Mommyblogosphere" in a post wherein she warns against what she perceives as a plethora of mommybloggers positioning themselves as victims in order to elicit sympathy and page hits. Here, she seems to address recent issues with the *MckMama* blog, and certainly, such measures are more retrograde than radical. Woman as object, as victim, as locus of sympathy, goes down with the smooth edges and satisfying taste of myth, and the narrative of a momtrepeneur suggests something that may just stick in one's throat

The narratives of separate spheres and the concomitant infrastructure of literacies of capitalism and patriarchy demand careful maintenance, constant vigilance, and diffusion of potential threats. While there is freedom in saying motherhood is work—that it is messy or hard or physical or boring—there is not the freedom to make motherhood work, in embodying that reconciliation between work and motherhood, in reconciling those spheres, in making money from mommying, even among fellow mothers. The liberation offered by this new location of performing motherhood is just a fantasy. For the pre-text of mommy myths has been interpolated, has been so well synthesized, and causes the fantasy to collapse from cultural pressure. In Marxist terms, and as Patricia Hill Collins deftly and most notably articulates, the worker is alienated from her "motherwork" and is, thus, reified. Capitalistic society demands it, consumers guard against anything otherwise, and the false consciousness, this ideology or mythology, is preserved. When that perimeter is breeched, therein lies the rub: there lies the transgression that must be punished and the discourse that must be silenced. In this logic, the blog, like Anne Bradstreet's and Mary Shelley's bastard children, the mother's word work, comes to threaten the legitimate offspring. Finally, the ideological implications of this new frontier as a space that may allow for a rewriting of the narratives of motherhood, simultaneously deems such alternatives not only illegible but also illegitimate.

WORKS CITED

Armstrong, Heather. *Dooce*. Armstrong Media, LLC. Web.

Arreola, Veronica. "Mommy and Me." *Bitch Magazine* 40 (Summer 2008): 48-49. *Academic Search Complete*. Web. 1 Nov. 2011.

Blakeley, Kiri. "Power Women: Dooce's Dilemma." *Forbes*. Forbes.com, 15 July 09. Web. 1 Nov. 2011.

Bradley, Alice. "Here is where I get all preachy. You can skim this one." *Finslippy*, 20 Feb. 2005. Web. 1 Nov. 2011.

Carr, Kelby. "Newspaper Bias Against Mom Bloggers." *KelbyCarr.com*. N.p., 14 Mar 2010. Web. 1 Nov. 2011.

Chase, Kristen. "Not All Bloggers Are Like That." *Motherhood Uncensored: The Seedy Underbelly of Motherhood*. 25 July 2009. Web. 1 Nov. 2011.

Damen, Ilyka. "Mommy Bloggers and the Hating of Them." *Ilyka Damen*. 1 Aug. 2006. Web. 1 Nov. 2011.

DoubleX Staff. "Fact-Checking the Franzenfreude." *Slate*. The Slate Group, LLC, 2 Sept. 2010. Web. 29 Mar. 2012.

Faludi, Susan. *Backlash: The Undeclared War Against American Women*. New York: Anchor Books, 1991. Print.

Foucault, Michel. "The Repressive Hypothesis." *The Foucault Reader*. Ed. Paul Rabinow. New York: Pantheon, 1984. 301-329. Print.

Franklin, Ruth. "The Read: Franzen Fallout." *The New Republic*. TNR.com, 7 Sept. 2010. Web. 1 Nov. 2011.

Franzen, Jonathan. Interview by Terry Gross. *Fresh Air*, NPR. 9 Sept. 2010. Web. 1 Nov. 2011.

Fulton, Ben. "Utah Blogger Makes Forbes' Influential List." *The Salt Lake Tribune*. The Salt Lake Tribune.com, 17 July 2009. Web. 1 Nov. 2011.

Gumbinner, Liz. "The Year that Shame Died." *Mom101*, 27 July 2009. Web. 1 Nov. 2011.

Gumbinner, Liz. "Honey, Don't Bother Mommy. I'm Writing a Mildly Annoyed Letter to *The New York Times*." *Mom 101*.

N.p., 14 Mar. 2010. Web. 1 Nov. 2011.

Haraway, Donna. "A Cyborg Manifesto: Science, Technology, and Socialist-Feminism in the Late Twentieth Century." *Simians, Cyborgs, and Women: The Reinvention of Nature.* New York: Routledge, 1991. 149-182. Print.

Hartmann, Heidi. "The Unhappy Marriage of Marxism and Feminism." *Capitalism and Class* 3.2 (Summer 1979): 165-196. Print.

Howerton, Kristen. "Dooce Trip to Bangladesh Provokes Twitter Clash and Blogger Backlash." *ShePosts*, 2 July 2011. Web. 1 Nov. 2011.

Jesella, Kara. "Cyberhood is Powerful." *Ms. Magazine.* Summer 2009: 27-29. Print.

Kirby, Carrie. "'Mommybloggers' turn their hobby into profits." *SFGate.com. San Francisco Chronicle* 22 July 2008. Web. 1 Nov. 2011.

Lauck, Jenny. "Mommybloggers: Integrity, Community, and Taking Back the Respect We Earned." *Mommy Needs Coffee*, 1 Aug. 2009. Web. 1 Nov. 2011.

Lopez, Lori Kido. "The Radical Act of 'Mommy Blogging': Redefining Motherhood through the Blogosphere." *New Media and Society* 11.5 (2009): 729-747. Web. 1 Nov. 2011.

Marsh, Julie. "Don't Call Me a Mommy Blogger." *The Mom Slant.* N.p., 25 July 2009. Web. 1 Nov. 2011.

Mendelsohn, Jennifer. "Honey, Don't Bother Mommy. I'm Too Busy Building My Brand." *The New York Times* 12 Mar. 2010. Web. 1 Nov. 2011.

O'Rourke, Meghan. "Can A Woman Be a 'Great American Novelist'?" *Slate.* The Slate Group, LLC, 14 Sept. 2010. Web. 1 Nov. 2011.

Quindlen, Anna. "A Teachable Moment: Being a parent is easy and intuitive, correct? Well, no—it's just customary to pretend that that's the case." *Newsweek* 153.17 (27 Apr. 2009). Web. 1 Nov. 2011.

"Rise of the 'Daddy Blogger.'" *The Week.* The Week, 17 June 2009. Web. 1 Nov. 2011.

Scott, A. O. "In Search of the Best." *The New York Times* 21 May 2006. Web. 1 Nov. 2011.

Shellenbarger, Sue. "The Blogger Mom, In Your Face." *The Wall*

Street Journal WSJ.com, 10 Apr. 2008. Web. 1 Nov. 2011.
Smith Jr., George. "Threatened at Blogher." *The Personal Blog of @GeorgeGSmithJr*, 27 July 2009. Web. 1 Nov. 2011.
Tatum, Christine. "Mommy Blogs Prove Market Might." *The Denver Post.com* 23 Oct. 2007. Web. 1 Nov. 2011.
Thompson, Stephanie. "Mommy Blogs: A Marketer's Dream" *Advertising Age*. Crain Communications, 26 Feb. 2007: 6. *Academic Search Complete*. Web. 1 Nov. 2011.
Viehle, Anna. "Commodification of Victimhood in the Mommy Blogosphere." ABDPBT, 3 Aug. 2011. Web. 1 Nov. 2011.
Viehle, Anna. "Possible Signs the Mommyblogging Bubble is Bursting." ABDPBT, 25 July 2011. Web. 1 Nov. 2011.
Waters, Darren. "Pick of the Blogs: Dooce" *BBC News.com* 20 July 2005. Web. 1 Nov. 2011.

15.
King Solomon's Semiotic Chains/Inner Division and the Literacy of Motherhood

TERESA WINTERHALTER

IN AN IMPORTANT STUDY of women who perform acts of political violence, Patricia Melzer posits that, "the crisis female terrorists pose to our cultural understanding of [them] builds on a long tradition of dissociating women from violence in Western thought" (82). She further argues that, in nearly all cases, those women who have claimed political agency through acts of violence have been summarily accounted for by declaring them "inhuman." This designation, she claims, allows the anxiety that surrounds these women to be resolved by aligning them with the "unnatural," a term that conversely relegates "natural" women to the private sphere where they produce and take care of life. Because the prevailing story that accompanies female terrorists' lives is that they have abandoned their lives as mothers, they are repeatedly characterized as "possessing an identity that exists outside the limits of political and moral discourse" (Hacker, qtd. in Melzer 82). Thus, Melzer concludes, there is far more going on here than simply condemning these women for being unfeminine, unnatural, and inhuman creatures: in the absence of a linguistic framework in which to construct their stories, they become effectively unreadable as women.

   I take this study of terrorist women as my starting point, not so much because I am interested in their motivations or transgressions; rather, I begin here because our attempts to account for them at all point toward a set of pre-existing cultural assumptions, beliefs, and discursive practices about women and motherhood. Because these women's actions and their expressions of personal conviction challenge our prevailing assumptions about their primary roles as mothers, they are unable to be deciphered within the existing rhetorical parameters of women's natures. The linguistic economy that surrounds them, then, constitutes what I consider a *de facto* cultural literacy of motherhood, arising out of a habitual way of understanding women and filtering the broad field of our perceptions and attitudes about their legitimacy. Women, both as mothers and non-mothers, are read through a relationship to concepts of motherhood, a relationship that polices their points of entrance into the public sphere, where the pervasive discursive constructions of western society cast "good" women and motherhood as synonymous.

In common parlance, however, literacy is most often equated with skills-based conceptions of having the ability to decode print and the power to encode speech into written symbols. While such skills of literacy are vital to women's definitions and self-definitions, I want to stress that I am invoking the term in an expanded sense, as a collection of cultural and communicative practices that govern the way we view the world, talk about it, understand its operations, and produce its discourses. This enlarged conception foregrounds the relationship between the maintenance of existing structures of power and common representations of identity. Or as Antonio Gramsci might argue, it highlights how we conform to existing configurations of power as we recognize that our own lives are read through (and that we in turn learn to read through) its terms. In this dialectic, such practices of reading point out the hegemonic function of language in the circulation and production of dominant ideologies. The creation of a shared cultural literacy, then, must be seen to occur simultaneously through the processes of acquisition (as in the acquisition of a foreign language through prolonged association with it) and learning (as in receiving explicit instruction in the prevailing rules and structures of a foreign tongue). Through these simultaneous processes, motherhood, as the authoritative legitimating language for women, becomes a shared and intimate discourse that shapes the course of women's private and public lives.

It is no wonder, then, that the social monitoring functions of this cultural literacy become apparent as women attempt to move out of the maternal home its discourses have provided for them. As numerous social critics have pointed out, if women have occupied any place in the political and civic world, they have, for centuries, been accommodated through expanding the common parlance of motherhood to encompass a nurturing role for society, not through changing women's definitions within it. Typically women's public presence has been tolerated so long as it is associated with matters of social welfare, safety, morality, and children; and consequently "women's connection to the state has historically been centered on their roles as mothers" (Greenlee 406). This connection has vested the social pressure that compels them to retain their identities as mothers as they move into the public sphere with the power to control their self-expressions and determine the implications of what is said about them. It is not surprising, then, that many women in the contemporary political world continue to fashion themselves through the discourses surrounding motherhood; they borrow upon and reinforce a time-honored tradition of negotiating their entrance into the public sphere through reintroducing, reframing, and even reinforcing the traditional rhetoric of motherhood that circulates in the wider culture.

As the campaign rhetoric of a public figure such as Sarah Palin suggests, the literacy of motherhood serves to legitimate even her "rogue" status. In her rallies to call women to Republican voting booths, for example, she invoked her role as a mother as her credential to hold public office, implying that mothers have the ability to see the world a bit differently from other women. Throughout her campaign for the vice presidency, Palin traded upon the notion that women with children have different political priorities and relied upon voters accepting a seamless connection between maternal parenting and being qualified to run a country. As she called upon women to protect their cubs—to reincarnate themselves from "pit-bull hockey moms" into "momma grizzlies"—being a mom became a pervasive trope throughout the 2010 mid-term elections. It served as a ready synonym for being one of the people (someone real, authentic, someone you don't want to cross) and as code for a native, even instinctual, wisdom (as Palin's appeal to the common sense of women "moms just kinda know" demonstrates). In this claim for the power of intuitive motherhood, Palin deflected anxieties about usurping male power by assuming widespread agreement among her constituents that raising a brood of children does, without question, naturally provide the job training necessary to be president of the United States (Jaffe 18).

It is important to stress here how deeply these notions of maternal authority tap into public sentiment. In effect, by invoking motherhood as her rallying cry, Palin slips the noose of public reproach for her personal goals and ambitions. Although she is a mother of five children, one of whom has special needs, her rhetoric reinforces, rather than challenges, the self-interest for which her constituents might scold her by establishing her platform squarely within the terms of the prevailing literacy of motherhood. In fact, the acceptability of Palin's incitements to stand alone on one's hind legs—to protect family values and to strike out against any encroaching collectivism endorsed by the state—is plainly legible to her followers. We see how clearly they read her script in the testimonials of the "Pink Elephants," a group of women also known as the SarahPAC, who rally for political revolution under a flag of maternal instinct. Unlike terrorist women who are condemned as they dissociate themselves from maternity when they turn to violence, the SarahPac women claim a moral high ground for their violent actions by invoking their "duties" as mothers. In effect, motherhood serves as a shorthand justification for embracing violence, even a vigilante gun-culture, if the state is seen to place one's own kin in danger (Rosin). One blogger writes:

It's instinctual: my job as a mother is to raise up, nurture and protect my children, to protect their interests, to protect the interests of my family. In a society where my first line of defense, my husband, has been compromised by the self-victimization of the female sex, and I do it for my children.

Clearly this mother justifies herself as an aggressor because she senses that her children are in danger. Thus the legitimating discourse of woman as protective mother allows her to posit even violent action as acceptable, perhaps even obligatory. What this rallying cry also points out, however, is the larger linguistic context in which the cultural literacy of motherhood occurs and how this literacy is dependent upon preserving a traditional separate spheres ideology of proper roles for men and women.

Overall this rhetoric reveals a consensus among a broad swath of the public that contemporary alterations in traditional separate-spheres ideology are to blame for our political, even moral, decline. This reification of traditional gender binaries becomes even more apparent when we pair Palin's supporter's remarks with those from someone like Sharon Angle, who was also a political contender in 2010. Recall that Angle boasted that she is "not a career politician" but "a mother and a grandmother" while she scolded Harry Reid to "man up." Rather than enter the public arena as a woman who could potentially dismantle sexist stereotyping and make the divisions between men's and women's roles more porous and supple, Angle (supported by many likeminded women) entered the public eye under the aegis of biological motherhood, suggesting that (what Foucault would term) our disciplinary training in gender need not be transformed. Rather those time-honored roles needed only to be valued and appropriately assumed. In all of this, there was no acknowledgement of the damage this rigidity has wrecked on men's and women's lives for centuries; rather it championed and idealized traditional gender roles to such an extent that they became, once again, interpolated as the principle architectural fixtures of our social lexicon.

The inveterate nature of this literacy is especially apparent when we look across party lines and consider someone like Michelle Obama, who as the First Lady, stepped into the public eye not as an Ivy League educated lawyer and hospital executive, but as someone concerned primarily about what public policy might "mean for [her] girls." Numerous social critics have pointed out, however, that Mrs. Obama's highly public presentation of her maternal role may be read as keenly diplomatic. As a black woman entering the public arena, she was doubly susceptible to perceptual penalties should she not offer some reassurance that the dominant superstructure of white paternal authority would not be jeopardized by her presence. In her case in particular, we see that one of the only ways for a woman to legitimately claim public power is to do so under the shield of motherhood. To shun it has been to commit political suicide, as many have argued Hillary Clinton did when she scoffed at the idea of "staying home and baking cookies." From that point on, Clinton was repeatedly

Fig. 1. Hillary Clinton, Spy Magazine Cover 1   Fig. 2. Hillary Clinton, Spy Magazine Cover 2

denigrated as a woman. No longer just a blonde with thick glasses and poor taste in headbands, she became sexually monstrous, as these covers from *Spy* magazine graphically illustrate (see Fig. 1 & 2). Here she is no Tammy Waynette ("standing by [her] man"); she is rather the dominatrix taming male power by usurping it, or an even more startling abomination: she is someone who really hides male power under her skirt. Much like the women who participate in armed struggle or violence, who are similarly characterized as "unnatural" and who frequently report the daunting effects this participation has on their internal states, Clinton tells us of the "guilt involved" in making the choices she did.

Palin and company, however, skirt such inner conflict. Although they indirectly tap into the contemporary rhetoric of the working mother who can juggle both career and family, as they parade both across political stages (even to some degree co-opting a residual 1960s "sisterhood is powerful" ethos, where we want to support them because they do not shirk one calling for another), they never challenge the prevailing discourses of their legitimacy. In a profound manner, their example makes plain that the cooption of the maternal shield as women enter the public realm has far less to do with meeting the needs of one's children than with catering to a public neurosis about women in power, a neurosis that is quelled by maintaining the linguistic constructions through which women have been read as mothers for centuries.

It is important to point out, however, that these negotiations of women's entrance into previously restricted realms not only occur within conservative frameworks that operate largely to maintain the rhetoric of the past; they also occur within feminist frameworks that have been working for decades to rewrite many of the limiting terms of that past. As feminists have come to understand that the cultural production of identities conforms to existing configurations of power, they have also seen literacy as a powerful tool to create new meanings and conditions. Yet even within feminism's attempts to reframe fixed dogmas, motherhood repeatedly emerges as an identity of irreconcilable contradictions and impossible demands. It remains a concept that is riddled with assumptions about maternal practices; it seems incapable of escaping the larger semiotic structures that operate like a vise grip on women's significations. Thus, even the literacy of feminist motherhood allows little room for re-envisioning a future of the sort that Donna Haraway describes, which is "an ocean of semiotic currents in which non-monological ethics, politics, and mutual accountability might take lovely forms, promising to differentiate us from the established order" (xii).

Consider, for example, the way certain thinkers within feminist theory look with unease at women's direct participation in political arenas such as military organizations. Important feminist ethicists such as Sara Ruddick and Virginia Held make discerning claims for rejecting these forces. Instead, they want women's energies to be directed toward reforming masculinist models of duty, justice, and autonomy by reclaiming concepts of care, nurturance, and relatedness from their denigrated status as "women's work." According to Ruddick, reexamining maternal practice helps us endorse the values of protection and responsiveness in a way that need not be confined to child rearing alone. She argues that these values ought to infuse public policy for men and women alike. Her concept of "feminist maternal peace politics" is representative of a large body of feminist texts that expand the notion of our political work as primarily nonviolent by citing the *practice* of care giving and nurturing that is available to both men and women and deemphasizing biological maternity (220-242). Similarly, other feminist thinkers link women's social consciousness directly to their physical experiences. Foremost among them, perhaps, is Caroline Whitbeck, who locates women's potential for ethical reform explicitly in the experience of pregnancy and childbirth. By prioritizing biological motherhood, Whitbeck claims that the mother's host relationship to the child inside her and her vulnerability in the moment of birth enables her to identify with the powerlessness of others and thereby forge deep social bonds and attachments (189-191). Yet even while arguing for social reform through maternal practices, none of these thinkers seems to move us into a literacy of motherhood that does not reinforce the established order.

Indeed feminist attempts to embody their own language of motherhood have a history as complicated as it is long. Even a cursory glance across modern history reveals numerous examples of women who were explicitly restricted from holding public office, but who nevertheless attempted to claim public agency. Because these women were (more often than not) relegated to the domestic sphere, it is not surprising that one of the only ways they could circumvent the conditions of their confinement was to write. Given the perils of social censure these women faced when they dared to raise their voices through their pens, however, it is also not surprising that the trope of motherhood frequently served to filter the dangerous autonomous agency lurking in their expressions. In fact, because women so often claimed the rights to public discourse through the metaphoric valences of motherhood, I suggest that the tensions inherent in this pairing essentially reinforced the very cultural literacy they were attempting to challenge. The reading and writing of motherhood continued to frame women within sternly regulated codes of legitimacy and created self-sustaining myths of maternity as the appropriate model for women's power.

Let me explore the implications of this linguistic entanglement by borrowing upon the words of twentieth-century psychoanalyst Helene Deutsch who offers a keen diagnosis of the double bind in which women writers found themselves. Deutsch tells us: "Mothers don't write, they are written" (479). At first glance, there seems something shrewd in her discernment. She identifies the division that many mothers experience (both internally and culturally) when they attempt to write in societies that have already adjudicated their legitimacy through pre-established discourses and discursive practices. Recall, for example, the sense of internal conflict mothers in the eighteenth and nineteenth-centuries felt when they wrote in societies that extolled them as "virtuous and true" only if a concern for the wellbeing of others defined their salient occupations. As numerous critics have pointed out, the sense of being split between writing and being written often figures as the explicit subject matter for mothers who produce both children and words.

Even within the strident codes for goodness and motherhood in early Puritan America, for example, there is more than a whiff of ironic disingenuousness when Anne Bradstreet refers to her book of poems as:

> Thou ill-formed offspring of my feeble brain,
> Who after birth didst by my side remain,
> Till snatched from thence by friends, less wise than true,
> Who thee abroad, exposed to public view... (ll. 1-4)

Bradstreet's governing maternal metaphor demonstrates that she has already been interpolated into the social equation between godliness and selflessness for mothers. But there is also a transparency in her characterization of her book as a misbegotten child that offers an implicit critique of the conditions that cast her as transgressive if she is to be a writing mother. As the subject of her poem becomes her attempt to reconcile her urge to create (through organs other than her womb) with the demands of her society to shun those desires, something subversive in her pretense at poor mothering and piety emerges. This diagnostic irony is wielded even more subtlety by Mary Shelley, who in the preface to her novel *Frankenstein*, refers to her tale as her "hideous progeny." *Frankenstein*, itself a series of narrative epistles encircling Shelley's own struggle to claim simultaneous rights to creation and self-expression, repeatedly grafts one tale onto the next. So doing, she gives a form to her novel that replicates the suturing Dr. Frankenstein performs as he brings his monster to life. As does the doctor, Shelley creates from the carrion her culture has left her, and chillingly she foreshadows the horrific consequences as she bids her text "go forth." Writ large in the novel's Gothic scale, Shelley's irony is scalding as it shrewdly announces the prohibitions that surround her.

I invoke these examples not only to isolate the verbal veils such women donned to camouflage their self-involvement, but also to suggest how such rhetorical maneuvering denotes the concealed assumptions about motherhood that must be identified if new semiotic possibilities for women's agency are to be conceived. To this end, Deutsch's comma splice ("Women don't write, they are written") marks the center of what has commonly come to be understood as "feminist motherhood." For here—graphically represented in the sentence's punctuation—there is internal conflict. The idea that mothers don't write is not an independent clause; it is rather a concept that is wholly dependent upon the fact that women are already written. This linguistic precondition suggests why much of the theorizing about the problem of mothers defining their own realities develops around the concept of inner division.

Throughout their groundbreaking study of the trope of double-voicing that recurs throughout women's literature, for example, literary critics Sandra Gilbert and Susan Gubar (1978) have famously termed this inner division "split subjectivity"; indeed this term has gained such wide usage that is now almost common parlance in feminist criticism. Additionally, psychoanalysts Alice Balint and Nancy Chodorow point out the pervasiveness of this trope in their case studies. Chodorow refers to this divide as a "masochistic-feminine willingness to sacrifice" (77), and Balint claims: "it remains self-evident that socially the interest of the mother and the child be identical, and it is generally acknowledged as a measure of the goodness of the mother how far she really feels this identity of interests. The mother who considers herself before the child is no longer deemed 'good,' even by herself" (qtd. in Chodorow 39). Similarly legal theorist Martha Fineman, in her important study, *Mothers in Law*, shapes her argument clearly within the terms of this division, pointing out that in legal writing motherhood itself is "a colonized concept, an event physically practiced and experienced by women, but occupied, defined, and given content and value by the core concepts of patriarchal ideology" (12). For several decades, then, as women have renegotiated the spaces wherein they mother and work, feminist theorists have pointed out that the woman who defines herself outside of patriarchy's terms not only splits herself against herself, but also against the whole weight of the culture that enshrines her in definitions. Cultural theorist Susan Suleiman powerfully refers to her as the mother who is "split in two" (42).

Yet I am troubled by my willingness to accept summarily the consequences of this "sentencing." Although the terms through which mothers are split are critically analyzed in artistic expressions, psychoanalytic theories, and legal reviews, all of these discourses share a fundamental concern with representing "the natural mother," albeit one who is *not* allowed to hold herself together. Even in the act of resisting the punishing rhetoric of instinctual motherhood, contemporary feminist theorists reinstate the "split in two mother" as a natural by-product of ideology and biology. As a consequence of her pervasiveness, in fact, the self-divided mother has also come to stand as an unproblematized term, and perhaps once again functions as a naturalized category that is unaware of its own constructedness. To a large extent, women themselves and the cultures that superintend them do internalize this division as a natural consequence of the conditions in which they live. But this is, I maintain, the legacy of the way motherhood has been so mythologized that we no longer recognize it as a myth. As Roland Barthes makes clear in *Mythologies*, the further we get from the complications of narrative (with its subtleties of situation, ambiguities of meaning, and ethical snarls) the closer we move into myth as patented explanation for conceptions of world order (142).

Consider, for example, these two iconographic Judeo-Christian stories: "The Sacrifice of Isaac" and "The Judgment of Solomon." In the first image, according to the narrative, Abraham sets out to obey God's command to sacrifice without questioning. After his son Isaac is bound to the altar, an angel stops Abraham at the last minute, at which point he discovers a ram caught in some bushes and sacrifices it instead of Isaac. If we are to conclude that the angel that stays his hand is God's reward for his obedience, then there is no judgment levied against him for his attempted infanticide.

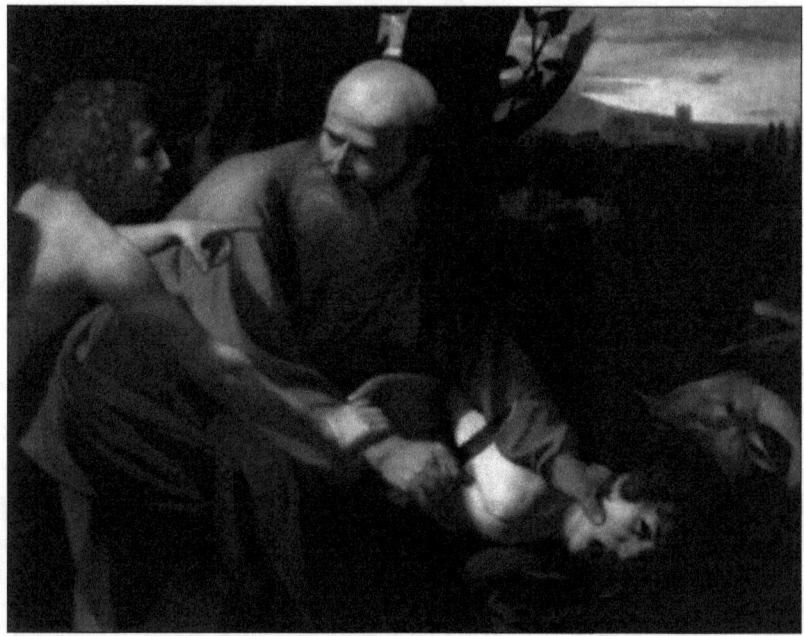

Fig. 3. Caravaggio, The Sacrifice of Isaac, 1603, Oil on canvas, 41 x 53

In the second image, two new mothers approach their king, Solomon, bringing with them one dead baby boy. Each mother presents the same story and accusation: She and the other woman live together and have both recently given birth to baby boys. One night soon after the birth of their respective sons, the other woman woke to find that she had smothered her own baby in her sleep. In anguish and jealousy, she took her dead son and exchanged it with the other's child. That is the accusation to which Solomon must respond. After some deliberation, he calls for a sword to be brought before him. He declares that there is only one fair solution: the live son must be split in two, each woman receiving half of the child. The boy's true mother cries out to give the other woman the child and save its life, and Solomon instantly gives the baby to the real mother, realizing the mother's selflessness is the woman's first identity.

What we find here is the psychic patterning on which so many of our assumptions about motherhood rest, and why women can today use this trope to gain traction in the political arena, or conversely why women not as prone to swapping dirty diapers for

Fig. 4. Rafaello Sanzio, The Judgment of Solomon, 1518, Fresco, The Vatican

congressional bills are themselves quick to characterize themselves as driven. No doubt the doubling in this depiction of Solomon's wisdom should give us pause, for the woman's divided self defines the trial of the "true mother." What has fallen out of the story as it has moved into the realm of myth is the understanding that motherhood is socially constructed by the dominant ideology of paternal authority: in this case the laws of Levirate marriage, where the baby was actually the lying woman's brother-in-law, whom she was obligated to marry when he reached the age of fifteen. Therefore, the lying woman, seeing that the result of Solomon's decision to split the baby in half would better serve her interests to be free to remarry, agreed. This piece of the tale merely lurks in the margins, and we often forget to remember that women's powerlessness to alter conceptions of legitimate and illegitimate sexual relationships also patrols the parameters of true motherhood.

What this example illustrates so usefully is that the myth of the mother who is split in two not only is, but also has been for ages, profoundly engrained within and among us. And even when we leverage critical theory to recognize that the metaphor itself denotes a site of rending, we reaffirm the division between the self-interested and the selfless mother as a necessary condition of motherhood. The split-in-two mother thus acquires legitimacy as a real mother, and leaves us reproducing the very value systems we purport to critique.

Our predisposition to naturalize this division is, I think, clearly deconstructed for us in Rosellen Brown's short story "Good Housekeeping." Of course the title is double-edged. In the story, the mother puts her baby down for a nap. She is a photographer, working again after her child has been born. Having taken a commission for a photo spread for a women's magazine, she spends her day isolating and stylizing the quotidian aspects of her world. Focusing her lens on the baby's bottom, the sludge in the coffeepot, the mountain of laundry, the vegetable peelings in the sink, the rumpled bed-sheets, a handful of condoms found in one of her husband's shoe boxes, a dirty window, and a welcome mat caked with mud, she moves through her own landscape. But then the baby wakes, and is screaming. With the shades up, she sees the back of the baby's throat quivering "like an icicle about to drop." When the baby sees the camera, however, he stops crying, fascinated. He then smiles, reaching for his mother through the slats of the crib. The mother's next action closes the story:

> She put her head in her hands. Then she reached in and, focusing as well as she could with one hand, the baby slapping at her through the bars, wheezing with laughter, she found one cool bare thigh, the rosy tightness of it, and pinched it with three fingers, kept pinching hard, till she got that angry uvula again, and a good bit of very wet tongue. Through the magnifier it was spiny as some plant, some sponge maybe, under the sea. (70)

It is important to examine the narrative tugs in this passage in order to weigh our judgments. The infant's thigh is not rendered in personalized terms, rather in aesthetic ones. Like the baby's tear, the wet upper lip that is envisioned as "an icicle about to drop"; the baby's leg is a "rosy tightness," and thus the language that propels the story is cast through the point of view of the photographer.

The concept of "free indirect discourse" from narrative theory is especially pertinent here, for while the story is ostensibly told from a third-person point of view, the terms of narration compel us to enter the perceptions of the world through the mind of the character being portrayed. As it passes into free indirect discourse, the story actually resists the ethical certainty that third person narration wants to impose.

Read solely from a third person point of view, the mother is split by the reader's judgments of her behavior. It seems impossible, in fact, not to want to reach a verdict on her actions. The passages of descriptive language, however, carry a different tug of allegiance. If we follow them, once the mother has picked her head up from her hands, Brown compels us to witness that she is no longer divided. Indeed the metaphoric compression into organic forms that flows throughout the story's conclusion suggests that she is at one with the world she sees. It is rather from the outside perspective of the reader that the question of "hurting" the child comes into play. In order for us to resolve our ethical queasiness, we return her to the split within herself Solomon relies upon, and along the edge of that paternal sword, there is no semiotic space available to us to provide her with something like a voice in the clouds that justifies her actions for a higher purpose. It is her raid on undivided power itself that distresses us. For torn between the pinch and the shutter speed, we remain in deficit of alternative possibilities through which to ratify her actions; our judgments are inadequate to the task of seeing the woman in a way that does not divide her against herself. But if we focus on the "rosy tightness" in these images, we may also see that the mother selects her own lexicon to record her world and that in the story there is no self-reproach. How easily we forget that this woman is, in fact, most clearly claiming the power to articulate her self as a mother in non-maternal stereotypes.

What I want to stress here is how—as we consider the insights that critical theory and meta-narrative awareness have bequeathed us—the terms through which we formulate these insights have become our own mythologies. This mother *is* an artist. The problem is that even in feminist theory we cannot also call her a mother without dividing her within her body. If she threatens to be simultaneously a woman of agency and a mother, we cannot abide her. Therefore, given the psychic home our cultural literacy has created for her, she remains at war within herself and the dominant ideologies of our society. In this regard, the women of the Tea Party are particularly rhetorically savvy, for they have restored the body of the integrated mother as, once again, the legitimate body through with to leverage political power. Yet neither they nor feminist theorists have finally freed her from the semiotic chains that threaten to bind her to the wisdom of Solomon eternally.

WORKS CITED

Balint, Alice. "Love for the Mother and Mother Love." *Primary Love and Psychoanalytic Technique*. Michael Balint. New York: Liveright, 1965. Print.

Barthes, Roland. *Mythologies*. Trans. Annette Lavers. *Mythologies*. London: Paladin, 1972. Print.

Bradstreet, Anne. "The Author to Her Book." *The Norton Anthology of Literature by Women*. Ed. Sandra Gilbert and Susan Gubar. New York: Norton, 2007. Print.

Brown, Rosellen. "Good Housekeeping." *Bitches and Sad Ladies: An Anthology of Fiction by and About Women*. Ed. Pat Rotter. New York: Dell, 1976: 68-70. Print.

Chodorow, Nancy. *The Reproduction of Mothering: Psychoanalysis and the Sociology of Gender*. Berkeley: University of California Press, 1978. Print.

Deutsch, Helene. *The Psychology of Women*. New York: Bantam, 1973. Print.

Fineman, Martha. *Mothers in Law*. New York: Columbia University Press, 1995. Print.

Gilbert, Sandra and Susan Gubar. *The Madwoman in the Attic: The Woman Writer and the Nineteenth Century Literary Imagination*. New Haven: Yale University Press, 1978. Print.

Gramsci, Antonio. *Selections from the Prison Notebooks*. New York: International Publishers, 1971. Print.

Greenlee, Jill. "Soccer Moms, Hockey Moms and the Question of 'Transformative' Motherhood." *The Women and Politics*

Research Section of the American Political Science Association. Cambridge: Cambridge University Press, 2010: 405-431. Print.

Haraway, Donna. "Foreword." *Women Writing Culture.* Eds. Gary A. Olson and Elizabeth Hirsh. Albany: State University of New York Press, 1995. Print.

Held, Virginia. "Feminism and Moral Theory." *Women and Moral Theory.* Ed. Eva Feder Kittay and Diana Tietens Meyers. Savage: Rowman and Littlefield, 1987: 111-128. Print.

Jaffe, Sarah. "Tea Stained: Co-opting Feminism with the Gun-Toting Fillies of the Tea Party." *Bitch Magazine* (19 Aug. 2010). Print.

Melzer, Patricia. "Maternal Ethics and Political Violence: The 'Betrayal' of Motherhood among the Women of the RAF and June 2 Movement." *Seminar* 47.1 (Feb. 2011): 81-101. Print.

Rosin, Hanna. "Is the Tea Party a Feminist Movement? It's Becoming an Insta-network for Aspiring Female Candidates." *Slate* May 12, 2010. Print.

Ruddick, Sara. *Maternal Thinking toward a Politics of Peace.* New York: Ballentine, 1989. Print.

Shelley, Mary. "Preface." *Frankenstein, or the Modern Prometheus.* Ed. James Rieger. Chicago: University of Chicago Press, 1974. Print.

Suleiman, Susan Rubin. *Risking Who One Is: Encounters with Contemporary Art and Literature.* Cambridge: Harvard University Press, 1994. 39-50. Print.

Whitbeck, Caroline. "The Maternal Instinct (1972)." *Mothering: Essays in Feminist Theory.* Ed. Joyce Trebilcot. Totowa: Rowman & Allanheld, 1984: 185-98. Print.

Zwerman, Gilda. "Mothering on the Lam: Politics, Gender Fantasies and Maternal Thinking in Women Associated with Armed, Clandestine Organizations in the United States." *Feminist Review* 47 (1994): 33-56. Print.

16.
"What's a Mom To Do?"

Negotiating Public Health Literacies Through the Traffic between Motherhood and Mothering in School-based HPV Vaccination Programming

MICHELLE WYNDHAM-WEST

> This vaccine is a catch-22 because if I do not let her have it and if she ends up getting cervical cancer, I'll always blame myself because I had the chance to get her the shot. But, it is so new I am not sure what to think. It weighs heavily on my mind. (Carmen, college professor and mother of an eighth-grade daughter)

IN 2007, THE CANADIAN PROVINCE of Ontario introduced a voluntary, subsidized school-based vaccination program whereby all grade eight girls (average ages range from 12 to 13) could receive the vaccine in their public schools free of charge (Office of the Premier 2007). It is on the heels of this program introduction and the general release of the vaccine in Canada that I began my dissertation fieldwork. During this fieldwork period—which took place from 2009 to 2010—I interviewed almost 70 women regarding their perspectives on the HPV vaccine. The women were comprised of university students, women who were receiving HPV related medical interventions and mothers with daughters at or near the grade eight vaccination age. This chapter focuses upon my interviews with mothers and outlines their experiences negotiating this vaccine for their daughters. As such, in this chapter, I explore how hegemonic conceptualizations surrounding motherhood (Rich) are embedded in public health messaging surrounding the vaccine and how mothers creatively re-appropriate these tenets in agentive ways in order to reach a vaccine decision that they are comfortable with. Thus, tracing the process whereby motherhood and "doing mothering" (Glenn) come into contact, and its associated "traffic" (Rapp 185), allows insight into how women formulate their own "public health literacies" (Pleasant and Kuruvilla 157). The formulation of public health literacies, whether it be a decision to vaccinate, to abstain from vaccination, or to delay vaccine decision-making, all involve the strategic re-appropriation of the "good" mother discourse, which is carried out through a plethora of "intensive mothering" (Hayes) practices. These intensive mothering practices are complex, often contradictory and steeped in irony. It is, however, through these agentive and resistive entanglements that new possibilities, or hope, for the interrogation of motherhood ideologies embedded within public health initiatives and messaging emerges.

METHODOLOGICAL AND THEORETICAL FRAMING

It was not difficult to recruit 20 mothers in the Toronto-area to take part in interviews due to the topical nature of my research. I approached mothers in my own networks and many were kind enough to suggest friends and relatives, who were happy to participate. My positionality as a mother of two boys at a school offering the vaccine no doubt facilitated recruitment. Interviews were conducted in person over kitchen tables, in coffee shops near women's homes, and at their offices. All interviews were held on a one-on-one basis. I was cognizant to create a semi-structured interview format to allow the "space" for the emergence of "the complexity of women's responses to the medicalization, which may range from selective resistance to selective compliance" (Lock and Kaufert 2). In other words, while interview questions served as a guide, they were also flexible enough to accommodate women's own narrative directions as they emerged in our conversations. This approach facilitates grounded qualitative data collection (Strauss and Corbin). Once the interviews were complete, I unpacked women's narratives through a "categorical-content" analysis (Lieblich, Tuval-Mashiach and Zilber 13). This takes into account the overarching narrative before identifying themes to focus upon, which emanate organically and not in a pre-determined fashion from women's recounting.

As participant narratives reveal, mothers were highly engaged with issues surrounding the HPV vaccine. This engagement reflects the continually negotiated process whereby mothers create their own public health literacies by mediating between popularized notions of motherhood, as is exhibited in public health messaging, and enacting health practices they are comfortable with for their daughters. Thus, in my analysis I trace the creative energy that "erupts" (Stewart 245) when motherhood and mothering intersects (Rich). Adrienne Rich explains the motherhood/mothering dyad, "I try to distinguish between two meanings of motherhood, one superimposed on the other: the *potential relationship* of any woman to her powers of reproduction and to children; and the *institution*, which aims at ensuring that that potential—and all women—shall remain under male control" (13, emphasis in the original). Therefore, the intersections between motherhood and mothering produce a "traffic" (Rapp 185) as individuals work to strategically accommodate, reject and hybridize the institutional directives that are embedded in HPV vaccine public health messaging. The noise, confusion and frustration of traffic, along with the mapping of your own route through this congestion, are all part and parcel of "doing mothering" (Glenn 5).

I consider doing mothering akin to Butler's performing or doing gender. Gender, says Judith Butler, "is always a doing, though not a doing by a subject who might be said to preexist the deed" (*Gender Trouble* 34). Doing gender is a continual process, not a discrete or concrete bodily motion, just as is experienced in doing mothering. And, when I examined women's narratives focusing upon doing mothering while engaging in vaccine decision-making, I found great variability within mothering strategies. Each woman draws upon her own unique set of experiences in order to chart her way forward in determining the best vaccination measure for her daughter. Correspondingly, doing mothering is a practice that allows for multiple forms of agency and resistance, even in what may seem as echoes of dominant motherhood directives. In this vein, the conceptualizations of agency and resistance that I draw upon are not to be characterized as an outright attempt to overthrow, but measures that can cause short- and long-term fissures in the "systems of domination" without its actual dismantling (Gledhill

287). This is what James Scott refers to as "everyday resistance" (xvii)—resistance that is quiet, subtle and can be hard to spot.

In the case of the women interviewed, agency and resistance are enacted through an individual's re-framing or "resignification" (Allen 3): creatively re-formulating their identity, self-ascription and sense of self within existing power frameworks. Whilst doing mothering within the context of vaccine decision-making, mothers creatively harnessed the "good" mother discourse and enacted "intensive mothering" (Hayes) to productive affect/effect. Their resignifications reveal the complicated and often ironic nature of agency and resistance. As such, women may initially appear to echo dominant discourses surrounding motherhood, but a closer examination reveals they are re-fashioning the good mother precept in novel ways, which diverge from intended institutional meanings. As discussed henceforth, mothers' narratives demonstrate how negotiating one's *own* public health literacies for another can, indeed, be a generative process (Zaloom). Engaging in re-signification while making a vaccine decision for a daughter provides the women interviewed with the opportunity to re-produce, re-create and re-enforce an aspect of their own sense of self—their sense of being a mother.

A SCHOOL-BASED VACCINATION CAMPAIGN, PUBLIC HEALTH LITERACIES AND HPV RISK-MAKING

My first interview of a fellow mother regarding the vaccine took place in September 2010. This meeting with Carmen is still a vivid memory for me. This poised and self-assured community-college professor was clearly a bit rattled. Besides the somewhat harried period of back-to-school time, Carmen's daughter, Emily, had entered grade eight. This is a transitional time for young adolescents, the last year of middle school before high school, but that is not what was bothering Carmen. In the large packet of forms to be signed that Emily brought home on the first day of school, which ranged from pizza ordering to school accident insurance requests, was an HPV vaccine consent form. Carmen brought a copy of the form to our interview. The two-page form contained a letter to parents, an HPV "fact" sheet and the boxes for the required dual consent—that of daughter and parent/guardian. The consent form needed to be returned in four days in order for Emily to be eligible for the three-phased shots. As Carmen stated, "we got it on a Tuesday and it had to be in by the Friday." The teachers explained the short turn-around time as an administrative matter—time was needed to process of all the paperwork for the timed vaccine. Carmen, however, felt the process was rushed. She explains:

> *I spent about three hours on the Wednesday night going back and forth saying should we have this done. It's so new. Looking up the side effects, looking up if there were any long-term studies done on it. It seems pretty safe, but everything seems pretty safe when they're trying to make everybody have it done.*

At this point in our interview Carmen paused, and the stress of the decision-making process was visible on her face. This was a look that became more and more familiar as my interviews progressed. Andrea, a pint-size and energetic entrepreneur, also commented on the narrow window for decision-making:

> *We didn't have a lot of time, I remember. We had little information and we had to make a decision. So I would imagine there were people who delayed that decision because they wanted to do their own research and they wanted to figure it out.*

After my interview with Carmen, I looked more closely at the public health documentation she had brought for me. The letter from the public health authority was short, as was the "fact" sheet. The half-page letter began by stating that the Ontario government was providing the vaccination service free of charge. The official logo of the public health authority and the endorsement of the vaccine by the provincial government, which are juxtaposed at the top of the letter, set an authoritative tone for this piece of correspondence. The next paragraph—a mere three and a half lines—provided information on HPV. This description states, "in 2006, there were an estimated 500 cases of cervical cancer with

10 deaths in Ontario." This paragraph is brought to a close by saying that Gardasil®—the Merck Frost vaccine purchased by the provincial government in Ontario—"can prevent the HPV infections that cause the majority of the cervical cancer and genital warts in Canada." The remaining information in the letter focuses upon logistical aspects of getting the three-dose vaccine and in-school vaccination procedures. The accompanying "fact sheet" offers half a dozen bullet points on HPV and the Gardasil® vaccine. The fact sheet emphasizes that there are on average 400 deaths a year in Canada due to cervical cancer.

The data surrounding HPV and cervical cancer, however, is more complex than is presented in this public health literature. HPV is found at a high rate among the general population (Braun and Gavey). And, only a fraction of HPV infections lead to genital warts (Vanslyke et al. 585). Additionally, the public health literature does not explain the transient nature of HPV: HPV can come and go without one ever being aware of it and infections may never manifest as abnormal cervical cells. Additionally, approximately two thirds of "abnormal" cells that do present also have the propensity to "correct" themselves without intervention (Posner 61). Thus, cervical cellular mutations can take various paths, ranging from eventually turning into cancer, going back to "normal" or staying in a dysplastic form *pour la longue durée* (Clarke and Casper 607). Moreover, if a woman/girl is vaccinated against HPV, screening protocols still suggest undergoing regularized Pap smears once sexual activity has started. One might then conclude that the information provided by Carmen's local public health authority is not balanced and wonder why the use of cervical cancer statistics serves little purpose other than to instill fear in readers.

I was starting to understand Carmen's stress about making a decision surrounding the HPV vaccine for her daughter. Information was missing. There were not answers to the following questions: Is it safe? Does it really work? If so, for how long? The mothers I interviewed attempted to answer their questions by engaging in active information gathering concerning the vaccine, or put another way, piecing together public health literacies. Carmen discusses how she sought more details regarding the vaccine online:

> *When we got the letter, the first thing that I did was go to the website that was on the letter, the public health authority website. It was kind of vague and it was sort of "yes" this is great, you should have it done, no problems, blah, blah, blah. So I started Googling. That's a good thing and a bad thing, because of course the first thing that pops up on any Google search is Wikipedia, which can be written and re-written by whoever wants to add information.*

Despite a critical examination of the ineffectiveness of fear in public health campaigns (Lupton; Johnson et al.; Gagnon, Jacob and Holmes), the fear leitmotif is not only laced throughout public health HPV vaccine materials distributed in schools, but embedded in the voluminous news media accounts surrounding the vaccine. Since the introduction of the vaccination program in Ontario public schools in 2007, there has been a steady stream of newspaper and TV news stories. The vaccine has been covered in national and regional dailies, such as the *Globe and Mail*, the *Toronto Star* and the prominent news magazine *Macleans* (Gordon; Picard; Gulli, George and Intini). While it was not surprising to see intense news coverage at the outset of the subsidized school-based program, mass media coverage has been ongoing and particularly noticeable each September as the new school year begins. Carmen discusses her own thoughts about the mass media surrounding the vaccine:

> *At first I thought it was just something to scare to people again. When the flu shot became really popular everybody was like, "oh you have to have a flu shot, have to have a flu shot." Everybody was saying you have to have a flu shot. Now it's not really that big a deal anymore. So I'm finding it's the same thing with this vaccine or this shot. You get a lot of—you have a ton of media coverage about it. They're playing on some of the worst fears that you can get. Either you getting sick and leaving your children or your children getting sick, which are your daughters getting sick.*

In addition to the mass media coverage of the vaccine, Merck Frost's Gardasil® advertisement campaign has been ubiquitous. Carmen talked about the messaging of both the Gardasil® TV commercials and print advertisements at length. In regard to the TV commercials, she felt messaging was, "all about protecting your family and protecting your daughter and sort of instilling that sort of fear in you that it's around every corner." Carmen recommended I look at a particular advertisement, which was featured in that month's *Chatelaine* magazine, a periodical aimed at women, which covers "family" issues such as recipes, housekeeping tips, fitness regimes, health information and offers a small fashion section. Carmen described the advertisement she encountered, "Yeah. So it's in the family section. It's a mother and a daughter. The mother's got her arms around her daughter." Carmen picked up on the messaging surrounding HPV vaccination promotion, whether through public health documentation or the Gardasil® campaigns: that is, "good" mothers vaccinate their daughters against HPV. These campaigns hinge on the gendering of HPV and positioning Gardasil® as a cancer fighting mechanism for women, side stepping the issue of sexual health and related cancers. In short, the Gardasil® campaigns and school-based HPV vaccination programming work in tandem to brand HPV as a "woman's issue." By extension, good mothers are squarely responsible for mitigating HPV risk for their daughters.

MOVING FROM MOTHERHOOD TO MOTHERING: THE TRAFFIC OF DOING MOTHERING IN ON-THE-GROUND HPV VACCINE NEGOTIATION

The school-based vaccination programs and the accompanying Gardasil® campaigns saliently re-presents Rich's (1976/1986) critical work on motherhood. However, Rich's writings on the institutions of motherhood represent one half of her theoretical framework, with the other half reflecting the everyday act of mothering. Motherhood is comprised of the overarching strategies through which women are kept under the thumb of the dominant—and, predominantly patriarchal—order. Order is a key word here. In contrast, mothering reflects the on-the-ground workings of being a mother—the chaotic (and, disorderly) processes as described and defined by women. While the former is a subjugable form of power and, as Diana Ginn argues, "is a form of social control exercised over women as they bear and raise children" (32), the latter can function within spheres of agency. Evelyn Nakano Glenn emphasizes the agentive aspects of mothering:

> Mothering occurs within specific social contexts that vary in terms of material and cultural resources and constraints. How mothering is conceived, organized, and carried out is not simply determined by these conditions, however. Mothering is constructed through men's and women's actions within specific historical circumstances. Thus agency is central to an understanding of mothering as a social, rather than biological, construct. (3)

When one is able to harness the everyday experiences of mothering on one's own terms, even for a fleeting moment of resistance—no matter how covert—power can be reconceived and the narrative of motherhood can be destabilized. This resistance is evidenced in narratives of the women I interviewed, which harness the good mother discourse by enacting "intensive mothering" (Hayes) to productive effect/affect. This creative appropriation of dominant discourses as one engages in the development of one's sense of self is the focus going forward in this chapter.

Pragmatically, HPV vaccine negotiation strategies tended to fall into three groupings: (1) mothers who opted to vaccinate their daughters, whether through the school system or their physician at their cost or via an insurance plan due to the daughter being older than 13 years of age; (2) mothers who did not wish to vaccinate their daughters due to their concerns regarding big pharma and the gendering of the vaccine; and (3) mothers who decided to put off the decision in order to take more time to reach a decision and for additional research to emerge. Primary concerns for these mothers centered on vaccine safety and the duration of vaccine effectiveness. Numerically this translated into more of the mothers I interviewed opting to have their daughter vaccinated, than those who decided not to. In addition, only a handful pursued the path of delaying decision-making, reflecting a small number who occupy a class location that allows for financial flexibility in decision-making. However, to place undue emphasis on decision-making outcomes would provide a shallow reading of the data. Decision-making is complex and reflects the tensions, contradictions and confluences of quotidian life.

OPTING TO VACCINATE

Andrea recounts a decision-making process that reflects narratives common to the mothers I interviewed who opted to vaccinate their daughters. Andrea worried that her daughter, when an eventual mother herself, may not take the precautionary steps to ensure that she does not develop cervical cancer. Andrea explains that mothers often "tend focus on the health of their families, so there may always be a time issue for women to be able to go out and get a Pap test. Women probably put it off, focusing on their children's health instead." Therefore, as a way to relay the importance of a woman's health, particularly that of a mother, Andrea incorporated her daughter's input into her decision-making process. Andrea explains:

> She certainly had input into the conversation. It wasn't my decision that said, "I'm making this for you." We certainly had conversations around what this meant. It was something where—and this is where technology is great—you can go and look at information like this on the Internet. You can e-mail people to find out their thoughts as well too.

As Andrea indicates, bringing her daughter into the fold was one aspect of her decision-making process. Andrea also consulted friends, conducted research on the Internet and spoke extensively with her family physician. This is a prime example of intensive mothering. In performing intensive mothering, Andrea spent a great deal of time and energy coming to the decision and consulted many others, including experts—her family physician and on-line medical sources—numerous times. Andrea details this process:

> I did talk to our pediatrician to get his thoughts. He is a highly experienced doctor and he has three daughters as well. He said that if he was in the situation where he had to make this decision for them that he would 100 percent go ahead and do this. I also did talk to other parents, not that I was going to let other people's opinions about what they would do for their child sway what I would do for mine, but certainly just to get a range of comments and discussions.

Central to Andrea's decision to vaccinate is her role, as a mother, in mitigating risk for her daughter. Andrea was acutely concerned about "what will happen in five years' time? What are the implications of doing something like this?" Andrea elaborates upon her assessment of HPV vaccine risk:

> It's very similar to things like Meningitis vaccinations or Chickenpox vaccinations, all of which my children have had because again, I felt comfortable looking at the risk around vaccination versus the risk of getting the disease or having an illness that could have been prevented or, at least, the impact reduced. So, we spent a lot of time talking about this because, it was just again—I think that with decisions like that, if they affect me only, are easier, whereas as the parent you take on that responsibility of "what if?"

Heather, a physiotherapist with one daughter in grade eight, like Andrea, was clear in expressing the potentiality of vaccines in bringing about risk. Heather explains:

> I think there is always risk with a vaccine. I think some people will react badly and I think always there is a risk that we are going to find out some day later, like with any kind of medication or anything like that, there are some long-term effects we didn't realize. I think that there is always a risk.

Thus, for Andrea and Heather, the vaccination could bring about substantial risk but there is a greater risk in not vaccinating their daughters. Neither mother wanted to procure an undesired outcome because they opted not to vaccinate. Potential risk is a scenario that requires action—therefore, risk can be generative process (Zaloom). In making her decision, Andrea enacted a form of intensive mothering that contributes to her sense of self as a mother. Saying "yes" to the shot allows Andrea to form her *own* version of public health literacy. Andrea's public health literacy is slightly different than that of Heather, who had HPV-related complications in her early 20s and made her vaccination decision based on her HPV-related treatment experiences. Alternatively, Andrea's public health literacy is linked to her very conceptualization of mothering. Andrea is wishing to protect her daughter when she is a mother in the future, as Andrea expressed concern that many mothers do not look after their health in the same strident manner as they do for their own children and families due to time constraints while mothering. Therefore, Andrea is seeking to shield her daughter from the pitfalls of being an intensive mother.

There is a sense of irony in this concern as Andrea clearly practices intensive mothering. However, Andrea is practicing intensive mothering with a resistive sub-text that is laced with a sense of hope. Andrea's decision may appear to be a mirror of dominant discourses and she will certainly not overthrow hegemonic notions of motherhood. But she is, for a brief while, attempting to disrupt future hegemonic conceptualizations whilst doing mothering. This may also filter down the line, when her daughter is doing the same. Andrea is enacting resistance for her daughter, but also for the other women (and these prospective mothers) who will eventually populate her family tree. It is then not a surprise that Andrea spoke of her decision-making process with a thoughtful, quiet confidence and the occasional wry smile.

NOT VACCINATING AND DELAYING DECISION-MAKING

Mothers who opted not to vaccinate re-fashioned the popularized conceptualization of the good mother to stand for mothers who did ample research regarding their daughter's health, did not wish for their daughters to be "test" subjects due to the timeframe the vaccine has been on the market, and cared enough to say "no." For example, Colleen, a neighbor with a home-based business and a daughter just approaching grade eight, emphasized that grade eight girls were being treated like "a case study. It seems like, let's track these girls and see what happens."

During our interview Colleen spoke passionately about how it was her duty to protect her daughter from the dubious interests of big pharma. When I arrived at Colleen's home for our interview, she had just gotten off her computer, conducting on-line research into the vaccine:

> *I looked into it and what, we have three to four hundred deaths a year from cervical cancer. We have a death every seven minutes from heart- and stroke-related disease. And we're spending $300 million and 300 people a year on average are dying from cervical cancer. Cervical cancer is quite preventable with regular Pap screening. So, what the heck. And this vaccine is only protecting, they say, 70 percent of the cases. But there's all these other strains of HPV it's not protecting against. So why are we spending hundreds of millions of dollars to vaccinate against a disease when this is one of the few types of cancers that is preventable with screening? So there's a huge disconnect. So who wins with the vaccinating? Who's winning?*

Colleen is referring to the pharmaceutical company that manufactures Gardasil®—Merck Frost—as the "winner" and questions the necessity and effectiveness of the vaccine. Colleen is not, however, anti-vaccine as she did have her daughter vaccinated with the routine infant schedule.

As our interview was conducted in the early winter of 2010, just after the H1N1 vaccination offering, she was quick to point out that she did not immunize herself or family members against H1N1. For Colleen, vaccines that she deems as non-mandatory present an unnecessary risk to one's health and in this case, the HPV vaccine would bring forth this risk for her daughter. Colleen's conceptualization of health risk has altered after having a child and as her daughter matures:

> *I think that since my daughter has been born, I've gotten much more interested, I've got more invested in my own health. So I'm a little more aware now of what goes into your body is going to affect how you feel. So I try to eat healthy and I try to avoid things that are going to have a negative impact on my health.*
>
> *You never know what is going to happen to you. And I could get in the car—I'm totally jinxing myself—to go to the doctor's and I might get hit by a truck. I don't mean I'm not going to drive. So, you have to maintain a certain amount of—you don't want to be complacent, but you can only do so much, right?*

In the quote above Colleen illustrates how she is more vigilant about health risks as she gets older and has become a mother. But her rendition of risk and public health literacy is different than is exhibited by Andrea and Heather. For Colleen, health risk is about taking in contaminants, like tobacco, or "unnecessary" vaccines. She also believes that, as a society, we have become hyper aware of potential risks, to the point of paralysis. In response to, and in resistance to, living in a "risk society" (Beck and Willms 2004), Colleen chooses not to over-think every potential risk. Thus, for Colleen, pharmaceuticals, which are manufactured by for-profit companies, bring about greater risk than the HPV virus itself and she is actively resisting Gardasil® advertising that, in her own words, is set to make all mothers "afraid" for their daughters. Therefore, in this line of thinking, Colleen is being a good mother by protecting her daughter from the HPV vaccine, both in terms of potential vaccine side effects and "doing too much" to avoid perceived and hyped risk. Both the vaccine and too much stress are deemed to be "unnatural" and, thus, unhealthy.

Colleen spends a great deal of time researching her daughter's health, from vaccines to the food that they eat. Colleen only serves organic fruits and vegetables to her family and abstains from eating white flour baked goods or white pasta or rice. Catriona Sandilands calls this type of food consumption "'green' consumerism ... [which is a] part of a process of environmental privatization. This process is problematic for both environmentalist and feminist politics: environmental privatization depoliticizes environmental problems, and does so in the company of a very conservative notion of gender" (45). Green or organic products are marketed to women and reinforce traditional notions of women as caretakers for their families. These marketing campaigns, not unlike the Gardasil® one, espouse the notion that environmentally sound and organically-oriented women are "protecting their offspring" (Sandilands 46). In essence, they are being good mothers. Colleen's disavowal of the Gardasil® discourse and the appropriation of the green consumerism discourse, which both exhibit similar messaging around motherhood, points to the contradictions of everyday mothering.

In my interviews, mothers generally took a firm position on whether or not they would vaccinate their daughters, but a few mothers postponed their decision-making. Those who decided to delay decision-making were also practicing a variant of intensive mothering. The decision to put off making a decision is based on the notion that current research is insufficient. For these mothers, they feel it is prudent to wait for more research. This requires a mother to make a commitment to monitor future research, demonstrating access to scientific informational resources and the time to collect and interpret future studies. Delaying a decision also marks one's ability to pay for the vaccine out-of-pocket

CONCLUSION

When mothers engaged in vaccine decision-making, they strategically re-appropriated the good mother precept and its dominant practice—intensive mothering—while formulating their own public health literacies. These forms of resignification, or re-constructing what it means to them to be a good mother, reveal the complex, contradictory and often ironic nature of agency and resistance while doing mothering. As is exhibited by Colleen, being a good mother is achieved by accepting certain public health literacies and disavowing others, even if they exhibit similar messaging surrounding motherhood. As Butler states the fact "that my agency is riven with paradox does not mean it is impossible. It only means that paradox is the condition of its possibility" (*Undoing*

Gender 3). Andrea also provides a salient example of formulating a public health literacy that is linked to her very conceptualization of mothering, but instead of contradiction, her decision-making is steeped in irony. Andrea is seeking to shield her daughter from the downsides of being an intensive mother some day, all the while clearly enacting these canons herself. Andrea's vaccine decision may mirror dominant motherhood discourses, but she is, momentarily, attempting to disrupt future hegemonic conceptualizations of motherhood so that her daughter does not have to do the same when she grows up. Thus, to form her own public health literacies within the context of vaccine decision-making and doing mothering is an act of hope. She is saying that while she needs to navigate the maze of motherhood, that doesn't mean her daughter should have to negotiate these ideological frameworks. While Andrea's creative mothering strategies will not dismantle the overarching structures of motherhood, she can begin to loosen their grip. Her approach is a move to "undo restrictively normative conceptions of sexual and gendered life" (*Undoing Gender* 1). What this undoing may look like is open to debate because changing one set of norms for another is inscribing a new set of restrictions for someone, somewhere. However, in the meantime, the acts of everyday agency and resistance exhibited by Colleen, Andrea and the other mothers featured in this chapter deserve a moment of pause. It is through this reflection that new possibilities for the interrogation of motherhood ideologies within public health measures become more and more likely.

WORKS CITED

Allen, Amy. *The Politics of Our Selves: Power, Autonomy, and Gender in Contemporary Critical Theory*. New York: Columbia University Press, 2008. Print.

Beck, Ulrich and Johannes Willms. *Conversations with Ulrich Beck*. Cambridge, UK: Polity Press, 2004. Print.

Braun, Virginia and Nicola Gavey. "'Bad Girls' and 'Good Girls'? Sexuality and Cervical Cancer." *Women's Studies International Forum* (1999): 22.2, 203-213. Print.

Butler, Judith. *Gender Trouble: Feminism and the Subversion of Identity.* New York: Routledge, (2007/1990). Print.

Butler, Judith. "Introduction: Acting in Concert." *Undoing Gender.* New York: Routledge, 2004.

Clarke, Adele and Monica Casper. "From Simple Technology to Complex Arena: Classification of Pap Smears, 1917-90." *Medical Anthropology Quarterly* 10.4 (1996): 601-623. Print.

Gagnon, M., Jean Daniel Jacob and Dave Holmes. "Governing Through (In)security: A Critical Analysis of a Fear-based Public Health Campaign." *Critical Public Health* 20.2 (2010): 245-256. Print.

Ginn, Diana. "The Supreme Court of Canada and What It Means to be 'Of Woman Born'." *From Motherhood to Mothering: the Legacy of Adrienne Rich's of Woman Born.* Ed. Andrea O'Reilly. Albany: State University of New York Press, 2004. 27-43. Print.

Gledhill, John. *Power and Its Disguises: Anthropological Perspectives on Politics* (2nd Ed). London: Pluto Press, 2000. Print.

Glenn, Evelyn Nakano. "Social Constructions of Mothering: A Thematic Overview." *Mothering: Ideology, Experience, and Agency.* Eds. Evelyn Nakano Glenn, Grace Chang and Linda Forcey. New York: Routledge, 1994. 1-29. Print.

Gordon, Andrea. "Gardasil Side Effects Examined; HPV Vaccine Causes Some Adverse Reactions, U.S. Study Confirms." *The Toronto Star* 19 August 2009: E1. Print.

Gulli, C., L. George, and J. Intini. "Our Girls Are Not Guinea Pigs: Is an Upcoming Mass Inoculation of a Generation Unnecessary and Potentially Dangerous?" *Macleans* 23 August 2007: 38-42. Print.

Hayes, Sharon. *The Cultural Contradictions of Motherhood.* New Haven: Yale University Press, 1996. Print.

Johnson, Joy, John Oliffe, Mary T. Kelly, Joan Bottorff, and Karen LeBeau. "The Readings of Smoking Fathers: A Reception Analysis of Tobacco Cessation Images." *Health Communication* 24.6 (2009): 532-547. Print.

Lieblich, Amia, Rivka Tuval-Mashiach and Tamar Zilber. *Narrative Research: Reading, Analysis, and Interpretation.* Thousand Oaks, CA: Sage, 1998. Print.

Lock, Margaret and Patricia A. Kaufert. "Introduction." *Prag-

matic women and body politics. Ed. Margaret Lock & Patricia A. Kaufert. Cambridge, UK: Cambridge University Press, 1998. 1-27. Print.

Lupton, Deborah. *The Imperative of Health: Public Health and the Regulated Body.* London: Sage Publications, 1995. Print.

Merck Frost. *New England Journal of Medicine Publishes Efficacy and Safety Data for Gardasil in Males.* Montreal: Author, 2 February 2011. Web. 4 February 2011

Office of the Premier. *McGuinty Government Launches Life-saving HPV Immunization Program.* Toronto: Author, 2 August 2007. Web. 12 September 2010

Picard, André. "How Politics Pushed the HPV Vaccine." *The Globe and Mail* 11 August 2007: A1. Print.

Pleasant, Andrew and Shyama Kuruvilla. "A Tale of Two Health Literacies: Public Health and Clinical Approaches to Health Literacy" *Health Promotion International,* 23.2 (2008): 152-159. Print.

Posner, Tina. "Ethical Issues and the Individual Woman in Cancer Screening Programs." *Journal of Advances in Health and Nursing Care* 2.3 (1993): 55-70. Print.

Rapp, Rayna. "Extra Chromosomes and Blue Tulips: Medico-familial Interpretations." *Living and Working with the New Medical Technologies: Intersections of Inquiry.* Ed. Margaret Lock, Alan Young and Alberto Cambrosio. Cambridge: Cambridge University Press, 2000. 184-207. Print.

Rich, Adrienne. *Of Woman Born: Motherhood as Experience and Institution.* New York: W.W. Norton & Company, 1976/1986. Print.

Sandilands, Catriona. "Consumerism: Environmental Privatization and Family Values." *Canadian Woman Studies* 13.3 (1993): 45-47. Print.

Scott, James C. *Weapons of the Weak: Everyday Forms of Peasant "Resistance."* New Haven: Yale University Press, 1985. Print.

Stewart, Kathleen. "Real American Dreams (Can be Nightmares)." *Cultural Studies and Political Theory* Ed. Jodi Dean. Ithaca, NY: Cornell University Press, 2000. 243-257. Print.

Strauss, Anselm and Juliet Corbin. "Introduction." *Grounded Theory in Practice* Eds. Anselm Strauss and Juliet Corbin. Thousand

Oaks, CA: Sage Publications Inc., 1997. vii-viii. Print.
Vanslyke, Jan G., Julie Baum, Veronica Plaza, Maria Otero, Cosette Wheeler, and Deborah L. Helitzer. "HPV and Cervical Cancer Testing and Prevention: Knowledge, Beliefs, and Attitudes Among Hispanic Women." *Qualitative Health Research* 18.5 (2008): 584-596. Print.
Zaloom, Caitlin. "The Productive Life of Risk." *Cultural Anthropology* 19.3 (2004): 365-391. Print.

Contributor Notes

Jill Bryant is a professor at Willamette University in Salem, Oregon. At Willamette she teaches literacy courses to K-12 preservice teachers. When she is not teaching, Jill can be found with her daughter and partner working on their flower farm, riding bikes, playing basketball, and, of course, reading great books

Rachel Epp Buller is a feminist-art historian-printmaker-mama of three who investigates critical issues of mothering and the maternal body through art, scholarship, and curatorial projects. She is the editor of *Reconciling Art and Mothering* (2012) and the co-editor of *Mothering Mennonite* (2013). She holds a Ph.D. in art history.

Ariel Cooksey, MA, is currently a Ph.D. candidate in sociology at Texas Woman's University studying the discourse and lived realities that make up identity and gender. She has worked in education and behavior intervention for ten years across a broad scope of curriculum and age levels, utilizing art within the context of therapeutic interventions for Emotionally Disturbed individuals. Her current projects include a co-constructed account of postpartum depression and an in-depth analysis of transgender mothering.

Stacey Crooks has worked as a literacy practitioner and researcher for the past 13 years. Currently, Stacey is a Ph.D. student at the Ontario Institute for Studies in Education at the University of Toronto. Her research focuses on family literacy programs as sites of regulation and empowerment. Stacey is also the mother of two school-aged children.

Lauren Cross is a Ph.D. student in Women's Studies at Texas Woman's University (Denton, Texas). Cross' background in the visual arts (BA in Art, Design, Media; MFA in Visual Arts) has influenced her current research, which takes on multicultural approach to gender in visual culture analysis.

Linda Shuford Evans is an assistant professor of TESOL teacher education at Kennesaw State University. Linda's interest in literacy was kindled as she studied for her bachelor's and master's degrees in Elementary Bilingual Education at Boston University, culminating in a master's thesis on teaching language through storytelling. She earned her doctorate in Literacy and Language Arts at the University of South Florida and engaged in literacy education through her work as a teacher educator of foreign languages and English as a second language; her research on language acquisition, reading, and giftedness; and her workshops for teachers on bilingualism, biliteracy and dual language education. The literacy work which made her rethink everything she knew and believed, however, came with the births of her children Abby and Zach over 20 years ago, and that rethinking continues today.

Marta Cecilia Gutiérrez-Restrepo holds a MS in Education and Human Development. She has worked as a Child and Youth Psychotherapist, Clinical Psychology Consultant for schools-parents, and Human Development Graduate Faculty. She Coordinates the Psychology, Health, and Society Scholars Team at Universidad CES and is the President of the BioEthics & Deontology Board of Antioquia, Colombia.

Jessica Smartt Gullion, Ph.D., is associate professor of sociology at Texas Woman's University where she studies the discourse construction of health and illness. She has published extensively on representations of health issues. Her writings on motherhood have appeared in the *Journal of the Association for Research on Mothering*, *Literary Mama*, the *Mother's Movement Online*, and in the anthology *Mama, PhD: Women Write About Motherhood and Academic Life*. She is currently conducting an ethnographic account of natural gas drilling activism.

Erin Hemmens served five years as an executive board member of the Midwifery Coalition of Nova Scotia, a consumer lobby group dedicated to improving access to publically funded midwifery services for all women and families in Nova Scotia. While writing this piece, she moved from Halifax, Nova Scotia, to Vancouver Island, to be closer to her family. She has a Masters degree in Social Anthropology and is employed as a Health Promotion Coordinator with the Canadian Cancer Society, BC and Yukon Division.

Elizabeth Howells has served in administrative roles as the Director of Composition and the interim Assistant Dean of the College of Liberal Arts and has taught courses in literature, composition, rhetoric, and gender and women's studies. Recent publications include an article on Charlotte Bronte and George Smith in *Bronte Studies* and a textbook entitled *Literature: Reading to Write* for Pearson, both fall of 2010.

Masako Kato holds a Ph.D. in Anthropology from the Graduate Center, CUNY, USA. She taught at Tsuda College in Tokyo, Japan, from 2010 to 2012, and is now an independent scholar and researcher, who lives in London, UK. Her research interests include linguistic anthropology, language and gender, language socialization, language and identity, and bilingualism.

Miriamne Ara Krummel is an Associate Professor in the Department of English at the University of Dayton. The author of *Crafting Jewishness in Medieval England: Legally Absent, Virtually Present* (2011), her creative nonfiction has appeared in *Embodied Rhetorics: Disability in Language and Culture* (2001), as well as *The Dayton Jewish Observer* and *Jewish Currents*.

Laura Newhart is Associate Professor of Philosophy and current chair of the Department of Philosophy and Religion at Eastern Kentucky University. Her areas of specialization are feminist theory, biomedical ethics, and twentieth century European philosophy. Her current research interests include mothering and philosophy, logic-based therapy, and philosophy for children.

Cara L. Preuss, Ph.D., is a language learner, educator, and scholar. She has taught Spanish and English in various settings and trained teachers in the U.S. and Azerbaijan. Her research interests include critical language and literacy investigations in and outside schools.

Amanda B. Richey, Ph.D., is an assistant professor of TESOL and Inclusive Education at Kennesaw State University in Georgia. Before her doctoral studies, she worked as a freelance travel writer, EFL teacher, and a health volunteer for the Peace Corps in Morocco. Her research and publications are focused on issues of gender and literacy, family engagement in urban schools, representations of Islam in educational contexts, and critical/social justice multicultural education. Amanda is mother to Noor (age six) and Lena (age four).

Cinthya M. Saavedra received her Ph.D. from Texas A&M University in Curriculum and Instruction. She is currently an assistant professor at Utah State University where she teaches bilingual/ESL and foundations courses in the School of Teacher Education and Leadership. Her scholarship centers Chicana/Latina epistemology and poststructuralist perspectives in bilingual/ESL immigrant childhood studies and teacher education. She also explores the possibilities of constructing critical qualitative (decolonizing) research methods with marginalized populations.

Suzanne Smythe is an Assistant Professor in Adult Literacy and Adult Education at Simon Fraser University in Burnaby, Canada. A long-time adult literacy educator, her current research explores mothers' literacy work for schools as well as policies that rely upon parenting work in the home to address inequalities in children's educational outcomes.

Blaire Willson Toso, Ph.D., conducts research at Penn State on the ways that literacy, schooling and the accompanying discourses shape—and are shaped by—adult learners' agency and literacy practices, particularly as the topic pertains to immigrant mothers. She publishes on a variety of topics pertaining to adult education and family literacy.

Elizabeth Trejos-Castillo is an Assistant Professor of Human Development and Family Studies at Texas Tech University. Her research interests include parenting, generational effects, context and individual characteristics on risk-taking and problem behaviors in minority, immigrant, and international youth. She is an Associate Editor of *The Journal of Early Adolescence.*

Paulina Vélez is a Research Assistant and a Fulbright Fellow who completed her Master's degree in Human Development and Family Studies at Texas Tech University. She has a B.S. degree in Psychology from Universidad CES (Medellin, Colombia). Her research interests include children's social and emotional development, parenting and motherhood.

Teresa Winterhalter is Professor of British literature and Director of Faculty Development at AASU in Savannah, Georgia. She has published numerous articles on modernist poetry, the representation of women in film, and Virginia Woolf. Two NEH grants have launched her current research on nostalgia as a recuperative force in Modern novels.

Michelle Wyndham-West is currently finishing her dissertation entitled *Gendered Risk: An Ethnographic Exploration of HPV Vaccine Policy in Ontario* at York University in Toronto, Canada. Michelle's research draws upon social science approaches to risk, post-structuralist theory, medical anthropology and feminist praxis. In addition to completing her Ph.D. studies, Michelle teaches gender-related courses on an adjunct basis at the Ontario College of Art and Design University (OCADU) and is in the midst of raising two teenage boys.